D1233034

GERRIT SMITH

A BIOGRAPHY

BY

OCTAVIUS BROOKS FROTHINGHAM

NEGRO UNIVERSITIES PRESS
NEW YORK

B
Smith

Originally published in 1878
by G. P. Putnam's Sons, New York

Reprinted 1969 by
Negro Universities Press
A DIVISION OF GREENWOOD PRESS, INC.
NEW YORK

SBN 8371-2765-3

PRINTED IN UNITED STATES OF AMERICA

CONTENTS.

LIFE OF GERRIT SMITH.

CHAPTER I.

PARENTAGE.

TO one who looks into the beginnings of any local society, the influence of individuals is apparent. The interest centres in a few men. This was the case in central New York. One of the men who made himself felt there in the first quarter of the century, was Peter Smith. He was born in Greenbush, Rockland Co., November 15, 1768. His ancestors, who were Hollanders, had lived and died there, for several generations. Petrus Smith died January 24, 1767, aged eighty years, two months, four days. Annitje his wife, died January 1, 1803. Gerrit P. Smith, their son, (born June 15, 1743, died October 7, 1826) married Wintje Lent (born July 16, 1750, died at her son's house in Schenectady, February 17, 1834). Peter was their oldest child. They lived on the farm near Tappan, which was made famous by the execution of John André. Peter was about twelve years old when that tragedy was enacted. At the age of sixteen or thereabouts he became clerk to Abraham Herring, an importing merchant in New York City. At this time, it is said, he exhibited the taste for theatricals that is usual with very young men, and, as an actor of subordinate parts on the stage of the old Park Theatre, gave signs of a faculty which if cultivated and directed might have enabled him to shine in another career. He was of sensitive temperament and quick emotions, easily moved to tears by consideration of his religious duties and by reflection on his relations to the Supreme Being and the destinies of the hereafter.

Versatile and persuasive, a man to impress himself on others, and win confidence, his clerk life was succeeded by a partnership with John Jacob Astor, a poor youth like himself, but like himself adventurous, and endowed with the qualities that ensure success—patience, endurance, industry, and the sagacity that divines, as by instinct, the way to wealth. They kept a little store and traded in furs which they procured at first hand from the Indian hunters at the North. It was their custom in the summer months to go to Albany by sloop, thence on foot to penetrate into the interior of the State, making their way as they could across rivers, swamps and other natural barriers, climbing, wading, swimming until they reached the tribes, Mohawks, Oneidas, Cayugas, Senecas, who held the treasures of winter spoil. The price paid was not dear, the " Indian money " as it was called, consisting of beads, shells, bits of glass, of no value except in savage eyes ;—but the Indians were satisfied, and helped the traders to transport the skins, on man-back and by canoe to Albany, whence they were taken down the river to New York. The business was profitable for those times. It was perhaps to make it more profitable that Smith took up his residence in central New York, in the valley of the Mohawk, and opened an Indian trader's store in a corner of his house,

on what is known as the Bleecker property at Utica
At this period the furs were sent to his partner in New
York. But other interests engrossed him, and the partnership with Mr. Astor was dissolved. Astor bought
real estate in the heart of the city, and Smith bought
acres in the centre of the State.

Two little pocket journals exist, written rudely in
pencil, containing notes of journeys northward from
Albany, in the summer and autumn of 1822. The descriptions suggest hardships of nearly every description ;
bad roads, scant accommodations, sparse populations,
hard climates, vile weather, but they disclose a sturdy
resolve, a keen vigilance, an appreciation of natural advantages and a foresight into future possibilities, an intelligent, humane interest, too, in the prospects of civilization, such as belong only to men of genuine power.
The purchases of land were, even at the start, immense
in extent. At this period the Indians in his neighborhood outnumbered the whites, who were mostly Dutch.
His native language was Dutch, but he was able to communicate with the Indians, and even to address them
effectively in their own speech. His frequent excursions
in search of skins had made him acquainted with the
land in different parts of the State and given him hints
in regard to the probable sites for towns and villages,
which he was quick to act on. As it was illegal to buy
land outright from the Indians, Mr. Smith leased a large
tract for the technical ninety-nine years, and then by
arrangement with the authorities obtained permission to
purchase a tract of some sixty thousand acres, for which
he paid three dollars and fifty-three and a half cents per
acre. Of this enough was sold at auction in 1802, to

repay the purchase money and still leave him a large estate. Mortgages on the lands that were sold on credit were transferred to the State in discharge of his indebtedness, and formed in part the capital of the Common School Fund. The tract of sixty thousand acres was divided into four parcels. The first contained seventy-four lots; fifty-five in Oneida County, in the present town of Augusta; fourteen in Stockbridge, and five in Smithfield. The second contained sixty lots; most of them in the present town of Smithfield; the rest in the adjacent township of Fenner. The third contained fifty-six lots, all but three in Fenner. The fourth contained forty-seven lots, mostly in the town of Cazenovia, then in Chenango County. Mr. Smith, then Judge Smith, was, it is said, the largest purchaser of land in the Oneida Reservation, embracing nearly the whole of the Second Assembly District of Madison County, and several large towns in Oneida County, which was sold in tracts of various sizes and shapes to speculators. He bought largely lands that were sold for taxes, often at a merely nominal sum, and either remained in his hands as permanent possessions, or were redeemed at enhanced prices. Among these later purchases, were eighty thousand acres in the then county of Oneida, for which he paid to the State three dollars an acre. Of the amount offered at auction in Utica, twenty-two thousand two hundred and ninety-nine and a half acres remained unsold. The highest price paid was eight dollars and forty cents per acre. Whole townships of unoccupied land were sometimes bought at a single purchase. Thus Mr. Smith became one of the largest landholders in the Union, certainly the largest in the State. His posses-

sions comprised acres by the hundred thousand, nearer
a million than half a million; they were measured by
square miles.

Judge Smith resided in the county of Madison and
presided at the County Court. The township where he
lived was named Smithfield, and the village Peterboro.
Here he kept open house and exercised generous hospitality. He was one of the burgomasters of his day
when the Dutch Huguenots and the active merchants
of Holland were colonizing and civilizing the central
portion of the State. The Vanderkemps and Schuylers
and Van Rensselaers and Kips, were welcome guests.
The great landholder could be social and even jovial.
His latch-string was out for his friends ; and he was too
wise if not too kindly to make enemies. To the last he
remained on good terms with the Indians ; the Oneida
chief, Skenandoah, was a friend so fast ·that Mr. Smith
named his first born son after him, Peter Skenandoah.
In fact, his influence with the Indians was so great as to
cause uneasiness to the general government, which dis-
patched an agent to break up what threatened to be an
embarrassing intimacy. The danger however was imaginary. The agent reported accordingly, and the savage
associations continued as long as he lived in the neighborhood. The Indians made free with the hospitality
of the Peterboro mansion, camped in the halls and out-
houses, and lay loose about the piazza, not always desirable, though still useful visitors.

To those who knew Judge Smith casually, he seemed
a hard, sharp, shrewd man, close at a bargain, selfish and
grasping, too much occupied with himself to make others
happy, or to be genial of intercourse. He was heavy in
1*

build, but not tall, with large eyes that had in them a gleam of wildness which was at times almost fierce. In reality he was a man of quick feelings, and sensitive. The rude note books above referred to contain incidental touches which reveal a sense of justice, a homely kindness of heart ; and several passages display the presence, and fitful working of religious emotion, more impetuous than constant. *July* 31, 1822, "I feel much relieved, though sick and feeble still! Thank the Lord, O my soul, for all his mercies, in whatever shape they may come! I am snatched as it were from the grave! O let it be another incentive, so to number my remaining days that I may apply my. heart unto wisdom! Man times and plans, God disappoints! Yet, O my soul, praise and thank his holy name for all his mercies!"

Aug. 1, "Have had a comfortable night, much better than could have been expected. I hope by Saturday to be able to start for the Plain. O heavenly Father, fill my heart with gratitude, in consideration of all the blessings and comforts I still enjoy, and more especially that thou hast thus far sustained me through this violent attack of a dangerous disorder. Elder Churchill has just been with me. O, what pains do the people of God take to cause me to see and pursue the right way! How vile, how hardened must I be! Rev. Mr. Comstock has just left me, prayed for me. O, what can all this mean? Is the Lord about convincing me that the last opportunities are now offered?"

Aug. 2, "Not quite so comfortable, yet I hope by to-morrow morning to move. O, may all these dispensations of Providence, though somewhat afflictive, only cause me to take and keep my latter end in mind!"

Aug. 5, " Have had a comfortable night, and still no heart to thank a most merciful God for this mercy."

Aug. 24, " Just now saw two smart Vermonters going as settlers upon Hoffman township. They give twenty dollars an acre. I am very much worried and fatigued ; very little attention to make me comfortable at this tavern. O, may I be resigned to all my trials ! Give me, heavenly Father, a contented mind."

Sept. 8, *Sunday,* " Have not had a comfortable night, spirits too much agitated this morning ; intend going to meeting at —— five and a half miles north ; may the perturbations of my mind be allayed ! May I hear attentively and profitably ! "

Monday morning, " Still at Esq. Johnson's ; am not very well ; mind is much perplexed regarding concerns here. Heard two sermons yesterday, from Rev. Mr. Comstock ; the one in afternoon was funeral sermon, a daughter of Mr. Catlin, about — yrs. of age, had died suddenly—croup I expect. ' Work while it is day, for the night cometh,' etc. O, could I be persuaded so to do ! But this stupidity ! This unbelief ! "

Sept. 30, *Monday,* " Yesterday we had reading and prayer-meeting here ; all seems to have no lasting effect on my slothful, sluggish mind. I read much and good books, but when I lay them down, the world is instantly uppermost ! Were we but prepared for death ! We read : ' A Christian's death is the best part of his existence !' What *is it* keeps me from embracing the proffer of the Saviour ! O, the hardness of heart ! ' Heaping up wrath against the day of wrath.' O, what consummate folly ! O, had I but faith in the Lord Jesus Christ ! What shall I do to obtain it ! O, might I but firmly be-

lieve in that Jesus who is the resurrection and the life!
O, for grace, for saving, divine grace!"

Feeling and intellect were at strife in the man. He
was sincere, but could not make up his mind.

It was his habit to leave tracts as he journeyed on
his land expeditions. His approach to a settlement was
announced by small placards set on way-side posts, announcing the message of "Eternity." The gospel
trumpet, in the similitude of a horn, blown by himself,
heralded his near presence. Thus he plied the business
of two worlds at once.

Aug. 8, 1822, "I have here, as well as heretofore on
this journey, distributed many tracts, but not half as
many as I could have wished. I was not sufficiently
supplied; must hereafter on my journeys be more attentive to this. At Plattsburgh I presented *No Fiction* to
the Misses Davidson, and for other ladies, Mrs. Judge
Platt, Mrs. General Moers, Mrs. R. H. Walworth to read.
May they receive good from it, and may all I do in this
way result in good, and O, might it to my own soul!"

On his removal from Peterboro to Schenectady, in the
spring of 1825, he made systematic arrangements for the
continuance of this pious work.

"We arrive, with view to take up residence at Schenectady, April 9, 1825.

"For several years past, I Peter Smith of Peterboro,
have from time to time supplied myself with great variety of religious tracts, and some larger works, and in
the habit of distributing such, in my frequent excursions
in various directions, mostly within this State, from
which have *myself* derived much satisfaction, and I hope
many *others* have been, and will be benefited from it!

My intentions are, *God* allowing bodily and pecuniary ability, to continue doing the like ; may *He* bless the recipients and distributors !

" In addition, I intend to make deposit with suitable person, in neighborhoods (more particularly where the gospel is not statedly presented) in the northern and western counties, of tracts, *say from one hundred to one thousand*, according to circumstances, with request that to each head of a family, one tract be given, the like to schools, and to single persons not attached to a family, with desire they may be exchanged at the depository, from time to time ; (to deliver to such *only* who intend to make the exchanges,) the receivers desired to keep the tracts neat and clean as may be, list to be kept of the names to whom tracts *in first instance* are delivered —it is also my intention from time to time, to make additions to the deposits, especially in neighborhoods where most read.

" The person with whom deposits are made, to make report at the end of every year, stating whatever may have come to his knowledge, regarding the effects (if any observable) produced by the reading, and what the encouragement for the future.

" And further my intention is (God willing) to send to friends in destitute neighborhoods, from time to time, bundles of twenty-five, thirty or forty tracts for themselves and families to read, with request to loan to such of their neighbors as will read them."

NEW YORK STATE TRACT SOCIETY.

Albany, 1st *June*, 1825.

Peter Smith Esq. having submitted to us a circular letter to accompany deposits of tracts in various places in the interior of the

State, we are constrained to express our great gratification in his *original* and *systematic* efforts for *planting* tracts. We persuade ourselves, the plan will lead to the establishment of auxiliary tract societies in those places where his deposits may be made : and we hope that the persons to whom he shall entrust the pleasing labor of circulating the tracts, will set that desirable result before them as the object of their aim. No matter, in the first instance, how small the societies may be.

Another pleasing view of this subject is, that these deposits will, in many instances, be the *germs* of *lending libraries* : a plan of operation which has been extensively adopted, within a year or two, in Europe ; and the happy effects of which are spoken of in the highest terms, in many of the annual reports of religious societies of the past year.

W. A. Tweed Dale
Nath'l Davis
Aaron Hand   Executive
Nahum Rice   Committee.
John Willard

EBEN'R WATSON, Corresponding Secretary.

To ——

Dear Sir — I take pleasure in making an addition to the deposit of religious tracts heretofore made with you ; accompanying are standard tracts, *all* different from the former. I not only hope that yourself will take pleasure in reading, and in putting and keeping *these* with the former ones in lively and continued circulation, but that your neighbors near may, by their attentive perusal of them, manifest a *due sense* of the opportunity afforded. The more these, and the like books, are read, the more we may expect the cause of religion and morality to be promoted.

I am gratified in having it in my power to inform, that the New York State Tract Society have resolved to forward you a copy of the *New York Tract Magazine,* without charge to yourself, save the postage.

I am greatly encouraged in the prospect (having communication from different quarters) that our expense and labor, in these matters, will not prove in vain.

Wishing you happiness in this world, and in that which is to come,   I remain your friend,

PETER SMITH.

My Dear — Herewith be pleased to receive the tracts and books specified below, as an addition to my former deposits, for loaning to families and others in your place and neighborhood. I anticipated much satisfaction from the effects of my former deposits of tracts, but I make the present addition with increased satisfaction, from the great avidity with which (I am informed from many quarters) they have been sought after and read, and the decided good which, in some instances, they have produced. And why should they not be sought after, and why should they not do good? Though in form, of all things the most unpretending, they are, in fact, most powerful preachers to the heart and conscience. In their subject they are second to nothing that can be presented to the mind of an immortal, for they treat of his eternal happiness or misery. In their execution they may be justly styled the elegant extracts of theological literature ; for they are the productions of some of the soundest heads and the purest hearts which bless our world ; a greater proof of excellence can hardly be given of a man's writings, than to honor them with a place in the series of the American Tract Society. When, therefore, their worth is considered on the one hand, and their necessity on the other, from the destitution of the stated ordi-nances of the gospel, with which the heart of every man of proper feelings is pained, who traverses any considerable portion of the State, (particularly the northern and south-western sections,) it is no matter of surprise that they are almost universally interesting and extensively beneficial. Much has my heart been rejoiced by the re-lation of the effects produced by those I have deposited, in many places, destitute of almost all religious privileges.

With these views, I am very desirous of extending their circula-tion much beyond my deposits. One of the principal designs in planting a few tracts and books in various places is, that they may, in due season, bring forth fruit, in the establishment of Auxiliary Tract Societies. There are many important advantages to be de-rived from such societies, which will readily occur to your reflection. While, therefore, I confirm my former instructions, for the mode of circulating the deposits entrusted to your kind care, I now propose, for the purpose of encouraging the establishment of Auxiliary So-cieties, that the tracts and books in your charge, *as my depositary,* shall be considered as a donation from myself, to any society that shall hereafter be established in your neighborhood, auxiliary to the New York State branch of the American Tract Society, which shall raise by an *annual* subscription, in the outset, a sum not less than — dollars. To facilitate that measure I send herewith a printed form of a constitution, which has been recommended by the Ameri-can Tract Society : you will readily perceive the propriety of my being apprised of the measure when adopted. Should a county Branch Tract Society, be hereafter established in your county, which I hope may shortly be done, it will doubtless be expedient for the local auxiliaries to connect themselves directly with the county Branch.

Those justly and highly valued publications, the *New York Tract Magazine,* and the *Children's Friend,* will be continued to you. Should your sets from any means not be complete, state in writing, by private opportunity, what numbers are lacking, to *Ebenezer Watson,* Esq., Corresponding Secretary of the New York State Branch of the American Tract Society, in Albany, he will forward the deficient numbers by return of the same person.

May the blessing of God accompany the labors of those who strive to supply the needy with spiritual food, is the prayer of

Your sincere friend and very humble servant,

PETER SMITH, *of Peterboro.*

Standard Tracts,
4 Page do.
Broad sheet do.
Hand bill do.
Children's Books,
And one Christian Almanack.

N. B. It is hoped you will cause such of the tracts as are not covered, to be so before you loan them.

Dear —— Herewith you will receive —— standard tracts, —— four page do. —— Christian Almanack. Although I am constrained to confess, I have not *generally,* within the last year, received that encouragement from my various depositories that I had anticipated, and did for previous years, and although I sometimes feel *almost* inclined to give up the expense and labor of obtaining, depositing and distributing tracts, in manner I am doing and have done in years past ; then again, we may hope for good account of bread cast upon the waters (if not immediately) after many days —— so try again.

Let me entreat you, my dear —— to manage the books and tracts in your charge to the best advantage; put and keep them in lively circulation, and let us pray *with hope,* that good may proceed from our exertions. If we do not observe the *good* effects in time, that we may in eternity.

Affectionately,

I am your friend,

And exceeding well wisher,

P. SMITH, *of Peterboro.*

Dear Sir —— Since I last sent you a package of tracts, another year has passed, admonishing us by its rapid flight, that our " time is short," and that we must do quickly what remains for us to do.

I trust that the tracts you have hitherto received from me, have not been without some good effect in arresting the careless sinner, and in quickening the zeal of the pious believer. May the Lord's blessing accompany the *little preachers* I now send you, and make them the messengers of comfort, and joy, and salvation to many.

It will afford me great gratification to receive from you an occasional letter, telling me of some good thing in the history of your tract depository. Especially will it gratify me to hear, that Christians in your neighborhood prize this little establishment, and commend it to the blessings of Him who hears and rewards prayer.

With affectionate regard,

Your sincere friend,

PETER SMITH, *of Peterboro.*

Dear Sir, Through the providence of God, I am again permitted to address you upon the subject of tracts ; I have confidence it is a subject that, with yourself has not become stale. We are greatly encouraged to persevere in furnishing and circulating these silent unassuming preachers. We have accounts, almost daily, through the newspapers and otherwise, where the use of tracts has been greatly blessed. Myself am favored with communications from several depositaries, stating that under God, great good has been produced through the means of tracts in their respective neighborhoods. If within the bounds of your circulation, no material effects are as yet discernible, do not therefore be discouraged nor slacken your hand, but continue to distribute. In some ground seed lies longer than in other, before it springs up and yields fruit ; we must sow in hope.

The publications with which I furnish my depositaries are in the language of an able and faithful minister of the word of God, " free from everything sectarian. Instead of exciting the jealousy of the different denominations of Christians, they are eminently calculated to strengthen the bonds of brotherly love among the friends of truth, and make them feel they are disciples of the same master."

Herewith I forward to you —— standard tracts, from twelve to forty-four pages each, —— of four pages, and one on cholera. I trust you will make them productive of the greatest good *in your power*, by lending out, receiving in, and lending again and again ! By frequently conversing with your neighbors upon the subject of their contents ; and above all, by prayer to God for his blessing upon our doings in this behalf.

May we live to see great beneficial results proceeding from our labor in this cause, and that it may be sanctified to our souls, is the prayer of   Your sincere friend,

PETER SMITH, *of Peterboro.*

Dear Sir — Let us continue in well doing, and not be wearied. Having laid our hands to the plough, not look back.   Although the fruits of our labor and *expense*, may not show itself as frequent and abundant as we could wish ; yet we *must* hope it *will* appear, not only in the present. but in generations when we and our doings shall be forgotten.   In this belief, I continue to furnish the *Silent Preacher*.   Herewith you will receive —— standard tracts, —— four page tracts, and —— Christian Almanack.   I again take the liberty of soliciting that yourself may not cease striving to cause them to be read by all classes and ages.

May you be abundantly rewarded for the faithful discharge of your agency, in time and in eternity, is the prayer of

Your friend and exceeding

Well wisher,

PETER SMITH, *of Peterboro.*

Be pleased to cover such of the tracts as are not, before you loan them.

Dear Sir — Another year has gone by since I penned my tract circular number six, and five years since number one.   How many I may still be permitted to write and you receive, is, *for wise purposes*, hid from us ; may we but do *our* duty while it is *to-day*, of the *morrow* we are not assured.

Let me entreat you, my dear sir, to make the most of these silent preachers, which, from time to time, I am putting into your charge. Let them have free circulation.   We have numerous accounts of religious tracts having been the means, *under God*, of showing the sinner the true state of his heart, and of producing in him a right mind.

Herewith are   covered tracts,
                                      four page do.
                                      Christian Almanack,

I will esteem it a favor, *occasionally*, to hear from you upon the subject of tracts ; the more especially, if any good effects from the reading, in any instance, are visible. I am very desirous that all the families in your neighborhood should *in turn* have the use of *all* you receive from me. May God's blessing accompany our labors in this cause ! I am, indeed, your well wisher for time and eternity, and very respectfully,

Your ob't servant,

PETER SMITH, *of Peterboro.*

Dear Sir — I now deposit with you, and under your particular charge ———— RELIGIOUS TRACTS. I beg the favor that you give ONE to each head of a family in your neighborhood, to teachers of schools, and to single persons not attached to a family, with request that they be read and exchanged, one for another, from time to time. Deliver them to such only as engage to make the exchange and entreat that the tracts be preserved neat and clean. You will keep a list of the names to whom tracts, *in the first instance,* are given and annex the same hereunto.

My intention is to continue this deposit, and occasionally to make additions to it ; especially, if you shall deem that so doing may be profitable. Hence I must beg that at the end of ——— you make report, in writing directed to me at ——— stating, as far as you are able to ascertain, the effects the tracts have produced, and any other facts you may think proper.

May the Lord prosper this the labor of our hands.

I am very respectfully,

Your friend and well wisher,

PETER SMITH.

Mr. Smith, on the 5th February, 1792, married Elizabeth, daughter of James Livingston, of Montgomery County. She was born in Lower Canada, May 18, 1773. Col. Livingston her father was born in New York, March 27, 1747. He was a graduate of Columbia College, and a lawyer in Montreal until the outbreak of the Revolutionary War, when he fled to the United States with three hundred men, and joined the American army. He was colonel of a New York regiment, fought against Sir William Johnson at Johnstown, and assisted Montgomery and Arnold in the assault on Quebec, leading the diversionary attack on Fort Diamond ; was at the head of his regiment when Burgoyne was taken, and shared in other actions of the war. His ancestors for four generations had lived in America, the first Livingston, Robert, coming in 1674. The Livingstons intermarried with the Van Rensselaers, the Schuylers, the Tenbroecks. The wife of Peter Smith was second cousin to Chancellor Livingston. She died in Utica, Aug. 27, 1818. Mr. Smith married a second time Sarah Pogson, of Charleston, S. C., a lady of English birth. Her tastes were literary, and more social than suited the reserved, taciturn and fractious man. The union was an unhappy one. The wife, after the experiment of an absence in England, finally left her husband and returned to her old home, where she died at an advanced age, after the close of the civil war. The references to her in Mr. Smith's letters to his son, indicate a bitterness of feeling that was long and keen, but give no clue either to the nature or the occasion of the alienation.

Judge Smith had six children ;—Cornelia Wyntje, Peter Skenandoah, Gerrit, and Adolphus Lent, were the only ones that reached maturity. All are now dead.

At the time of his first wife's death,—a woman for whom one at least of her children cherished a warm affection and had a tender reverence to the last of his life—Judge Smith became melancholy and disinclined to business. In October, 1819, he made arrangements to put out of his hands, into those of his second son, his whole estate real and personal, valued at about $400,000, on condition that his debts, amounting to $75,000 should be paid, that he should receive the income of $125,000, and that one half of the remainder should be divided equally among the children of his other son and the children of his daughter. This done, the active man, then scarcely past the prime of life, left the family mansion in Peterboro. In April, 1825, he took up his residence in Schenectady, where he died of heart disease, April 13, 1837. His second wife brought him no offspring. His last years were outwardly tranquil, but as a force he was no longer felt. The nick-name "The saw-mill" bestowed on him by the Indians, hardly applied to the quiet man, who, alone in his age, withdrew more and more within himself, brooding over the other world, which, in his active years, he felt he had too much neglected. He was far from happy. His frequent letters to Gerrit prove that the natural infirmities of his disposition increased when the pressure of active business was taken off. The same curious mixture of worldly with other worldly anxieties that characterized the journals, is prominent here, only the former are more peevish, and the latter more helpless. Complaints of loneliness, pious ejaculations, lamentations, regrets, reproaches, restless desires to be elsewhere, groans over the vanity of his life and of all life, morbid uneasiness about the health of his body and the destiny of his soul, remonstrances with Gerrit for giving too much to the missionaries, make strange confusion in the sentences. He was on the verge of hypochondria, a trouble to himself, and a vexation to those about him. The example of such a man is a warning to active men not to let go the practical interests which keep their powers in vigorous play. Most of all does the warning come home to those who need the weight of earthly affairs to counteract the illusions of fancy, and the teasings of an emotion that is untrained and unreconciled with the realities of human existence.

The fourth child of Peter Smith and Elizabeth his wife was born in Utica, March 6, 1797. About five years after, the family removed to Whitesboro, Oneida County. In January, 1806, Gerrit and his brother, accompanied by a domestic, Mary Thomas, went to Peterboro, Madison County. The rest of the family followed in February. On the first of January, 1813, the two brothers left home for the academy at Clinton, Oneida County, to spend some years in a course of education. Peter, in a year or two, went back to his home; but Gerrit, whose bent was intellectual, and in whose mental training his father seems to have taken a peculiar interest, encouraging especially his oratorical powers, staid in Clinton, entered Hamilton College, (an institution that grew out of the academy, and received its charter from the State in 1812,) and was graduated with honors in 1818, under the presidency of Rev. Henry Davis, the successor of Dr. Azel Backus, who had died two years before. On the day of graduation the class of twenty-three was reduced to ten. Smith delivered the valedictory oration, which was allowed a length of fifteen minutes, the other parts being limited to ten. In college Smith was an excellent scholar, not recluse, but faithful; he had a fine mind, interested in the newest letters and opinions, was an enthusiastic reader of the books of the period, especially the Letters of Junius, which were making a stir just then, a warm partisan in the discussions of the day, hospitable in his literary tastes, with a hearty appreciation of the best things in prose and verse and an enthusiastic sympathy with generous sentiments. It is quite likely he referred to himself when in after years he describes some who aspired to the fame of possessing genius, on the strength of " flowing hair and the broad Byron collar," the latter being one of his own peculiarities to the end of his life. As a youth he was remarkably handsome in person, the admiration of all beholders. His manners were open, his bearing was cordial, his action graceful and winning. His popularity was universal, and the social turn of his disposition carried him into the games, entertainments, collegiate and extra-collegiate amusements of his companions. He was gay and sportive, but never vicious, or in the vulgar sense, " wild." He was an innocent, joyous youth, not averse to noisy but harmless pranks, having no prejudice against a game of cards, but rather a passion for them. He records, himself, that in a club of card players " to which," he wrote afterwards, " it was my unhappiness and wickedness to belong," his nick-name was " Old Mariner," and that he played cards for stakes on Sunday. It is related that on one occasion when uproar was at its height, the tutor's ominous rap was heard at the door. There was another door at which the young rioters made hasty retreat. Smith remained, and flung himself, face downward, on the floor behind a desk. The tutor espied the prostrate form, and demanded an account of it. Who is it ? " Gerrit Smith, sir." Well, Smith, what are you about ? " Meditating on the mutations of empire." The tutor, not pausing for admonition, retired, professing briefly his satisfaction at finding Smith so profitably employed. The character he bore among his mates is indicated by an inscription on the fly leaf of a copy of Byron's

" Siege of Corinth," presented by his bosom friend, F. W. Haight, " to his sincere, affectionate, sentimental, poetic, ambitious, superior-minded, noble, generous, honest, honorable, jealous, deceitful, hoaxing, partial, epicurean, gambling Smith, as token of high esteem. Hamilton College, July 23, 1816." The piety that was so fervent in his later years, was not conspicuous in these college days. The son of a rich man, he dressed carefully, lived well, and was becomingly free in expense ; but it is not in the memory of his mates that he spent money in hurtful dissipations of any kind. It is clearly in their recollection that he detested meanness, niggardliness, selfishness, injustice ; that he invariably took the part of the weak against the strong, of the wronged against the wronger, of the oppressed against the oppressor, and never failed to win the hearts of the noble in soul. His destination was the profession of law, for which his abilities and general mental aptitudes peculiarly qualified him, but domestic events changed his career.

Mr. Smith's interest in Hamilton College continued hearty throughout his life ; so hearty that he could not bear to have it seem unfaithful to the highest concerns of education, and during the presidency of Dr Dwight—1833–1835—his discontent reached the point indicated by the following entry in his Journal. "*Aug.* 12, 1834. I went to Clinton to attend the meeting of the trustees of the college. Returned next day, not having remained to attend Commencement. Probably this is the last meeting of the trustees of the college which I shall attend." But in 1835, at the resignation of President Dwight, we find him proposing a plan for paying the debt on the institution, and loaning the college five thousand dollars for the scheme. He also accepts a place on the committee for obtaining a new president. The following letters tell their own story.

Hamilton College, Clinton, N. Y., April 22, 1872.

HON. GERRIT SMITH, LL.D.

My Dear Sir — I reached Clinton last week after an absence of eight months in Europe. One of my first walks was to our college cemetery, where I always find some good inspiration. I was pained to see the monument to President Backus is falling to pieces. It is a cheap and *hollow* structure, made of marble slabs. If it were durable, it would be wholly unfit to stand by the grave of a hero, whose solid greatness would be more fitly symbolized by solid granite.

How shall this wrong to the memory of our first and greatest President be righted? The college is so needy that the grave of its founder, Dominie Kirkland, still waits for an epitaph in marble. The monument to President Davis was erected by his son, Hon. Thomas T. Davis. It is costly, massive and permanent. The monuments to Dr. Noyes and Professor Catlin were erected by their executors.

You see whither I am drifting?

I write to ask if you could make a worthier use of five hundred or a thousand dollars, than to perpetuate the memory of Dr. Backus in marble or in granite? The inscriptions on the marble slabs now broken and crumbling are very appropriate. These could be transferred to the new monument. Then all who visit the cemetery would be spared the pain of seeing in the Backus monument a crumbling satire on the Scriptural promise that

" The righteous shall be in everlasting remembrance."

If I seem to be rude or intrusive in what I suggest, I beg you will forgive me and place it to the account of my reverence for one of

" The few immortal names that were not born to die."

With the highest esteem,

Yours very sincerely,

EDWARD NORTH.

Peterboro, April 24, 1872.

PROFESSOR NORTH,

My Dear Sir — Your esteemed letter of 22d instant came this evening. As I take the Utica Herald, I was aware of your visit to Europe and of your return to your home. I am sorry to learn of the bad condition and unfit material of President Backus' monument. I agree with you that there should be a solid structure in the place of it. I shall be willing to pay for it, if it be such a monument as meets my sense of fitness. It must be plain and simple and costing not more than five hundred dollars ($500), I have no sympathy with mourning apparel, nor with expensive coffins, nor with the display of wealth in gravestones.

Very respectfully your friend,

GERRIT SMITH.

Hamilton College, President's Room.

Clinton, Oneida Co., N. Y., February 19, 1874.

HON. GERRIT SMITH.

My Dear Sir — I have just received this evening, your letter of yesterday containing two checks of five hundred dollars each for the use of Hamilton College, and I cannot sleep without thanking you most sincerely for this most generous and timely gift. The college, I am sure, is worthy of the love of its friends. It has done already a great and good work for the State, and needs only somewhat better means and appliances to take a position still more advanced, one of which her sons may reasonably be proud. These means, my dear sir, your gift will help to furnish.

Let me thank you also personally, for without knowing it, you have done me a great service. None but those intimately acquainted with the necessities of the Institution, can understand the anxieties of those who have to bear, rather more directly than others, the burden of administering its affairs, a burden which you have done much to lighten.

Mrs. Brown and myself have both been greatly disappointed in not having been able to visit you, or to welcome you at our house. I trust that both these pleasures are yet in store for us.

Wishing you health and every prosperity, with much regard from Mrs. Brown as well as from myself,

I remain sincerely,

Your obliged friend and serv't,

S. G. BROWN.

Hamilton College, President's Room.

Clinton, Oneida Co., N. Y., Nov. 17, 1874.

HON. GERRIT SMITH.

My Dear Sir,—I hardly know in what terms to acknowledge your large-hearted liberality to Hamilton College, not more distinguished for its generosity, than for the kind, hopeful and affectionate words with which you accompany it. If the old proverb be true, *bis dat qui cito dat,* I think it is no less true that he who gives with the spirit of love doubles the value of his gift.

You are good enough to leave the disposition of your munificence to the trustees of the college. I do not know to what use they may think it wise to put it, but whatever it be, no one who loves the college can help remembering with gratitude the generous giver.

I am happy to add, my dear sir, that Mrs. Brown seems to be the better for her ride to Peterboro, and neither she nor my daughter, nor myself, shall soon forget our exceedingly pleasant trip. The rest of us are well. With affectionate regards from them all, I am,
Dear Sir, your greatly obliged friend
and ob't serv't,
S. G. BROWN.

The second of these letters is an acknowledgment of two subsequent cheques for five thousand dollars each, given without solicitation and without conditions, making in all twenty thousand dollars to the institution.

The day after his graduation, Aug. 27, 1818, his mother died. This brought him back to Peterboro, where he remained the rest of the year. On the 11th of January, 1819, he was married, in Rochester, to Wealthy Ann, the only daughter of Dr. Azel Backus, first president of Hamilton College. They had been engaged since the spring of 1817. This wife was taken from him by dropsy of the brain, on the 15th of August, 1819, seven months only after marriage. On the 3d of January, 1822, he was a second time married, to Ann Carroll, daughter of William Fitzhugh, who lived about four miles from Geneseo, Livingston County. She was born in Hagerstown, Maryland, January 11, 1805. Early in November, 1819, he had begun to keep house in the family mansion in Peterboro. At this time, his household consisted of his mother-in-law, her son Robert H. Backus, who was in his employ as clerk, and Laura Bosworth, who remained a member of the family for more than twenty years. Thus early in life began his household care, his personal sorrow and responsibilities and his abounding hospitality.

The arrangements above alluded to, by which his father placed in Gerrit's hands his whole estate, real and personal, under conditions that required the careful administration of a large property, decided his residence and occupation. He was to be a man of business. The act showed on his father's part a remarkable confidence in the young man's practical ability and personal integrity, and on the part of the son a consciousness of power, and a readiness to accept responsibility, not singular, it must be confessed, for many a youth jumps at opportunities he cannot· meet, and accepts trusts he lacks moral force to discharge—but in this instance, more than justified. From that hour the young man's career was determined. The necessities of business, the care of much land and of many people, the claims of kindred who were made dependent on him, duty to his father who trusted him so entirely, held him strictly to his locality. He could not wander from it for any purpose; he could not travel; he could not amuse himself. The life of enjoyment and dissipation was forbidden. Had he felt ever so keenly the young man's desire to see the world and taste its pleasures, he was as powerless to do so as the poorest man in the village. Remote from the small centres of American society; far from New York, far from Albany even, his days and years went on with noiseless unremitting energy, undistracted, unwasted. The talent for affairs which his sagacious father noticed, and which even his elder brother had to confess, was trained until he became, by the best testimony, one of the ablest business men in the country, by all admission, the most competent manager in the State. He was regular, exact, systematic, far sighted, bold and just. His working power was immense, and shrank from no burden that was laid upon it. The passion to acquire land which actuated his father, never possessed him in the same degree, though in early life he purchased largely. His purchases were never made with a view to accumulation, but to ensure profit from the rise in value of real estate, or to oblige debtors. The Michigan tract of six thousand acres bought in 1858, on account of James Backus, the brother of his first wife, was sold ten years afterwards, at a handsome advance. It cost six dollars an acre and brought thirty-two, more than five times as much ; but the taxes and other expenses during the ten years he held it, made the profits of the sale much less than these figures report. He was scarcely more than twenty-one years of age, when he bought eighteen thousand acres of land in Florence. In 1827, the State of New York, sold in lots at public auction, the site of the then village of Oswego, about a mile square on either side of the river, the Welland and Oswego canals being at the time nearly finished. The expectation that the canals would build up the little village of seven or eight hundred inhabitants into a thriving town, raised the price of the land, though the surrounding woods concealed much of it from any but speculative eyes. Mr. Smith was one of the largest purchasers on the east side of the river, where lots were valued one-third less than on the west side. The sum invested was not great, about fourteen thousand dollars ; but the purchase proved to be important. In a few

years his property equalled in valuation that on the opposite bank of the river, and half a million of dollars
would not buy what a few thousand secured at first. Soon
after this, the acute speculator bought nearly the whole
stock of the Oswego Hydraulic Canal Company, put the
canal in good order, leased the water privileges at low
rates, and in connection with his brother-in-law and
others built flour mills, which after a time changed
hands. In 1831–2, he improved what was called the
East Cove, a marshy, unwholesome district, for which,
after renting it several years from the town, he had paid
five thousand dollars, by digging a ship basin and ship
passage from the river.   The land purchased was sold in
lots. By October, 1835, all the property was sold at
moderate rates, except the canal and cove property.
Then began the disastrous speculations in real estate,
which carried away nearly every man in the town.   A
general bankruptcy followed, and a large portion of the
property which Mr. Smith disposed of in 1835, being but
partially paid for, fell back into his hands. The panic
of 1837 brought him to a strait pass.   An accumulation
of debt distressed him, and there seemed no way out of
bankruptcy, except by incurring new obligations.   The
large sum obtained of John Jacob Astor, mentioned
elsewhere, barely enabled him to pay interest and taxes,
leaving the principal undiminished.   He left his large
house, and retired to a smaller one called " The Grove,"
about a mile distant, reduced his establishment, called
on his wife and daughter to take the place in the
office of discharged clerks, and toiled terribly to
lift the burden—a heavy one at that time—of six
hundred thousand dollars. His predicament at this

period, is hinted at in a letter to his wife, dated
Dec. 11, 1839.

"Never, my dear wife, have I been reduced to such
straits in money matters. I have some fifteen hundred
debtors, but I receive almost literally nothing, and I
can borrow nothing. I shall find it difficult to keep you
and Libby at Philadelphia,—difficult even to get money
enough to visit you." The lands coming into the market
about 1843, gradually put him in funds; the debt was
rapidly reduced, and in 1850 was all paid. Misfortunes
never come singly; neither do persecutions. In 1837,
he had taken, in part payment of a very heavy debt
from a relative,—one hundred and seventy-five thousand
dollars,—a mortgage on an undivided fourth part of the
steamboat "St. Lawrence." It was good for nothing,
and had been put down as practically good for nothing,
a worthless piece of property. In the summer of 1844,
it happened, that the village of Sackett's Harbor took
fire, and was nearly destroyed. The fire began by
the lake, and soon after the "St. Lawrence" had left
the port; whence it was ingeniously surmised that a
spark from her smoke stack had done the damage. A
certain Mr. Dodge, well named, caught at the idea, and
brought suit against the owners of the boat, Mr. Smith
included, to recover the loss on his hotel. It was an
absurd suit, and was almost immediately dismissed.
But it cost time and lawyer's fees, and indefinite vexation
of mind. Counsel thought the case looked dark, quoted
the deceitful adage that where there is smoke there must
be fire, and advised a composition, even an assignment
of property! Poor Mr. Smith! he might have been
extinguished entirely, but for his own pluck. Of the

debt of one hundred and seventy-five thousand dollars, he recovered perhaps thirty or forty thousand.

The submarine improvement of " Grampus Bay,"— so called from the fate of the " Grampus " which disastrously went ashore there,—the building of six wharves, slips and a river pier, and the reconstruction of the dilapidated " East Pier,"—work begun in 1852 and completed in 1854 at a cost of nearly one hundred thousand dollars, quite doubled the value of wharf property in the city. Through his influence at Washington a custom house was established at Oswego, the third custom house in the State, and the Act of Canadian Reciprocity pressed by his friend Alvan Bronson, owed much to his instance, while in Washington. Thus by degrees the business interests were centered in Oswego, which became the principal source of his pecuniary supply. The income of course, varied much with changing seasons in the business world. The best average for twenty-five years was from fifty to sixty thousand dollars a year ; not an enormous income for these days, but very large thirty years ago. During the last ten years of his life, it was not far from eighty thousand dollars. The work of husbanding and securing all this was by no means light. Many hours daily were spent in the office with his clerks and books. It was his custom, in the busy period of his career, to devote to these affairs nine or ten hours a day ; often twelve or fifteen were no more than enough; for he superintended the whole, and performed much labor with his own hand. He was a model of minuteness and exactness, a model too, of fairness and consideration. The business agent in Oswego, who was in his service forty-three years, cannot recall a single unpleasant passage, or a single unkind word written or spoken to him in all that period of time. His openness of dealing is illustrated by such a public notice as the following, which was issued Nov. 22, 1849.

" *The Directors and Stockholders of the Canastota and Morrisville Plank Road Company,* and indeed, all other persons, are desired to feel themselves to be at perfect liberty to call at the office of Gerrit Smith and examine the maps, profiles and reports of the engineers who have been employed upon the several plank road routes between Morrisville and Canastota."

The only records he was not willing the public should examine were the records of his benefactions. His reputation for integrity in financial transactions could not be better illustrated than by the incident here related. The Journal of Aug. 10, 1837, contains this modest entry. " I this week receive a letter from my friend, and my father's friend, John Jacob Astor, in which he consents to loan me for a long period the large sum of money which I had applied for to him. This money will enable me to rid myself of pecuniary embarrassments, and to extend important assistance to others, and especially to extend indulgence to those who owe me. This is a great mercy of God to me. It relieves my mind of a great burden of anxiety. My pecuniary embarrassments, growing out of my liabilities for —— and out of my liabilities for, and advances to —— have often, and for hours together, filled me with painful concern." The sum requested was, in all, two hundred and fifty thousand dollars. The application, in general terms, was made by letter. The letter was answered by an invitation to dinner. As the two sat at meat, the

2*

host was full of reminiscences of former years when he went in search of skins with his guest's father, now little more than three months deceased. There was no talk of business till the cloth was removed, and the two were by themselves. Then the visitor opened a tale of distress which was short, but heavy. It was a season of panic. The banks had suspended specie payments and could afford only feeble and precarious relief. Business was at a stand-still; real estate had fallen to a nominal value; land was unproductive. The legal adviser and brother-in-law of Peter Smith, his son's counsellor too, urged an assignment of property for the benefit of the creditors. How much do you need? asked the millionaire. The visitor named the sum. Do you want the whole of it at once? I do. Astor looked grave for a moment, then said: "you shall have it." A mortgage was pledged on the Oswego purchase, made ten years before, and the relieved guest went home to Peterboro. Astor's cheque for two hundred and fifty thousand dollars came in a few days. The mortgage was executed and duly recorded, and Smith went on with his affairs. Here comes the most remarkable part of the transaction. The county clerk neglected to transmit the papers to Mr. Astor. Weeks elapsed, and Smith's part of the bargain was unfulfilled. A letter from New York, sent Mr. Smith to Oswego. The clerk's stupidity was reprimanded, and the papers, with satisfactory explanations, were sent to their proper destination. Mr. Astor had parted with a quarter of a million of dollars on the bare word of Gerrit Smith, and had been content with the bare word, for weeks !

To multitudes Gerrit Smith is vaguely known as the

man of wealth. Some think that without his wealth he
would not have been known at all, that his purse was his
power, that his fortune was his fame. That the wealth
was a most important factor, that it always is and must
be an important factor, it were idle to deny. It provides the material basis for character. It is opportunity, patronage, influence. The rich man is sure of a
hearing and a welcome. He can control the press; he
can maintain a press of his own; he can back his opinions with gold, and carry his policies with bounties. He
withdraws his support and enterprises fail; he lends his
aid and undertakings thrive. His argument prevails;
his jest is applauded; his frown is confusion; his smile
makes glad. Gerrit Smith had this power; had he not
possessed it, he certainly would not have occupied the
place he did. The remarkable thing is that possessing
the power he did occupy the place; that the wealth was
his help, not his ruin; that it was his opportunity not
his temptation; that it furnished a solid base for his intellectual and moral operations, not a grave in which his
manhood was buried; that he could wear the purple,
and still be a king. It must be a grand figure that looks
grand on a high pedestal.

Let it be granted that in the remoteness and seclusion of Peterboro he looked and felt larger than he would
have done in a city like New York. Let it be granted
that he *was* larger there than he would have been in
the city, by reason of the greater leisure allowed him,
and the exemption from wasting interruptions and the
dissipations of social life. All this is no prejudice to the
man, but it was his advantage. It did not make him, it
simply permitted him to be all he was meant to be; but

the spontaneous energy of mind which made him what he became, was all his own. Circumstances supply opportunity for this, but do not originate it. Most men require the excitement of stimulating conditions to provoke their latent vigor. They that can dispense with these, and grow in thin soil, are the few. Daniel Webster defined genius as the power to kindle one's own fires. The elm tree that stands in the field, apart, with all the air and soil there is for its sustenance, is not to be depreciated on this account; it can appropriate only what belongs to it, and its size and symmetry attest the fidelity of its obedience to the laws of its nature.

Let it be remembered too, that small places have their disadvantages as well as large ones. They feed conceit. So that the man's apparent gain from the solitariness of his position may be more than counter-balanced by the injury he suffers from the flattery of villagers. The small man will look, in the city, smaller than he is. In the country he will be smaller than he might be. The genuine man will prove his value by extracting virtue from whatever circumstances he may be thrown in. The circumstances will shape the form of the qualities and determine their proportion, but the manliness must decide the character. It is idle to discuss the relative advantages of social and private, of city and of country life. Either may make and either may mar the man. To grow great, or continue great in either is an achievement to be honored. The special type of greatness may be subject for comment, the greatness speaks for itself. The unique or peculiar man will distinguish himself wherever stationed. In large places he will be regarded

as an oddity, because so unlike the multitude about
him. The tall underbrush conceals from view his massive qualities. In the small place, his height will seem
to be greater than it is, but he will at least display his
full proportions.

CHAPTER II.

HEALTH.

THE promise " in health and wealth long to live "
was given to Gerrit Smith at his birth. He came of
strong, mixed races. His father's father and mother
were Low Dutch. His mother's father was half Dutch
and half Scotch ; his mother's mother was, though born
in Ireland, of Scotch parentage. In temperament he
might be classed with the sanguine-lymphatic, not a
fortunate combination, as a rule ; implying as it does the
union of great vitality, ardor, and swiftness of blood,
with a certain doggedness of purpose and moral obtuse-
ness which bode ill for elevation of aim or humanity of
achievement. In this instance, the confidence and elas-
ticity gained more than they lost from the alliance with
a resolute persistency that never knew discouragement,
and never confessed defeat. The frame was stately ; the
countenance noble ; the massive, well-proportioned head
was superbly set on broad shoulders ; the chest was
deep ; the face was expressive ; the eye was large and
brilliant ; the voice was sonorous and rich, remarkable
for compass, musicalness and power ; the brown hair,
worn long in youth, fell in strong masses over the collar,
which, open in front, displayed the round, smooth throat.
The man possessed the great advantages of stature and
weight. He was six feet in height. In 1865 he weighed

two hundred and one pounds, against George Thompson's one hundred and forty-six,—a difference that awakened reflections on the subject of light and heavy people. At the age of seventy, in mid-summer, in thinnest clothes, he weighed more than two hundred pounds, two hundred and eight pounds and a half. In his college youth, he was the image of health; a model of manly beauty and power. And so he always seemed to those who saw him in society or in public. They who knew him intimately in and after middle life were aware of physical ailments that would have pulled down a weaker man, and daunted a less resolute one.

In November, 1832, so the Diary records, he gave up the use of tea and coffee ; he had previously " abjured the castors," meaning spices and condiments. In March, 1835, he began a course of abstinence from " fish, flesh and gravies." On the following month all the products of slave labor were excluded from his diet. In 1840, when transcribing the journal of 1835, Mr. Smith remarks " I continue to abstain from flesh. I have, however, eaten fish very frequently during the last four years. For the last few months I have abstained almost entirely from fish and butter."

The reasons assigned for these rules are that they were deemed salutary to sedentary people, and that the supply of human food, consequently the increase of the human family, would be vastly augmented by the abandonment of flesh diet.

" The myriads of China could not be subsisted, if they were extensively flesh eating. God authorizes the eating of flesh. But it is an interesting question whether he would have us eat it now, when the world's population is so comparatively dense, and when the eating of it interferes with obedience to his command to multiply and replenish the earth. Canals and railways, by saving the necessity of much animal power,—say, millions of horses,—make great room for the increase of the human family. But how much more room would the relinquishment of flesh food afford ! "

That the adoption of these practices was harmful is not here asserted. The ailments just alluded to may have been due to the confinement of a laborious and sedentary life ; some of them tormented his father, and were probably ancestral inheritances ; the most agonizing of all clearly was. A youth less confined and harassed might have eluded them. As it was, his occupations furnished the conditions for their early manifestation. It is interesting to note that signs of weakness and illness occur in close connection with the asceticism. The brief diary makes distinct records of sickness and disease for almost every year between 1836 and 1863. Not ten times is the mention omitted. Severe colds and rheumatism ; feverish attacks, giddiness, are often spoken of. Surgical operations at home, in Philadelphia, New York ; for hydrocele, hemorrhoids, tumor in the back, hernia, caused great suffering and weeks of confinement. Applications of blisters and ointments severely tried his patience and fortitude. In June, 1839, the moxa was applied to the back to correct a weakness which he feared might imply or involve a curvature of the spine. For several years,—from 1842 to 1847,—the condition of his eyes was unsatisfactory; cataract was predicted ; he himself apprehended complete or partial blindness. At the most important public crisis of his life, the congressional episode, the rush of blood to the head troubled him so greatly that he kept his place with difficulty, and was all but compelled to desist from his meditated purpose. The following letter is of interest in this connection.

Philadelphia, Nov. 29, 1853.

D. H. FROST.

My Dear Sir—Although it is a fortnight since I left home, I am but so far on my way to Washington. I mean to be there at the opening of the session; but it is very far from certain that I shall take my seat in Congress at that time.

The disease in my head continues unabated. My New York physicians (how justly I do not know) believe it is a consequence of the surgical operation to which I submitted last summer. That skilful operation relieved me entirely of a painful disease; but it is perhaps a worse one which has now come upon me. However this may be, I am, at least for the present, disqualified for reading or writing or public speaking.

I do not intend to resign my office immediately. I presume that my constituents would prefer my holding to it for a month or two longer, in the expectation that, during this time, my health may be either so improved as to allow me to engage in the duties of my office, or so much worse as to make it my obvious duty to resign it.

Excuse my brevity. The sensations in my drumming head make it no small task for me to write even so short a letter as this.

Your friend,

GERRIT SMITH.

Fifteen years before this, Mr. Smith had doubted whether his bodily ailments and business occupations would permit him to attend public meetings, or make speeches any more. Ten years earlier still, his friend, Theodore D. Weld, expressed deep concern about his health, and recommended a mode of treatment for spinal affections, which had proved efficacious in cases of his own knowledge. In 1840, he thanks Elizur Wright for a warm-hearted letter, " a cordial to my spirits, which are sometimes a little depressed by my long confinement with sickness ;" tells him that he has been in the hands of his physician for seven weeks, and expects to be for

some weeks more. Gerrit Smith did not welcome sickness. Pain he shrank from and faced unwillingly. It is
possible that his extreme sensibility to it increased the
dread of it, and gave rise to morbid fears of danger,
though nothing of this appears in the brief mentions he
makes of his sicknesses, in his diary. That he was a sufferer from local disease, that he lost much time through
it, and was considerably weakened in force by it, may be
set down as certain. How often the infirmities of the
body baffle and hinder the man's purpose and energy!
How common it is to disregard their effect! We read
history, as if the actors on the scene were exempt from
ill; as if headache and dyspepsia were things unknown;
as if food was always digested and sleep never lost; and
when the man fails to justify himself in an emergency,
we ascribe the failure to lack of genius or valor, whereas,
were the truth known, both genius and valor never shone
more brilliantly than in the effort to contend against
some nervous disorder which undermined the moral
power, and balked the foresight of the intellect. Is it

> Strange that a harp of thousand strings
> Should keep in tune so long?

It is equally strange that a harp so easily put out of
tune, should give forth the noble music it does. Some
have ascribed Mr. Smith's impaired constitution to an
ascetic and notional way of living. But those who knew
him most intimately did not. He himself was certain, that
to features of it, its simplicity and temperance, he owed
his life at critical periods; and so it may have been. He
was no ascetic in the ordinary sense of the term. He
practiced a generous diet such as it was, ate as much as

he wanted, and what he thought agreed with him best. He knew what health was worth, for he wasted no moment of it. Had he known how to obtain more, or how to heighten what he had, he was not the man to let pleasure or whim stand in the way of such a privilege. Life to him was more than meat.

CHAPTER III.

RELIGION.

To understand the character and life of Gerrit Smith, it is necessary to have a clear view of the religious principles on which he built. His early years gave no signs of spiritual emotion. Though free from stain, kind, friendly, generous and just, he was not distinguished for the personal consecration to impersonal objects, which was so remarkable a feature in his manly career. But from his father he inherited a quick religious sensibility, which declared itself as soon as the call for it came. On March 17th, 1826, so the Diary informs us, he and his wife connected themselves with the Presbyterian church in Peterboro, making public profession of their faith in Jesus Christ as their God and Saviour. He had already for one year, acted as superintendent of the Sunday school. The journal which he began in 1826 contained, he remarks, nearly all the texts of the sermons he had heard, for thirteen years. In 1839, this journal, which covered upwards of four hundred pages, was condensed into less than a quarter the space; was made, in fact, exceedingly curt and dry; yet even then, the space given to sermon texts, names of preachers, Sabbath incidents, records of conference and prayer meetings, is out of all proportion to that given to any other subject. Expressions of religious feeling similar to those quoted from his father's diary, are of very frequent recurrence. A few are given to illustrate this peculiar element of character.

April 3, 1828, " She was prepared to die. In the whole circle of our friends, there was not one person more precious and estimable than herself. Her religion was emphatically the religion of Jesus. It exalted the Saviour and abased the sinner. It made rèdeeming love all in all. She was eminently a woman of prayer."

September 14, 1828, " The first Sabbath after they left us, they spent on their way from Albany to New York, and now they have profaned a great part of this holy day. May I truly lament this sin in members of my family ! "

January 7, 1833, " Our church assembled agreeably to the re-commendation of the General Assembly. The day was observed by us as a day of fasting and prayer for the conversion of the world."

January 16.—" I, this Wednesday, attended the church confer-ence. It was a solemn meeting. The question considered was, whether we would set about promoting a revival of religion."

March 6, 1834, " This Friday evening, my dear wife and I, under a sense of our sins, resolved to spend the following day in fasting and prayer and searchings of heart."

April 6, " The past week has been a week of great mercies to our church, of great humblings of heart, of sincere repentance, of many confessing to God and man. My dear son manifested yester-day more religious tenderness, more concern for his soul than I ever knew him to do before. He even hopes that he is a Christian. O God, leave him not to fall under delusion, but may his hope be a good hope through grace."

April 10, " The protracted meeting closed this afternoon. It has been a season of great mercy to many out of, as well as in the church. I suppose that upwards of one hundred persons have taken the ' anxious seats.'—Probably not more than one-fourth of them have obtained consolation in Christ, but many of the others are very serious."

February 10, 1835, " I find that my dear wife has had great struggles with sin and Satan during my absence. But the Lord has, in His great goodness, brought her triumphant out of them, and she has now more Christian confidence and peace than she has had at any previous time for years."

September 6, " I fear that I have lost that increased interest in religion which the death of my dear baby was the occasion of producing in me."

April 21, 1836, "How deficient is my interest in the Bible! Since my dear baby's death, I have not allowed myself to read on the Sabbath any other book than the Bible, excepting sermons in church, or, occasionally and unavoidably, a few paragraphs. Still, how little relish I have for the pages of God's Book!"

April 4, 1837, "Previous to my leaving home, there were indications that the Lord was about to revive his work among us. The expected blessing has come. During my absence a shower of grace has fallen on this village and neighborhood. It is supposed that not less than sixty have found the Saviour precious. Amongst them is ——, who has been a member of my family for six months. Thus is salvation again brought to my house."

Aug. 5, 1848, "In the interval of worship Mr. and Mrs. B ——, my dear wife and I were baptized. Mrs. B. was sprinkled, and the others were immersed. Though sprinkled in infancy, I had not, either in the judgment of Baptists or Pedobaptists, been baptized,— neither of my parents being pious at that time."

Nov. 1857, "I am an unspeakable debtor to God for my recovery from this painful and perilous sickness. Oh, that it might be proved that I am a still greater debtor to Him for my religious thoughts and purposes and many prayers during my sickness. This can be proved only by my better heart and better life."

Notes of like import occur to the end. Thus on *March* 6, 1871, he writes: "I am this day seventy-four years old. I thank my Heavenly Father for having spared me another year. I have not spent it as I should have done. I still feel that I need to be born again. My love of God and my love of man are both weak."

March 6, 1873, "I this day complete my seventy-sixth year, and yet, as I feel, my heart is not right in the sight of God."

May 19, 1874, "Black Friday was the name that the money changers gave two or three years ago to a certain day in New York. Friday the 15th inst. was my Black Friday. That Friday night my sins pressed heavily upon my conscience, and I got very little sleep."

No event of close personal application is mentioned without some suggestion of religious feeling; and pious usage to the last accompanied pious expression. The Sabbath was conscientiously observed. The Bible was diligently read; family prayer was constantly practiced. The custom of attending church, and interesting himself in evangelical movements stayed by to the last. A pious minister of the Methodist Episcopal Church, assigned to the parish at Peterboro in 1873, recalls with warm emotion Mr. Smith's presence and demeanor at the Lord's Supper, his devout manner of conducting service in his own free chapel, his grave dignity in rebuking unseemly harshness and looseness of speech in meetings for religious discussion, the evangelical tone of his occasional addresses at the Methodist meetings, his faithfulness and gentleness as superintendent of the Sunday School, his reverence for the character, and estimate of the mission of Jesus, his constant effort to impress on the young the type of goodness presented in the New Testament, the glowing testimonies borne on all occasions to the indebtedness of man, not to God alone, but to the only being worthy to be called His Son. They who have known Mr. Smith at home, bear out the witness of the good clergyman. No feature of that remarkable household was so impressive as its deep, living piety. The bible selection, recited from memory, the simple petition spoken with bowed head and tremulous voice, the tender spirit of trust and aspiration, are sweet memories in the minds of even unreligious people. Over his chamber door hung a framed tablet on which was embroidered the sentence " God is Love," and near the door was a roll of bible texts, called " The Silent Comforter," so placed that his eye fell on it as he went in and out, and caught a lesson of strength or consolation. The man's piety was simple, unaffected, unreserved. When the flood of feeling came

in, it bore him easily over all the barriers of mental misgiving, and made him at home in the company of those
whose life was wholly absorbed in God. In early life he
was scrupulous to comply with all the requirements of legal righteousness, in the observance of times and seasons.
He was a strict sabbatarian. He lent an ear to the
figurative arguments of the Millenarians, and was inclined to try whatever experiments in faith and practice
each new apostle might propose. In 1832, he attends
a public prayer meeting against cholera. In 1844, he
anticipates a near end of the world.

Peterboro, Oct. 21, 1844.   Monday Ev'g half past 8.

My Dearly Beloved,—We have just had family worship—perhaps
for the last time. To-day's mail brought me four copies of the extra Midnight Cry. It declares that the world will end at three to-
morrow morning. The Midnight Cry which came to-day says that
time may possibly continue until the 23d or even the 24th. There
are precious things in this number. I have read it this evening
with unusual solemnity and tenderness and prayer. . .

I know not my dear Nancy, that we shall meet in the air. You
will be there—for you have long loved and served your Saviour. I
cast myself on his mercy, like the thief on the Cross. I seek his
salvation, though it is in the last hour. And how my eyes have
flowed at the welcome thought that we shall meet our dear Fitzhugh
and Nanny! Oh, the treasures of religion! How mad have I
been to make so little account of them!

The sincerity of the piety it was that made him
break with pious organizations. There is no radicalism
like that of the spirit that is fully alive to real things.
Gerrit Smith's devoutness was rooted in his natural
heart and could not be transplanted. He took religion
seriously, held himself and others to their vows. In
1829, his reverence for the Sabbath impelled him to
draw up a petition to the Congress of the United States
praying that the laws regulating the post-office depart-

ment might be so amended, as not to require the transmission of the mail and the opening of the post-offices on the Lord's Day. The petition closes with these impassioned sentences.

" Essential as the Sabbath is, in the affairs of this life, it is, in relation to the things of the life to come, and in its office to prepare us for the blessedness beyond the grave, unspeakably more important. It is God's holy day ; and it is His own voice which commands us to ' remember it to keep it holy.' It is a day to be spent in the religious service of Him who declares that ' the kingdom and nation that will not serve Him shall perish.' Let us conjure you then, by the memory of those holy men who planted this nation, because they preferred the savage wilderness to a land of profaned Sabbaths and corrupted Christianity ; by the memory of our fathers, whose piety, as emphatically as their wisdom and blood, contributed to secure the independence, and to frame the government under which we live ; by your regard for the hundreds of thousands of your constituents, to whose religious faith the Sabbath is even more dear than their lives ; and lastly let us conjure you by that final accountability, which will be no less rigid in the public and official, than in the private acts of men, to spare the Sabbath, and the inestimable temporal and eternal blessings that are bound up in it."

This was quite consistent with the belief that the Sabbath was of divine ordinance, however uncomfortable to luxurious Christians who would worship both God and Mammon by driving to church in private carriages, or by spending the hours between services in reading business letters. He took his religion seriously.

The same stern consistency dictated this bible Christian's conduct on the question of excluding the Bible from the public schools. In December of 1869, he printed and distributed a sheet on " The Common School Compromise," in which occurs this sentence:

" The billows of agitation are rising fearfully high ; and in order to sink them to repose, the Bible, like another Jonah, must be

3

thrown overboard. Since it is rending the school, it must, like the evil spirits of old, undergo exorcism. . . . Surely, surely, the loss in such a compromise would be greater than should be incurred. The poor sort of peace which the school would get in exchange for the Bible would not pay for the loss. . . But it is said that the school will fall if the Bible is allowed to remain in it. Then let it fall. However great might be this loss, it nevertheless can be better afforded than the insulting of God by singling out this book, and this only for expulsion from the school. But must not our children be educated ? Not in a school which proscribes the Bible."

In 1873, he returned to the subject in another sheet entitled, " No School and State, as well as no Church and State," and there repeated the sentiment in almost the same words.

" Any institution may be regarded as near its end when to prolong its life it falls to compromising. One of these proposed compromises is to forego prayer in the school. Another is to forbid all religious teaching in it, and especially to exclude the Bible from it. Nothing could justify the ostracising of Shakespeare and Milton from the schools, still less can anything justify the ostracising of the Bible from it. For admitting all that may be said of the errors in the Bible, no other book equals it in specimens of the truest eloquence, and in the wisdom and purity of its precepts."

The last clause shows how the heart could be tenacious of positions which the head abandoned ; the concession that there might be error in the Bible, being fatal to the chief argument in favor of retaining it, namely, that it was " God's book." Mr. Matthew Arnold's doctrine that the Bible is invaluable as literature, had not, at this time, become familiar.

Mr. Smith was early brought to see and condemn the evils of sectarianism. Among the first entries in the journal is the following :

October 12, 1828, " The church have resolved to meet Wednes day next to consider the subject of intemperance, and to take such steps regarding this vice as shall appear proper."

October 16, " Agreeably to appointment, a number of the members of our church met this Wednesday, and discussed the subject of intemperance. I presented a paper which binds the subscribers to abstain totally from drinking ardent spirits except in cases of sickness. It was signed by all present but two."

October 19, " I find that many members of our church are opposed to our measures for suppressing intemperance. Their eyes are not yet opened to the nature and magnitude of the evil. Oh, that God would give us all a spirit to inquire of Him what is our duty in this matter."

It was Mr. Smith's habit to preserve in scrap books everything he printed in papers, whatever the substance or form. In the first of these volumes is the following remarkable letter:

Peterboro, June 22, 1839.

REV. LUTHER MYRICK :

My Dear Sir—Instances are continually occurring to remind us of the evil influences of sectarianism in the church of Christ, and to strengthen the desire for the abolition of all religious sects.

One of these instances is the disposition which was recently made of the slavery question by the New School General Assembly. It will not be denied that a majority of the members of that Assembly believed that American slavery is sin—enormous, heavendaring sin. Why then did they refuse to declare this to be its character? The debates of the Assembly on the question of slavery show why. They conclusively show, that, whilst as men, as abolitionists, and as Christians, the majority of the members were ready to ascribe to slavery its own awfully and transcendently wicked character ; nevertheless as Presbyterians, they were not. The debates show, in other words, that the Assembly were willing to merge their humanity, their morals and their religion in their Presbyterianism. They had the Presbyterian church and the New School General Assembly to take care of ; and they were just starting on a new career of glory to God and advantage to man. That they should, in these circumstances, make a declaration of the sinfulness of slavery —that they should freight their scarcely righted New School Presbyterian ship with odious abolition—in a word, that they should exceedingly prejudice their cause in the very outset—all this seemed in their eyes most inexpedient. It was in this wise, that they conferred with flesh and blood, leaned to their own understanding, instead of trusting in the Lord with all their hearts, took counsel of expediency, and, as a matter of course, came to the conclusion, that they would " suffer sin upon " their countrymen, and refuse to " cry aloud and spare not, and show the people their transgression, and the house of Jacob their sins."

I will mention another instance, in which good men have suffered their concern for a sect to control their Christianity and Abolitionism. In the Anti-slavery Convention held at Auburn the present week, I referred to this dereliction of principle in the New School Assembly to illustrate the corruption which the doctrines of expediency have wrought in the American church. I did not take the ground, that the Assembly was bound to discuss the question of slavery. For the sake of the argument, I yielded, (what truth forbids) that it was not. But I insisted, that, having agreed to discuss it, they were traitorous to the cause of truth, for refusing to express their opinion of its moral character—as much so, I said, as I should be, if, having consented to discuss the subject of intemperance, I should confine myself to the economical and political bearings of the vice, and refuse to declare its wickedness. I might have said, more so, since it is expected of ecclesiastical bodies, when they discuss the merits of an institution or practice, that they will pronounce, not only mainly, but almost, if not quite, exclusively, on its moral character. I might also have said, that their omission to decide upon the moral character of slavery implies that, in the judgment of the Assembly, slavery is not condemned of God.

Now, will you believe it, that some of the dear, ay and of the very dearest of the brethren in the convention, were greatly pained at my complaints of the New School Assembly? Will you believe it, that they even justified the Assembly? " What," say you, " Abolitionists justify it ! and that too, in an anti-slavery convention ! '

It is even so, notwithstanding the cause of humanity is bleeding and dying for the lack of the testimony of our ecclesiastical bodies against the wickedness of slavery ; there are, nevertheless, good men, good Abolitionists too, who justify the withholding of that testimony.

Do you ask me whether any Baptists or Methodists were pained at my censures? None, so far as I know. Though had I visited similar censures on Baptists and Methodists, there would very probably have been Baptist and Methodist murmurs. I believe none but Presbyterians, and they of the New School only, were grieved at my plain dealing.

I need not say, that it made my heart sad to see the dear men, who were dissatisfied with me, suffering their religion, their love of impartial and universal liberty, and their very manhood, to bow to their sectarianism. The Lord hasten the time for the breaking of all party cords in the church! The word can never have free course and be glorified in the midst of sectarian predilections. Baptists, Methodists, Presbyterians, Episcopalians, etc. etc., must embrace a common and unsectarian Christianity, before they will permit the truth to do its perfect work.

One thing more. What right have they to present themselves as ethical instructors and spiritual advisers, who have not the discernment to see, nor the honesty to say, that slavery is sin? Common sense revolts at the attachment of authority or the manifestation of respect to any of the opinions of an ecclesiastical assembly, that refuses to pronounce as sinful the system which forbids marriage and the reading of the Bible, and that markets men, women and children as beasts. Whether the refusal proceeds from ignorance or dishonesty, it equally argues the unfitness of those who are guilty of it, to be our religious teachers.

I trust you will not suppose from what I have said, that I have less respect for the New School Assembly, than I have for the Baptist National Convention, or the Methodist General Conference, or other ecclesiastical bodies. Least of all, would I have you think, that I hold it in less esteem than I do the Old School Assembly. It was creditable to the New School Assembly to discuss the question of slavery. But, on the other hand, there is no term of reproach too severe to bestow on that Resolution of the rival Assembly, which as it commends to the support of the churches that wicked and infamous society, whose leading doctrine is, that perpetual slavery is to be preferred to unconditional and immediate emancipation, does virtually sanction slavery.

Your friend and brother,
GERRIT SMITH.

How vital this matter is becoming appears from the ensuing note in the journal of May 7, 1843.

Sabbath morning. "I did not attend the preparatory lecture yesterday, and I do not propose to partake to-day of the Lord's Supper. I have come to the conclusion that the company of men and women with whom I formerly worshipped, do not perform the office, and exhibit the character of a Church of Christ. It has long been a grief to me that they preferred their sectarianism to Christian Union. I was amazed that the churches of Peterboro should show themselves to be no better than the world in respect to the mob which disgraced Peterboro last summer. But still I could not bring myself to look upon the Presbyterian Church of Peterboro as not a Church of Jesus Christ. Last fall, however, and the early part of the winter, it was urged to pass resolutions against slavery and intemperance and forbore to do so. I then inquired of my heart: can the Presbyterian Church of Peterboro be such a company of reformers,—such a ' light of the world,'—such a ' city set on a hill,' as a true Church of Christ must necessarily be?—and long since my heart has answered: It cannot be. It is distinguished indeed, from the world in that it statedly prays, sings holy songs, and listens to sermons. But is this distinction sufficient to prove that its spirit is not the spirit of the world and that it is a Church of Jesus Christ? It surely is not.

" I trust that it is in no spirit of self-righteousness that I have separated myself from my fellow worshippers, ' I know I'm guilty,—know I'm vile.' There is no part of my life,—not a day—not an hour—on which I look back with complacency. I know, too, that there are precious friends of God in that church; and when I say that collectively, they do not resemble and do not perform the office of a Church of Christ, I wish not to be understood as condemning this, or that, or the other member of the church. If it be said that it does not become one whose sins are so numerous and aggravated as mine, to condemn a church, my answer is that the fact that my sins are already so numerous and aggravated is a sufficient reason why I should not add another to them,—especially the great sin of countenancing as a Church of Christ, that which, in my heart, I do not believe is a Church of Christ.

" I shall here mention that one of the greatest trials of my heart, in respect to the Presbyterian Church in Peterboro, is its continued, though oft remonstrated against connection with the General Assembly,—a body so exceedingly wicked as deliberately to refuse to say that slavery is sin. I must not omit to mention that the dismission of Mr. —— for no other reason, as I think, than his faithful preaching on slavery, intemperance and some other sins, argues strongly against the character of the church."

Many years later, writing in 1865 about the rebellion, he said:

" We need a better religion. Our laws have been on the side of oppression. Our religion has gone to the polls and voted for the buyers and sellers of men. How shall we get better laws and a better religion? Only by getting juster and higher conceptions of the dignity and grandeur and sacredness of man. Our laws and our religion will conform precisely to those conceptions. Contemptible will be the laws and religion of every people, who think contemptuously of man. But beautiful and blessed will be the laws and religion which reverence human nature, even when in its lowest condition—even when in ignorance and rags and chains. This is the religion which Jesus taught."

The evils resulting from sectarianism struck deep, and roused in him the reformer's zeal.

Dec. 29, 1840, " This, Tuesday evening, some sixty persons met in the session room. Elder Maddock opened with prayer. Captain Myers was appointed chairman and Loring Fowler secretary. Rev. Mr. Schofield was not present. He is unwilling to countenance it. Introduced the following series of resolutions.

1. " Whereas the Bible teaches that the union, the oneness of Christians is important ;—even so important that the world might be convinced by it that Jesus is sent of God, and that his disciples are beloved of God ;—Resolved, therefore, that the division of Christians into rival sects or parties is unscriptural and wicked.

2. " Whereas the Bible teaches that a person who is rightfully excluded from the fellowship of a Church of Christ should no longer be regarded as a Christian,—Resolved, therefore, that it is manifestly anti-bible to exclude from such fellowship or to receive into it any person who is admitted to be a Christian.

3. " Resolved, that Christians have but to adopt and carry out the obviously true propositions of the foregoing resolutions, and a common christianity and a common church would take the place of the Methodist and Presbyterian and Baptist and other sects which now divide and afflict and corrupt Zion."

These resolutions were discussed at frequent meetings and found more or less favor, but were never adopted. No church was ready for so radical a reform as they implied. Outside of Peterboro the mover of them received such welcome as usually awaits the reformer. This, from the " Presbyterian " of Philadelphia, is an example :

"Gerrit Smith's anti-sect meeting has just been held in Oswego, New York, and resolutions denouncing the churches of every name were adopted. Beyond that, it was of course, impossible to go, as it would not be strictly consistent to form a new sect on the ground of hostility to all sects. Mr. Smith made a strenuous effort to get the convention to avow his peculiar views on the subject of slavery, war, etc. ; but the most of the members thought it best to confine themselves to the single business of breaking down church walls. The following resolution was discussed by several Presbyterian, Baptist, Unitarian, and Universalist clergymen and laymen ; the two latter sects in its favor, the two former against it. The Rev. William Max, Gerrit Smith, and an old Quaker, named McClintock, spoke in the affirmative and it was passed.

"Resolved, that the Gospel of Jesus Christ makes abundant provision for the closer and closer union of His disciples with each other ; but makes none at all for their separation from each other ; and that the dividing of Christians into parties and sects does no less violence to that mythical body of which they are all members, than it does to the natural or literal body by tearing asunder its constituent parts."

"We do not know an instance in which is exhibited with more clearness and melancholy interest, the downward tendency of ultra-ism than is afforded in the case of Gerrit Smith. We remember well when he was an eloquent and powerful advocate of every good cause, a noble philanthropist and a leading man. Possessed of a large fortune, a commanding person, and a persuasive eloquence, with a generous spirit and a warm heart, he was evidently endowed with the gifts essential to the highest degree of success in the path of usefulness and honor which he had marked out for himself. Probably the impulses of his benevolence were too strong for his judgment, and he was consumed in his own zeal. He was naturally an enthusiast ; he soon became fanatical. And of late years there has scarcely been a scheme of moral reform too visionary for his adoption and patronage. A Sabbath lecturer on political abolition, and an anti-church preacher on week-days, he now devotes his wealth and his mind to the overthrow of institutions that he once regarded with the most filial reverence and devoted love.

"Such a career is worth looking at. It affords a sad illustration of the instability of man, and of the power of truth. What has Mr. Smith done during the years of his war upon the churches of God ? He has made himself conspicuous as a beacon ; but what good has he done ? We might also ask, what harm has he done ? Have any of the people believed on him? We do not ask if any of the rulers; but have the people been led away by him? In the midst of a region where fanaticism has flourished, he is comparatively alone. Few, if any, will be persuaded to adopt his vagaries, and he himself may yet be brought to see the folly of the views he sought to propagate. It is painful to contemplate such a career as his, and yet we have no doubt that God will take care of his own cause, and make even the efforts of such men to result in the establishment of truth and the furtherance of His own glory."

Mr. Smith has this clipping in his scrap book. It is without date.

The 29th day of November, 1843, was observed as a day of fasting and prayer by persons of Peterboro and vicinity who believed that the Christians therein did, —merely by force of divine organization, all human arrangements to the contrary notwithstanding, simply because they were Christians,—constitute "The Church of Peterboro." In the afternoon they held a public meeting in the session room in Peterboro, and spent the time in prayer, reading the bible, singing and conversation. A statement of principles and resolutions was submitted to the meeting, with the request that they should be made the subject of earnest thought, conversation and prayer until the time for definite action on them. The meeting was adjourned to the second day of December. On that day, after deliberation and prayer, the statement and resolutions were read, commented on, and unanimously adopted. Near the close of the meeting the request was made that all who, approving the principles and the language in which they were expressed, believed themselves to be members of "The Church of Peterboro," would give their names to the secretary of the meeting. The following is the statement of principles:

3*

" We learn from the Holy Scriptures, which are the only infallible guide in all questions of morality and religion, that Christian and church relations spring not from external fellowship and human arrangements, but from the union of those who are the subjects of such relations with Jesus Christ. who is 'the Head of the body, the church.' (Col. i. 18 : Eph. ii. 20 : iv. 15, 16 : v. 23, 30 : John xv. 5 : 1 Peter ii. 4, 5, 6 : Rom. vii. 4 : xii. 4, 5.) Hence we believe that the Church of Christ on earth is composed of all the Christians on earth ; that the Church of Christ in any nation is composed of all the Christians in such nation ; and that the Church of Christ in any smaller community, even down to a single family, (Rom. xvi. 5 : 1 Corin. xvi. 19 :) is composed of all the Christians in such community. Thus believing, we declare that the Christians of Peterboro and its vicinity compose a church ; and that following apostolic usage, we may properly call it ' THE CHURCH OF PETERBORO.' The propriety of this name, and also the propriety of declaring that *all* the Christians of a given locality constitute the church of said locality, are justified by the following and other texts : Rom. i. 7 : 1 Cor. i. 2 : Eph. i. 1 : Phil. i. 1 connected with Phil. 10. 15 : Col. 1. 2 : in 2d and 3d Rev. ' church of Ephesus,'' etc., etc. As a consequence of the beliefs which we have expressed, we acknowledge ourselves bound, not to vote into our local Church, for we can neither vote into it nor vote out of it, but bound to recognize as a member of it any person within our territorial limits who affords satisfactory evidence that he is a disciple and friend of Christ, and bound too, to do this even in the case of those who do not consent to our thus recognizing them, and even in the case of those who, in their doctrines and practices, or both, are peculiar, unscriptural, blameworthy be it whatever extent it may ; and the consequence of the beliefs which we have expressed is, that whilst we are to maintain a strict church discipline, and to admonish and rebuke each other as occasion may call for such fidelity, we are to deem no persons worthy of being disfellowshipped by us, but those whom we have ceased to regard as Christians "

And here are the resolutions that accompanied the statement and were adopted with it.

RESOLUTIONS.

1st. *Resolved*, That ———, ———-, be deacons of this church.

2d. *Resolved*, That Samuel Wells, of Vernon, is affectionately invited to remove into this community, and thereby become a memb of this church ; and that in the event of such removal, he be expected to officiate as its elder or bishop, and to assume that share of instructing and feeding it, which is appropriate to one whom the Holy Ghost hath made an overseer, (Acts xx. 28).

3d. *Resolved*, That in view of the abundant means of living in this neighborhood, we hope our elder may always be in circumstances to give himself " continually to prayer and to the ministry of the word." (Acts vi. 4.) But, whether such shall be his circumstances, or whether he shall be compelled to " labor, working with his own hands," (1st Cor. iv. 12), we can not without guiltily shutting our eyes to the glaring evils of the practice of subscribing salaries to preachers of the gospel, promise him a salary. We trust that contributions in money will be made in our place of worship from Sabbath to Sabbath, and that the deacons, in their appropriation of these contributions—a part to this needy disciple and a part to that—a part to one object and a part to another—will pay especial and constant regard to the wants of the elder and his family.

4th. *Resolved*, That the elder be expected to keep an account of all the contributions, whether in money or otherwise, which shall be made to him by his church and congregation, and that he be expected to make a public and full report thereof, at the expiration of every three months.

5th. *Resolved*, That for the edification both of its members and others, for the honoring and establishing of the truth—this church will, as there shall be occasion for it, express its convictions in relation to doctrines and practices.

6th. *Resolved*, That a Church of Christ is a company of moral reformers ; and, therefore, that a church which refuses to engage in the prosecution of moral reforms, especially those that are nearest at hand and most urgent, is, however excellent may be the character of individuals in it, not a Church of Christ.

7th. *Resolved*, That sectarianism, guilty as it so clearly is of rending the seamless garment (John xix. 23) of the Saviour—of dividing the Church of Christ into mutually warring parties—of tearing asunder those who should esteem themselves to " be one," even as the Father and the Son " are one " (John xvii. 22) ; guilty also, as it so clearly is, of making the strongest and most successful appeals to the pride, bigotry, and intolerance of the heart ; is, therefore, the mightiest foe on earth to truth and reform, to God and man ; that is, in its features and spirit, one of the most marked children of its " father, the Devil."

8th. Whereas there is a prevailing delusion, that a Union Church requires a surrender of private judgment and a compromise of truth ; and that but for this surrender and compromise, the contentions in such church would be too great to be endured : *Resolved*, therefore, that the members of a Union or Gospel Church are not only free to entertain their respective views, both of doctrine and practice, but are bound to inculcate them on their brethren, and to rebuke the rejection of them ; Resolved, further, that while, on the one hand, such freedom and faithfulness do not only not engender fatal strife, but do actually produce assimilation of character and that true peace which follows purity (James iii. 17), the barriers which sectarianism erects do, on the other hand, by hindering the mutual access, and fomenting the mutual jealousies, of Christians, obstruct the progress of truth, and maintain an increasing disagreement of sentiments and opposition between those who are commanded to be " perfectly joined together in the same mind and in the same judgment " (1 Cor. i. 10), and to merge their diversities of character even in oneness itself (John xvii. 21, 22, 23).

9th. *Resolved*, That although, as is evident from the 15th chapter of Acts, there are occasions which justify the assembling of Christians together from the different parts of a country, or from different parts of the world, to discuss and decide on questions of religious interest ; nevertheless, for a local church to refuse to come into an Association of Churches, is a wise precaution for preserving its independence and purity.

10th. Whereas the mob which, in the year 1842, disgraced this community, and which is justly supposed to be the most fruitful cause of the disorders and lawlessness that have subsequently prevailed amongst us, was approved, rather than condemned, by the great majority of our professing Christians : *Resolved*, therefore, that this church feels itself loudly called on to declare that mob to have been, what every other mob is, a most flagrant outrage on human and divine laws—on the rights of man and the rights of God.

11th. Whereas there are in this community professing Christians, as well as other persons, who defend the use of intoxicating liquors as a drink ; and who also defend the selling of grain to the brewer and distiller : *Resolved*, therefore, that this church condemns such defences as unscriptural and wicked ; and pronounces the selling of such liquors for a drink—the licensing sale of them for that purpose—the election of officers who license the sale of them for that purpose—and the furnishing of materials for the manufacture of them for that purpose—to be all parts, one of them as certainly so as another, in that great and horrid work of death, which has already destroyed the bodies and souls of millions of our countrymen.

12th. Whereas there are professing Christians amongst us who patronize missionary and other societies, which solicit contributions from slaveholders : *Resolved*, therefore, That such professing Christians cannot be sinless, unless God has repealed his declaration : " I hate robbery for burnt-offering." (Isaiah lxi. 8.)

13th. Whereas, there are in this community professing Christians, as well as others, who vote to fill civil offices with slaveholders, and with persons who wield their official power in behalf of the most murderous and diabolical oppression of millions of God's poor : *Resolved*, therefore, That it is the duty of this Church to declare such voting to be very guilty treason toward the cause of humanity and the cause of God. And whereas the criminality of such voting is partially, or entirely, hidden to many eyes by plausible excuses, such as that there cannot be great sin in voting with a large party, in voting as thousands and millions vote, such as that the person voted for, although on the side of the oppressor, will nevertheless, if elected, accomplish in his office more good than evil, and will wisely conform himself to the maxim which requires the securing of " the greatest good to the greatest number ": *Resolved*, therefore, That God has left his admonitions—" Thou shalt not follow a multitude to do evil," (Ex. xxiii. 2.) : " Though hand join in hand, the wicked shall not be unpunished," (Prov. xi. 21), for the very purpose of teaching men that they cannot hide themselves and escape from responsibility in a crowd ; and that, in the light of these admonitions and of other divine instructions, the whole sin of electing a tyrant, or an upholder of tyranny, rests on each of the votes, as well as on the sum of the votes which elect him. And *Resolved*, further, That so long as the maxim should be, not "the greatest good of the greatest number," but "the greatest good of the whole number ; " and so long as Christianity forbids our seeking the good even of a universe, at the expense of the least right of the least being in it, it cannot be proper to clothe a person with official power, when we foresee that it will be employed to wrong, though it may be but a single individual, and that too, the obscurest individual among the millions subject to such power. And *Resolved*, further, That if the consideration that he will exercise his official power justly towards others of his fellow-men, can authorize us to set up a tyrant over some of them, then by the like reasoning, can that tyrant derive from the justice of his dealings with some persons a license to be unjust toward others ; then can the adulterer, the slaveholder, the murderer, be able to vindicate their adultery, slaveholding and murder, if they can prove that the harm which they have done to some of their fellow-beings by these crimes, is overbalanced by the benefit which, in whatever way, they have done to others of them. To illustrate and justify the positions of this resolution, we say, that whoever would estimate the measure of his own sin against the tens of thousands of slaves in the District of Columbia and in the Territory of Florida, for having voted to fill the office of President of the United States with a tyrant who uses the power of that office to retain in slavery those tens of thousands, should hold out of view every other vote cast for that tyrant except his own, and make his own wholly responsible for the election ; and should also hold out of view all, however good or bad of the official acts and influences of that tyrant, save only such as bear on those tens of thousands of slaves.

14th. Whereas there is, even amongst professors of religion, a prevailing opinion that it is wrong to preach politics on the Sabbath. *Resolved,* That the correctness of this opinion turns wholly on the character of the politics which are preached ; for whilst it is clearly wrong to preach anti-Bible or unrighteous politics on the Sabbath or on any other day, nothing can be clearer than that no day is too holy to be used in preaching the politics which are inculcated in the Bible.

It would be hard to put thoughts into plainer words. To read them, running, is easy ; yet, from the amount of controversy they started, from the letters and leading articles, the criticisms and objurgations, the biblical, metaphysical, theological, christological effusions that deluge the folio pages of the scrap book, one would imagine that some problem of unknown depth and darkness had been thrown down for the confusion of an unsophisticated Christendom.   And such indeed was the case ; for to the believers of that time, as to the believers of ours, the mystery of mysteries was the secret of religious fellowship.   Mr. Smith's plan,—for he was its author, formulator and executor—was practical, purely and simply practical.   The evil he tried to avoid was sectarianism ; the good he hoped to secure was moral harmony and coöperation. He wished to detach the realm of doctrine, since all could not think alike, and of practice too, since all could not reason alike on questions of applied ethics, from the realm of desire, aspiration, motive, purpose, where all could agree; where at least, their disagreement was beyond dispute. To the questions: How are you to know that any particular person is a Christian? How are you to agree in recognizing any particular person as a Christian? What is your test? he gave no answer. And he was safe in giving none. It was timely to meet such questions when they arose. It was not likely that they would arise. None but earnest people, Christians at heart, would care to connect themselves with a church like this; and Christians at heart, who were sincere in their allegiance to Christ, would have no difficulty in clinging together when the purpose was to admit none but the most interior causes of separation. Mr. Smith was not inclined to take up the metaphysics of the matter, perhaps he was not competent to do it; whether he was or not, he did not care to. Theological dispute was precisely what he was determined to avoid.

Within the circumstances the experiment worked reasonably well. The little chapel erected by Mr. Smith, about the year 1847, for the use of the Church of Peterboro, was open for that purpose until within two years of his death, when failing health, pressing cares and the irksomeness of maintaining the interest, almost alone, compelled him reluctantly to close its doors. The membership had dwindled to a handful, and of this handful he was the soul. No change of theological views induced him to abandon the enterprise he had held dear for so many years, but simply the sense of inability to sustain it longer, and without him it was nothing. The church, in its palmiest days, had its troubles, but they were neither many nor serious. Internal divisions tried the patience and faith of the members. There were discussions on points of doctrine, and disputes on points of practice. There was occasional sharpness of speech and bitterness of feeling, but the principle was not broken. One of the preachers and pastors, (1848) broached doctrines in regard to the Sabbath, pronouncing it unscriptural, characterizing the popular observance of it as superstitious, and commending what would commonly be called its "desecration," by pursuing secular business and continuing the ordinary occupations of life, as on other days. He was listened to, replied to: the propriety of his holding the office of stated teacher was gravely disputed; the members of the church voted unanimously, with this one single exception, that the Sabbath was not a Jewish institution, but an institution for all men, and that its law is of universal and perpetual obligation; Mr. Smith himself offered the resolution that notwithstanding it is the duty of a church to acknowledge in each of its members the right to be faithful to his or her convictions, and to teach and exhort as he or she may have ability or opportunity; it nevertheless, does not follow that it may choose for its teacher—least of all, that it may single out for its stated and leading teacher—one who inculcates doctrines and practices which, in its judgment, are fatal to its prosperity, and destructive of Christianity. Still, the " beloved pastor " was recognized as a fellow Christian, a fellow church member, and confidence, respect and love were entertained for him, as before. The church passed resolutions of confidence in — —, and desired him to remain with them; but he, considering the question to be a vital one, tendered a final resignation, went to New York, and became clerk in a store. In June, 1849, he came to Peterboro and preached in the former place. It so happened that at this time he served in an establishment in one department of which intoxicating drinks were sold. This offence, in Mr. Smith's eyes, was exceedingly grave. He protested against an apparent and indirect participation of a preacher in the demoralizing traffic. A short and sharp exchange of letters ensued; but the controversy did not invade the members of the church. At the end of six years, the founder of the church was able to give thanks that with the single exception of the individual referred to, none, since their identification with the "Church of Peterboro," had been guilty of voting for anti-abolitionists, or of drinking intoxicating liquors, or of contributing to the manufacture of them, or of connecting themselves with stores or other establishments in which the traffic in intoxicating drinks was carried on.

In the Church of Peterboro the ordinances were observed—the Lord's Supper, Baptism, the preaching of the gospel, the assembling of Christians together, the discipline of offending members, the appointment of officials,—not, however, as necessary distinctions of a Church of Christ, but as "duties, which could not be innocently omitted;" duties "the discharge of which is among the principal means of giving visibility to the church, and of shedding its light upon the world."

The student of this passage is forced to believe that

3*

the " Church of Peterboro " owed its strength and its
harmony to Gerrit Smith. But for his dignity and
sweetness of character, his simplicity, earnestness and
sincere devoutness, his mental resources and practical
wisdom, the experiment, instead of lasting thirty years,
would probably not have endured as many weeks. Something no doubt, was due to his commanding wealth and
social position. But these might have been disqualifica-
tions in a less noble person. It is too often forgotten,
that wealth and social position make enemies as well as
friends ; that one must be himself unconscious of their
possession, if he would make others unconscious of it ;
and that none but the truly great because the genuinely
humble and humane, can reach that unconsciousness.
The great man of the village might have formed a sect,
built a church, and made himself a laughing stock by
his pious impertinence. The good man of the village,
the best man of the village, the massiveness of his character making his bulk seem adventitious, planned and
sustained a religious society on the most radical christian principles and made himself respected and beloved,
most of all by the sincerest and the lowliest. The early
meetings of the Church of Peterboro were held in a
room of the hotel. In 1846, or thereabout, Mr. Smith
built a plain, inexpensive place of worship, where the
meetings were held as long as the church continued in
existence. It was his expectation that this temporary
structure would be replaced by a worthier one when his
principle should meet universal acceptance, and sectarian organizations should be abandoned.

Thus in middle life, in the heart of a severely orthodox community, himself educated in Calvinistic beliefs

and trained in Calvinistic ways, Gerrit Smith clearly saw the distinction between substance and form, spirit and letter. The next step, to a practical recognition of the distinction between religion and theology, was unavoidable. In fact this distinction was already reached. Theology was the cause of sectarianism, and therefore, indirectly, the cause of indifference to moral reform. The first onward movement of the reformer brought him in front of the bristling doctrines that defended the stronghold of conventional behavior. The temperance advocate was confronted at the outset by the recorded conduct of Jesus at the marriage feast in Cana, and was forced to take issue with the opinion that the example of the Christ was good for all time. Being unwilling to equivocate, too clear minded to be puzzled or satisfied by the chaffer about the probable composition of the Saviour's manufactured beverage ; too sincere to take refuge behind the witty repartee that wine made from water could harm nobody ; too manly to keep conscience waiting in the ante-chamber of christology, he frankly said that the action of Jesus on that occasion was no model for modern men ; in a word that Jesus, however incidentally excusable, was humanly mistaken. The report of a speech made by Mr. Smith, at a meeting of the New York State Temperance Society, at Albany, April, 1836, puts into his mouth the following language, which is uncorrected in the scrap book:

"To account for the apostles' use of liquor as a drink, on any other ground than the ignorance I have imputed to them, is to make them guilty of doing what they must have known it is inexpedient to do, and of doing, therefore, what, by the proposition of our opponents, 'it is morally wrong to do.' If the apostles used intoxicating liquor as a beverage, they did so simply because they did not enjoy the light which has revealed to us the uselessness of such a beverage, and for us, therefore, to hesitate to pronounce as immoral our use of such a liquor as a drink, because the apostles may have made such use of it, is utterly unreasonable."

"There is something radically wrong, either in our religion or our notion of it. I have supposed that our religion is not only suited to the apprehensions of faith and of our spiritual perceptions, but also responsive to reason and common sense. I have supposed this religion to be adapted to man's nature. But there are not a few (and among them are those who deny that the use of intoxicating liquor as a beverage, and the holding of immortal, blood-bought, God-like man in slavery are morally wrong,) who would have us believe that the Bible runs counter to the plainest deductions of reason and common sense ; for what is plainer than that intoxicating liquor is useless, immensely pernicious, and unspeakably ruinous as a drink, and that to use it as a drink is therefore morally wrong ? And what is plainer than that slavery is an enormous and unequalled outrage on great, sacred human rights, against which the very instincts of our nature cry out ? Can it be possible that the Bible affords a legitimate retreat and hiding place for the rum-maker, rum-seller and rum-drinker, and for the guilt-crimsoned slaveholder? It is not possible. . . . "When the rum drinker goes to the Bible to learn whether he may drink rum, and when the slaveholder goes there to learn whether he may hold his fellow-men in slavery, they go there in ninety-nine cases out of a hundred, to make the Bible a minister of sin, and to avail themselves of its authority to continue in their wickedness."

In a published letter on temperance, addressed to Edward C. Delavan, three years later, 1839, the following language is used to explain the conduct of Jesus:

"Save that He was 'without sin,' the man Christ Jesus was like other men. As a man He differed from them in holiness only ; not in capacity and knowledge. . . . Jesus Christ was not a man of science ; the Bible is not a book of science. We are not to go to it for scientific instruction, for lessons in astronomy or mechanics or physiology. It requires us, however, under fearful penalties for disobedience, to improve all our opportunities for acquiring knowledge. The Saviour requires us of this favored age, and favored portion of the world, to be better astronomers than were He and His cotemporaries. . . . The question then which we are to put ourselves is not whether our personal habits are in all respects like the Saviour's, but whether we have responded to the concurrent and mutually explanatory teachings of the Bible and nature and providence. . . . It is our duty to eat and drink what the wisdom of our age pronounces good. If science and observation have settled the fact that one particular vegetable is healthful and another injurious, this conclusion, and not my palate or my knowledge of Jewish living, is to govern my choice between them. So too, if it be settled what drinks are and what are not healthful, and this is a point which like the other, is to be settled by science and observation, rather than by recourse to the habits of the Saviour, I sin if I make the demands of the palate, however fortified they may be by distinguished examples, of paramount authority to the laws of health."

This common sense strikes at the heart of authority as surely as any "philosophy" does. Mr. Smith does not discredit the deity of Christ or the divinity of the Bible; but in limiting the supremacy of Christ to the sphere of principles and in all human respects judging him by natural standards, he, for every *practical* purpose, erects reason and conscience above him; and in making the divinity of the Bible consist in concurrence with natural feeling, he sets its supernatural claims aside. To adopt the Bible *because it is on one's own side*, is to reject its authority as effectually as any "infidelity" does. In either case Nature is made the judge of Revelation.

Mr. Smith's habit of preaching politics on Sunday, illustrated the completeness of his emancipation from traditional views. For the politics he preached were live, radical politics, secular, practical, going down to the roots and touching all the applications of principle; and he preached them plainly without apology, qualification or reserve. In his opinion "the better the day the better the deed." He wished to make politics religious, and religion political. Bible politics were as dear to his heart as bible-temperance and bible-abolition; and all alike occasioned scandal. The question: " Was Gerrit Smith wrong in preaching politics on the Sabbath ?" was publicly discussed in Syracuse and other places; the religious papers took it up, and in the tone of condemnation invariably. But he persevered, how boldly appears in the following extract from an announcement, an example of many such.

LOOK ! !

According to the public notice which he gave several months ago, GERRIT SMITH is, Providence permitting, to preach politics in the town of Sullivan, Sunday, October 15th, 1843. The friends of the slave in that town having referred it to him to designate the place of the meeting, he has concluded that Bridgeport is the most suitable place for it. One of the considerations which brought him to this conclusion, is that he has never yet plead the cause of the slave in the north part of Sullivan.

Mr. Smith, besides speaking several hours at Bridgeport, must travel twenty-four miles to get there. Will not the friends of the slave in every part of Sullivan go to the pains of meeting him there ?

May thousands of people come to Bridgeport to hear Mr. Smith's kind of politics ; not the kind that binds millions of his countrymen in the chains of slavery, but the Bible kind, the kind that requires civil government to " deliver the needy when he crieth, the poor also, and him that hath no helper." Mr. Smith would like to see on that occasion some of those sham ministers, who are afraid that they would lose the public favor and their salaries, if they should preach Bible politics ; and who are not only guilty of conniving at, but even of voting for pro-slavery politics.

Mr. Smith is to preach politics in De Ruyter, 8th inst ; in Lebanon, 22d inst., and in Georgetown, 29th instant. October 3, 1843.

The sharpness of the fire that was opened on him, may be judged in part by the sharpness of his return volleys. This is from a letter written to Mr. Bailey of the " Liberty Press," in August, 1842 :

" I presume, that in the mighty contest between freedom and oppression that is now going on in this county, there will not be found ten men in all the village of Hamilton, of sufficient philanthropy and courage to vote for the slave. If I am told that they have notwithstanding, much religion, I reply that it is their religion from which we have most to fear. It is their religion which has suffocated their humanity. Could we substitute for that religion the religion which dwells in the pitiful heart of Jesus, or could we substitute for it even blank infidelity, the anti-slavery cause would quickly be crowned with triumph even in the village of Hamilton.

" How little I thought, when, many years ago, I was in the habit of giving money to this, that and the other theological seminary and college, that I was thereby contributing to place the mightiest obstacle in the way of the cause of liberty and religion. Look for instance at the college where I was educated, and to which I once loved to give thousands of dollars. In my gayest moments the thought of Hamilton College brings sadness over me. This is the same college whose faculty humbled themselves so far as to beg pardon of a pro-slavery legislature for the prevalence of anti-slavery sentiments amongst their students. And the churches which I have helped build, are not a few of them, the enemies of the slave, and of course of the true religion."

The following is from a letter addressed in the same month of the same year, " To the pro-slavery Ministers of the County of Madison."

" My declaration that I am willing to spend my Sabbaths in pleading for God's enslaved poor, has proved an occasion for a new and rich display of your pro-slavery and pharisaism. You are warning the people in your respective cages not to hear me " preach politics " on the Sabbath, that is, not to hear me explain how wicked and murderous is your pro-slavery voting. . . . You have influence enough with your trustees and deacons and elders, to get them to refuse me the use of the churches under their control. But, thus far, the skies have favored us ; and beneath the grateful shelter of God-made trees, we have felt no need of man-made houses. . . The extent to which you presume on the ignorance and stupidity of the people is amazing. . . . You rely very much on your sly and sanctimonious manner of slipping in your pro-slavery votes to exempt you from detection and censure. But the people are waking up to your disgusting and abhorrent wickedness ; and your successful imposture is fast drawing to a close. . . . I entreat you then, in the name of truth and decency, that you no more number your-selves with the preachers, but with the betrayers of Jesus Christ ; no more with the friends but with the enemies of God ; no more with the friends but with the enemies of man ; until you shall have repented and have taken your stand by the side of those who, in the face of pro-slavery politicians and pro-slavery priests, and of devils, are laboring in the strength of their God and of their own good cause, to deliver the millions of their enslaved country-men."

This is from a letter to Greene C. Bronson—an open printed letter, as all these are,—dated Oct. 18, 1854. "No man's religion is better than his politics. His re-ligion is pure whose politics are pure ; whilst his religion is rascally whose politics are rascally."

This is plain speaking, and the preaching abounded in plain speech. But it would be a mistake to suppose that it was rude, coarse or violent. Gerrit Smith's ora-tory was persuasive ; clear, forcible, correct, but sweet and reasonable ; free from logical entanglements and asperities ; absolutely free from vituperation. His deep human feeling softened his argument, which never had the spirit of acrimony, and never took on the air of tri-umph. He *talked*, in a dignified, open, confiding way, in the manner of one so full of his purpose, so deeply in love with the truth, so profoundly impressed with the importance of what he was saying, so sure of its power to command the assent of all considerate minds, that the extreme boldness of his positions gave no shock even to sensitive feelings. The nobleness of his presence, the manly grace of his bearing, the kindness of his temper, the melodious majesty of his voice, the frankness of his concessions, the simplicity of his language, the directness of his moral appeal, the burden of emotion that he carried, the practical drift of his aim, which betrayed no sign of the forensic gladiator, gave an apostolic character to his address. There was no rhetoric for the sake of rhetoric; the impassioned bursts of eloquence came not from the lips, but from the heart; the large stores of intellectual power were made tributary to the soul. He was no fanatic, understanding by fanatic, a man of dark, morbid, lurid, despotic and destructive temper, a hater of evil rather than a lover of good, a missionary of the gospel of Fear;—he was an enthusiast, hopeful, benevolent, sunny, expansive, nourishing, an ardent disciple of peace and good will, a hearty believer in the substantial rectitude of human nature, a prophet of the new and better age. So far from being a *doctrinaire* was he, that he never formulated his opinions, but allowed inconsistent thoughts to lie about in his mind ready for use, and seemed impatient of the philosophy that demanded a severe harmony among the different elements of his creed.

To such a man theology was an object of grave suspicion, as interposing a dogmatic barrier between the human heart and the divine principles it lived on, and preventing the truth from exerting its rightful authority over mankind. It was not the separate article in the creed that outraged him so much as the dogmatic character of the creed itself. The separate article might or might not be true;—that was not in question, or was but incidentally in question; he left all that to the Bible interpreter. The point at issue was, whether any article or body of articles was entitled to stand in the place of religion; whether belief in them could be considered primary; whether acceptance of them constituted one a

4

religious man, or was worth counting in the estimate of
a religious man ; whether the interest in them did not
rather detract from the value of the religious character,
and whether the stress laid upon them did not hinder
progress in the religious life. His suspicions and his
assaults were directed against the theological, ecclesiastical and clerical *spirit*, as leading to sectarianism, dog-
matism, assumption, intolerance, party pride and moral
indifference.

The hostile feeling towards theology began early and
increased steadily for many years ; but its outbreak was
later. What point it reached at last may be inferred
from the headings of an open letter to William Lloyd
Garrison, printed in 1865.

THE THEOLOGIES THE GREAT ENEMIES OF RE-
LIGION.

THE THEOLOGIES THE GREAT HINDRANCES TO
JUSTICE AND REFORM.

THE THEOLOGIES THE GREAT CURSE OF MANKIND.

The letter begins with a strong statement of the case
of Jonathan Edwards, " an unqualified, an unmitigated,
unrelenting slaveholder," and asks how this can be explained of a man so learned, deep and conscientious.
The answer is that, " his theology called for or permitted
the relation, and with him the claims were paramount
to all other claims." The letter continues :—" But it
will be asked, what shall we do with religion, if we throw
away the theologies ? I answer that they never were
religion, nor any part of it ; and that they never stood
in any other relation to it than that of its greatest hinderance and mightiest enemy. Were the theologies of
the whole world cast aside, the religion of reason and

nature would quickly bless the whole world. Were the historical and traditional religion cast aside, and were there in its place the religion of a present consciousness, —the religion of the present voice of God to the soul, and of the present voice of the soul to itself,—men would not need to go from earth to find heaven."

Then, referring to Mr. Garrison's own remarkable experience, Mr. Smith goes on:

" I have often thought of your great change in these things. You were brought up in a strict Calvinistic theology. You have lost your theology, but your religion remains. God and His spirit, and Jesus, and prayer, and the Bible and the law of goodness and the hope of immortality are certainly no less dear to you than they were when you dwelt in your theological prison, and assumed that you must dwell in it all your days. But, though you have not lost your religion, there is, judging from my own experience, one thing you have lost. This one thing is the *certainty* of the objects of your faith. Once we could say with the orthodox : ' I *know* whom I have believed,' etc. But now we find ourselves remitted to all the conscious uncertainty of human reasonings. Nevertheless, we would not, if we could, buy back this lost certainty. The price would be too great. It would be no less than ignoring the revelations of science and the laws of evidence, and turning our backs upon reason and nature, and again picking up and prizing the bundle of fictions and fancies and follies, which our convictions had compelled us to throw away. For one, however great the comfort which may proceed from this certainty, I deny the right of any man to the comfort, because I deny the right of any man to the certainty. Such certainty is born of ignorance and superstition, and only the ignorant and superstitious have it."

On the 21st of February, 1858, January 23, 1859, and June 19, 1859, Mr. Smith delivered discourses in the Free Church of Peterboro, which were afterwards published in pamphlet form, with the title " Three Discourses on the Religion of Reason." There we find a frank expression of his views on this matter. But before specifying them, it may be wise to give his general idea of religion as set down in argument delivered at a meeting of Liberal Christians held in Canastota, Oct. 27, 1869.

*   *   *   *   *   *   *   *

Nothing short of religion can satisfy the demands of our being. But is nature sufficient to teach and illustrate religion? Undoubtedly, we should find it so if, instead of having become so unnatural, we were still natural. All that religion requires of us is obedience to the laws of nature. To be perfect in this obedience is to be perfect in religion. Nature reveals religion to us ; and religion, in turn, bids us be true to nature ; and exacts nothing else from us than to be natural. But these mistaken religions, of which we have been speaking, have ever disparaged nature, and ever made war upon it. Some of them fight it on Shaker planes, and some of them fight it on Mormon planes. Some of them crucify it, and some of them plead its sacred name for all manner of licentiousness and excess. Devotees of some of these religions lacerate and macerate and mutilate themselves. With most religionists fasting is regarded as a high merit. Nevertheless, no fasting is meritorious, nor less than positively sinful which brings harm to the body. Nature protests as earnestly against wronging one as another of the elements or constituents of our being. There is no part of it that she does not sacredly cherish, and she will accept no plea for benefiting either the understanding or the heart, if the benefiting is to be at the expense of the physical health. The religion which sings :

> " Nature must count her *gold* but dross,
> If she would gain the heavenly land,"

fancies herself to have sprung from the wisdom of heaven—nevertheless, she is born of the fanaticisms of earth. Such a religion, in its representing nature to be the enemy of man, necessarily represents it to be, also, the enemy of God. But nature, being the work of God is (unless like man it has fallen away from Him) the friend of God, and can, therefore, be no hindrance to His designs and provisions for the onward and upward way of His children. More than all this, the position that nature is at war with man involves the absurdity that God is at war with Himself.

In this connection let me say, that people should stop talking about man's *lower* nature. He has no *lower* nature. His nature is all high, since whatever he does with it, even eating or drinking, he can and should "do all to the glory of God." It is true that men forsake their high nature, and often descend very low ; but their departures from it and their violations of it are anti-nature, and must not be confounded with nature. When Jesus bids us take up our cross, he bids us crucify not our nature, but only its corruptions, or rather that which we have put in the place of nature. He requires in this nothing else than that we return from deserting our nature and consent to abide in it. To be born again into that loving and beautiful nature which we have so widely and foolishly forsaken, and to get up again to those heights from whence our sins and, may be, the sins of our progenitors also, had carried us so far downward ; this, and this only is the regeneration he calls for. But who should wonder, if such a new birth cannot be accomplished without the help of those blessed influences, which we would fain believe are forever flowing from the bosom of God throughout His universe ?

I have argued that nature is the foundation of our religion. But do I give the Bible no place in this foundation ? None whatever. And is, then, the Bible of no value? It is of incalculable value. For, notwithstanding the things in it, which, because they are revolting to reason and nature, and, therefore to religion, should not have been put into it, it is, beyond all comparison, the best of books. Here, far more than in all other books, are the lessons that help us build up the true religion on the true foundation. And do I make no account of Jesus either in this foundation? None at all. Nevertheless, in respect to the superstructure upon it, I gratefully and lovingly recognize him to be the master builder. I often see him put by radical religionists into the same category with Confucius, Socrates, Plato and other eminent teachers. But he is a teacher so immeasurably above all other teachers, that he should never be classed with any of them. Never was there other teacher so taught of God. Never other teacher, whose moral and spiritual character so far realizes our highest conceptions of God's moral and spiritual character. In respect to such character, well may it be said of him that he is filled with his Father's fulness—that he is even "God manifest in the flesh." Nevertheless, preëminent teacher though he is, he did not teach a new religion. He but taught the spirit and principles and commended and urged the claims of the one unchangeable and everlasting religion of nature. Until human nature is changed, its religion cannot be changed. How emphatically Jesus recognized the competency of human nature to understand the religion of human nature, when he said to the people : " Yea, and why even of yourselves judge ye not what is right ? " Repeatedly, when he would prove to his disciples the loving and unlimited beneficence of God, he goes straight to the teachings of nature. He inculcates upon them the duty of being good to all by calling their attention to some fact in nature, which goes to prove that *God* is good to all ; such a fact, for instance, as that sunlight comes to the evil and the good, and showers fall upon the just and unjust. And it is in connection with his citing this proof in nature of God's impartial goodness, that he reminds them that such goodness on their part is one of the ways for them to become perfect even as their Father in heaven is perfect. When, too, he would relieve them of anxious care for their food and clothing, he again draws from nature the lessons they need. He bids them " consider the ravens and the lilies," and to derive from God's feeding and clothing them, the irresistible inference that he has not failed to put food and clothes within the reach of His children, of His own sons and daughters, who are so much " better," of so much more importance, than fowls and flowers.

There are other and very beautiful recognitions in the Bible, that nature teaches the existence and character of God. " The heavens declare the glory of God ; and the firmament showeth His handiwork." Creation teaches " even His eternal power and godhead, so that they are without excuse," who do not know Him. " The eyes of all wait upon Thee : and Thou givest them their meat in due season. Thou openest Thy hand, and satisfiest the desire of every living thing."

Miserable world has this ever been because of the conventional religions which have ever prevailed in it ! Every religion is conventional, contemptibly conventional, that overrides reason with authority and finds its foundation in books or anything else than nature. The hanging and burning of innocent women charged with witchcraft ; the burning of the intellectual, pure and brave Servetus, at the especial instance of the learned but bigoted Calvin ; the Inquisition with its three or four hundred thousand victims—all these came from ignorantly and superstitiously substituting for the study and guidance of unerring nature, misleading books and traditions—in other phrase, from substituting man's words for God's words. The slaveholding religion, which, so long, ruled our land, was a conventional or authority religion—not a natural one. For nature makes infinitely broad the difference between man and beast, and abhors to the last degree the making merchandise of man. Nature could never be twisted into the approval of such a religion. Books and traditions easily can be. So too, the rum religion which now rules our land, drenching it with tears and blood, defies and outrages nature, instead of falling in with it. Her bosom is exuberant to the end that food may not be scarce to the mouths of the poor. But the rum religion starves the poor. No small share of its professors, in addition to casting their votes on the side of the dram-shop, yield up the products of their fields to the demands of that devourer and murderer. And such professors, along with other professors, who are steeped in various other iniquities, flatter themselves that they are Christians; and find, as they believe, justification in their authoritative books and traditions for stigmatizing as infidels those who hold religion to be a life rather than a letter, and character instead of creeds to be its supreme test.

An authority religion, heeding none of the remonstrances of reason and closing its ears to all pleas for mercy; its bigoted disciples with their huge quivers filled with arrows of all manner of persecutions; and its fanatical and frenzied disciples striding over the earth, with fire and sword—such is the religion that has ever been the great scourge of mankind. But christendom is confident that it will never again see such within *her* borders. Groundless confidence! Only let the progress of science be arrested, and the lights, which it, far more than authority religion, has kindled along the upward way of our civilization, become dim and, very soon, in all the length and breadth of christendom, would the civil government again become subordinate to the ecclesiastical; and, here and there, inquisitions, *auto-de-fès*, martyr-stakes, and burnings and hangings for witchcraft and other fanciful crimes would re-appear. We often hear it said that the church saves the world. This would be well said were the religion of the church founded in nature—but, as the case stands, the common sense and science in the world are needed to save both the world and the church. The particular authority religion, which would work this sad change in christendom to which I have referred, might be the Catholic or Presbyterian or Methodist or some other. That it would be mainly accomplished by one of the sects, can hardly be doubted, since, in the retrograding of science, and the deepening darkness of ignorance, one of the sects would be like to swallow up all the others. That the present sectarian religions of christendom have not absolute sway over her is because, instead of being one with each other, they are all more or less antagonistic to each other. Infinite debtor to science is christendom, if it be only that from the freedom of opinion, which science has obtained for her, so great a multiplication of religious sects has resulted. Admit that this multiplication is in itself a great evil. Nevertheless, it has protected her from an immeasurably greater evil—from the over-shadowing despotism of some single, dominant, all-absorbing sect. But however true it is, that the freedom of opinion, begotten of science, has led to the multiplying of the types and sects of this authority or book religion, it must not be forgotten that such religion and science are the enemies of each other. Is this mutual enmity denied?—and denied on the ground that sectarian churches abound where there is most science? The answer is that such of these churches as are most imbued with science, are the least bound by an authority religion and are first to throw it off entirely. It is not possible that science can be on good terms with any other religion than that of nature and reason."

Mr. Smith's conception of the religion of Jesus is thus expressed in the " Discourses."

" The religion which Jesus so perfectly illustrated with His lips and life was no other than the religion of reason—that one and only true religion which is adapted to all ages and to all peoples, and which stands opposed to all those fabrications of the cunning, and all those superstitions of the credulous, which are called religion. These fabrications and superstitions, and in short, every other religion than that of reason, Jesus confronted. No cabalism or mysticism found any favor with Him. The religion He taught was so obviously true as to make its appeal to natural sense and universal intuition. So simple was it that He found no occasion for sending men to books and priests to acquire an understanding of it. On the contrary, He put them upon their own convictions for the solution of its problems and asked them : ' Why even of yourselves judge ye not what is right ? ' He found reason outraged by monstrous claims in the name of religion ; and the one work of His ministry—the one work which, amid all the storms of passion and prejudice and bigotry He pursued so unfalteringly and calmly and sublimely—was to reëstablish the dominion of reason. He found common-sense reduced to a ruinous discount by its concessions to religious tricks and fooleries ; and He undertook to restore it to par. Such was then and is now the whole of the religion of Jesus. It is a common-sense religion. Wide as is its realm, it is but commensurate with common-sense and one with it. To bring the whole man and the whole life under the reign of reason is its sole office. The true religion is nothing more or less than a ' reasonable service,' and wherever there is the most reasonable man, there is the most truly religious man.

We deny that Jesus made faith in certain doctrines essential to salvation, nor is it true that He made faith in His literal self thus essential. What He means by faith in Himself is faith in the Christ principle and Christ character. Hence, salvation may come to him who has never heard of Christ. Cordially to believe in that principle of divine goodness, and truly to possess the character which grows out of this cordial belief, is the sufficient, ay, and the sole salvation."

The special opinions held under this general conception need not be dwelt on. It will be enough to indicate them in the writer's own language.

"For one I would have the friends baptized with water and in the manner in which He was. For one I would have them partake of His appointed supper, and around a table, and with conversation as did He and His disciples. For one, I would have them observe a Sabbath, and choose for it the same day of the week which He and His disciples did. Even in things which are counted unessential, it is safer and happier to walk in His steps than to depart from them."

BIBLE MEN.

"It is charged that we are not Bible men. I admit that we are not any further than we live according to its great and everlasting principles. They are Bible men whose lives are in harmony with those principles ; not they who trample upon them, at the same time that they make great merit of their pretended or imagined faith in the Bible."

MESSIAH.

"Jesus believed not only that the Jewish nation would within a few years be overwhelmed and scattered, but that 'then would His kingdom be set up and with power and great glory.' The temple, Jerusalem, and Judea, did all meet their fate before the generation to which Jesus spoke had passed away. But His kingdom has not yet been set up, nor have the signs appeared which were to precede it. . . . In Matthew xxv. are we not informed of the reward of those Jews who welcomed the ministry of Christ and of the punishment of those Jews who rejected it—especially of the reward of those who, during His expected brief disappearance from earth, should honor His disciples—even 'the least' of them—and the punishment of those who, during that brief period, should neglect those disciples—even 'the least' of them? It is true that the word is translated ' nations,' but it is also true that ' nations ' is not among the primary meanings, and that ' multitudes,' ' companies,' ' tribes ' are. In the light of Matt. xix. 28, do we not see some evidence that ' tribes ' would be a proper translation, and that the judgment in view was not to be of ' all nations,' but only of all the Jewish tribes ?"

ATONEMENT.

" It is said that nature and the history of man abound in analogies to the atonement. I can not admit that any such analogies are to be found in either. It is true that oftentimes the guiltless suffer for the guilty—now of necessity and now of choice. But in no case is there a transference of character from one to the other. The guilty party remains no less guilty, and the guiltless party contracts no guilt literal or constructive. Remember too, that the human sense of justice revolts at visiting on the good man the penalty due to the bad man—a strong argument by the way, that the Divine sense does also."

HELL.

" Eternal hell ! No man does and no man can believe it. It is untrue if only because human nature is incapable of believing it. Moreover, were such a belief possible, it would be fatal. Let the American people wake up with it to-morrow, and none of them would go to their fields, and none to their shops, and none would care for their homes. All interest in the things of earth would be dead. The whole nation would be struck with paralysis and frozen with horror. Even the beginnings of such a belief are too much for the safety of the brain ; and every step in that direction is a step towards the mad-house. The orthodox preacher of an eternal hell would himself go crazy did he believe his own preaching."

BIBLE.

" The Bible is really the best book in the world ; though the present uses of it make it practically the worst. All other books put together are not, so much as the Bible is, the occasion of obstructing the progress of civilization, and of filling the world with ignorance and superstition. It is adapted as no other book is, to enrich the mind and expand the soul. But misapprehended, misinterpreted, and perverted to the extent it is, no other book,—nay, no number of books—does so much to darken the mind and shrivel the soul."

DEPRAVITY.

" Radical must be the change in our fallen and depraved nature, ere a thorough and gospel honesty can characterize us. I say *fallen* nature. Let me remark that I do not entertain the common views of this subject. Owing to ancestral violations of moral as well as physical and intellectual laws, we inherit a constitution morally as well as physically and intellectually impaired. This is all I mean by a fallen nature, adding thereto what we may ourselves have done to degrade it."

PRAYER.

" The doctrine of Divine influence admitted, there are prayers which all will see to be reasonable ; such as are in effect prayers for the opening of the mind to that influence. Do I pray for an increase of my physical or spiritual health ? If I pray intelligently, it is not that God may increase it, but that He may influence me to increase it by my improvement of the means to that end placed by His providence within my reach. In other words it is asking Him to dispose me to answer my own prayers ; and surely this is not ignoring any general laws with which we are acquainted ; nor is it asking Him to come into conflict with them. . . . A law is not impossible, which, the conditions precedent being supplied, shall compel even the sun and moon to stand still in answer to prayer. I confess that it is not for man to limit the Divine possibilities, nor to essay to number and comprehend all the laws of the universe. . . I will say nothing here of ' special providences ' except that, if they do occur, they must be the result of the unchangeable and eternal laws of the unchangeable and eternal God."

MIRACLES.

" To be frank, I suppose that all enlightened and broad-minded men do at least doubt the truth of miracles. They have never seen any, and hence they are slow to yield to even abounding testimony in their behalf. Had they ever seen so much as one miracle, they could easily be brought to believe in others, on the same principle that, having seen one city, men can be persuaded of the existence of others. Moreover, it is especially difficult for him to believe in the Christian miracles who reflects that Christianity has done more than all things else to dispel belief in miracles."

DEATH.

" It is not true that death is a curse ; nor that it is so much as a calamity. That it is a penalty is purely a theological fiction. Were the laws of life and health properly observed, the common age of man, reaching probably to a hundred years, would give ample time for making trial and reaping the enjoyments of this state of being. He would then feel death to be seasonable. Abundantly welcome would it be if he had observed the moral laws also—it being in his power to learn these as well as the physical, by studying the creation and providence of God. Abundantly welcome, I say,—for then his holy, happy life would afford him the conscious preparation for a succeeding stage of existence. I add that death is necessary to make room for countless millions of human beings, who otherwise could have no existence, and that thus it is to be credited with swelling indefinitely the sum of human happiness."

IMMORTALITY.

" I believe there are strong, I will not say conclusive, proofs in nature that man shall live again. One is that God made him in His own likeness, He put into him His own spirit, and made him to be His immortal companion and co-worker. Another proof is that God made him with wants that this life cannot satisfy. . . I have no doubts of another life. I do not believe that the noble thoughts which William Goodell has uttered, will live, and he not be permitted to live along with them ; . . . I will only add, under this head, that if the spiritualists are not deceived, they have discovered another and a conclusive natural evidence that man is to live again."

Mr. Smith was not a spiritualist. His wife was, and in company with her, he visited mediums and attended circles. But the " manifestations " did not convince him. It is probable that his absorbing interest in human affairs made him indifferent to the problem of the hereafter. This he confessed. It is probable also, that the moral confidence in God that was habitual with him, made him incurious in regard to details of evidence. Certain it is, that the subject presented to his mind little attraction, though his deep respect and affection for his wife forbade other than playful criticism of it. His own habitual insensibility to the claims of the hereafter was confessed in the remark made to a friend that he had not quite made up his mind whether he had a soul or no. His interest in character was vital to the last, and made up for all other interests.

REVIVALS.

"We believe in revivals of true religion and rejoice in them. But we confess that of revivals in general we are very suspicious. And why should we not be? It is true that they serve to fill up the churches; but do they increase the sum total of humanity, and holiness and happiness? The revival of last year was preëminent for extent and commended character. But I am yet to be convinced that it has proved a public blessing, through the length and breadth of our State. Is not sectarian and party spirit, that power so mighty to shrivel and sink the soul, as rampant as ever? Was there ever a year in which the use of tobacco increased faster, or in which there was a more rapid multiplication of dram-shops? In no year among the last thirty has so little interest been taken in the cause of temperance. Indeed, at the last election its professed friends seemed to delight in pouring contempt upon it. And, although there is still much talk (part sincere and part hypocritical, and nearly all nonsensical) against the extension of slavery, yet has there never been a year since the dauntless young hero, William Lloyd Garrison, first summoned the nation to abolish it, in which has been evinced so little purpose to abolish it."

CREEDS.

"A religious creed is proper. Every man should have one. But a church creed is improper. Fifty or a hundred people in Peterboro or Cazenovia, however much alike in views or spirit, should no more be required to adopt a common religious creed, than to shorten or stretch out their bodies to a common length."

THE CLERICAL ORDER.

"Many clergymen are among the best of men. Nevertheless such an order is wholly unauthorized, and exceedingly pernicious. Their assumption of an exclusive right to teach religion makes the teachers conceited, dogmatic, arrogant, tyrannical ; and their hearers lazy and slavish in spirit. . . Every true Church of Christ is a simple democracy. Its ordinary assemblies should be mere conferences, in which all persons, male or female, are to feel entirely free to speak as the spirit moves them. Faith in Christ is the warrant to speak for Christ. . . But in addition to this means of grace, and growth within themselves, the collective churches should have and should liberally support a powerful itinerant ministry. Tne Pauls and Barnabases of modern times should travel among the churches as did the Pauls and Barnabases of ancient times. The obscurest country church should be favored as often as every month or two with a discourse from a Finney, a Beecher, a Lucretia Mott, an Angelina Weld, a Chapin, a Parker, a Beriah Green, an Alonzo Potter, or an Abram Pryne."

Reason and Religion.

" It is true that the reason of most men is greatly perverted. It is true that in innumerable instances it is reduced to little better than a compound of passion and prejudice;—or to speak with perhaps more philosophical correctness, such a compound is allowed to take the place of reason. Nevertheless, reason, poor guide though we may make it, is our only legitimate guide. It may lead us to ruin. Still we are not able to give it up for any other leader ; no, not for church, nor pope, nor Bible. If we have debased and corrupted our reason, we alone are responsible for the wrong, and we alone must bear the loss. We cannot cancel our obligations by our crimes. . . But is reason sufficient for all these things ? It is. Not however unless the Divine influence on it be unceasing. Man, as much as the planet, needs to be set in motion and kept in motion by God. Vain is an enlightened reason unless there be also the God-given spirit of submission to its control. Vain is it that man is made with ability to will and to do, unless he allow his Maker to work in him to will and to do."

It is unnecessary to multiply quotations ; it is unnecessary to explain. Mr. Smith's thoughts are simply expressed so that no attentive reader can fail to comprehend their drift and reach. The discourses are scarcely more than notes,—the comments of an acute, clear, practical mind, quite free in its movement over the spec-

ulative field. They are loosely put together and not always carefully reconciled in their parts. They make no
claim to learning, depth, critical accomplishment, or
philosophical exactness. They are certainly open to
criticism on several sides. Men like Beriah Green and
William Goodell had no difficulty in finding the weak
places in these popular statements. Mr. Smith's method
was that of common sense ; and common sense, however potent as a guide through the labyrinth of practical
details, is at fault in the region of criticism and speculation. But the observations we have quoted are
wonderfully shrewd ; here and there they anticipate
by sheer strength of reason, results which criticism
has only recently obtained, though the writer does not
sufficiently define his terms for scientific purposes, his
main intention is so evident, his purpose is so honest,
his conclusions are so broad, that only they who
are determined to misrepresent can fail to understand him.

There is no good reason for thinking that Gerrit
Smith ever abandoned or even to the last modified his
theological opinions, though there may be good reasons for thinking that he made less account of them in
his latter days. In fact, he foresaw that he should ;
and he foresaw that his orthodox opponents would take
advantage of this diminished interest, to declare that he
retracted his opinions. Hence he was mindful to say to
members of his family and others, that his views were
the result of honest inquiry ; and he begged them to remember his words, that however, in later life, as his intellect might weaken and his feeling increase, he might
seem to abandon the beliefs he had promulgated, they

were nevertheless, his serious and fixed convictions, the conclusions of his mind at its strongest.

It must, however, be said that his theological opinions seem never to have affected the tone of his religious feeling or spiritual conviction. With him the heart was always uppermost, though, as is usual with men as they age, the heart increased in vigor whilst the intellect declined in activity. The discourses themselves contain expressions that show that he was substantially, as far as *feelings* went, orthodox, and during the last ten years of his life, feeling became more and more prevailing. It is quite possible that he lost interest in theological speculations, even to the extent of advising friends not to read his discourses of Reason. This would not be at all inconsistent with his entertaining these views and promulgating them. Nay, it may be that some unwillingness in latter years to distribute his publications on the doctrines of the creeds arose in part from an opinion of their crudeness and inadequacy to convey his thoughts in a systematic and effective form. At all events it is certain from the following facts that within a few months of his death, his interest in the cause of reasonable religion continued. He was near seventy when he wrote the following note to the Boston " Investigator," the well known organ of what is called " infidelity."

Peterboro, Oct. 26, 1866.

Mr. J. P. Mendum :

Dear Sir,—Your paper has been sent to me for several months, I now wish to subscribe for it. Enclosed are seven dollars to pay for two years' subscription.

I was brought up to look only at one side—*my side*. Hence I entered upon my manhood a political and a religious bigot. But, for more than the latter half of my life, I have trained myself to look at all sides and to seek knowledge from all sides. Hence, badly as most people think of your paper, I nevertheless read it ; and what is more, I think I read it with profit.

Respectfully Yours,

GERRIT SMITH.

Mr. Smith was a subscriber to the " Index," a weekly paper devoted in general to the cause of religious emancipation, specially devoted to the complete separation of religion from the State, and opposed to " Christianity " as a system of intellectual oppression. In 1873 — May 1, he wrote a remarkable letter to his kinsman, Doctor Fitzhugh, of Livingston County, N. Y. It began thus :

" You like ' The Index.' So do I. Its vigorous reasonings and its beautiful candor and fairness make it a very attractive and useful paper. Its leading position, however,—that Christianity is not the true and ultimate religion and that our duty is to stand outside of it, —I cannot, as yet, fall in with."

Then follows a restatement which it is unnecessary to copy, of his vindication of Christianity on the ground of its identity with the religion of reason and nature. In conclusion he says :

" Perhaps I have done wrong to ' The Index.' For perhaps I have unduly magnified the difference between it and myself. This difference may be wholly in our definitions of Christianity. My definition does not include its unchristian mixtures. But ' The Index ' includes them all in its definition and holds Christ's religion responsible for them all. Were its definition just, there would be no ground to complain of its war upon Christianity. But in my view it is exceedingly though unintentionally unjust. Christianity is what its constructive principles are. It is what these always and everywhere call for,—nothing more, nothing less. If they call for any moral wrong, then Christianity is wrong, otherwise not. These principles determine its theoretical scope and practical character ; and it is unreasonable to hold it responsible for anything which violates them. It

is true that Jesus said something more than sufficed to enunciate
these principles,—but it was only to illustrate and explain them. It
was certainly not to overthrow nor invalidate them. In other
words it is not supposable that Jesus should speak against the tenor
of the religion He taught,—against the principles of His own
religion."

In 1872, Mr. Smith accepted the position of vice-
president of the "Free Religious Association," which
was offered to him as being one of the foremost champions in the country of the principles it asserted. In
1871, he had been a sympathetic participant in the discussions held at a convention of the association in Syracuse. That his interest was unabated in 1873, appears
from the following note addressed to the secretary of
the association :

WILLIAM J. POTTER :
Sept. 30, 1873.

My Dear Sir, — I have your esteemed letter. The request that
I preside over the approaching convention of the Free Religious Association, does me great honor. But I am too old (76) and infirm to
serve in this capacity, and your committee must therefore excuse me.
Allow me to avail myself of this occasion to say that my confidence
in the association continues unabated. It cannot fail to be eminently
useful so long as it shall continue to be characterized by its candid
and earnest seeking after truth. Moreover the promise " seek and
ye shall find " is to just this kind of seeking. Please use the enclosed in defraying the expenses of the convention. With great
regard your friend, GERRIT SMITH.

It was Mr. Smith's custom, when passing an occasional Sunday in New York, to attend the religious
service of the president of this very "Free Religious
Association."

Must we charge with inconsistency the man who
was thus faithful to two interests so widely separated
in the common mind, as those of religion and reason?

It will be more just to say that he, more vitally than perhaps any other conspicuous man, found their harmony in admitting their difference. The distinction between religion and theology was not, thirty years ago, as familiar as it is now. And even now, they that make the distinction are seldom so entirely at home with it that they preserve the freshness of their religious feeling while allowing free play to their understanding. But here was a man whose simple, unaffected piety was an example to members of the " evangelical " faith, and whose utter frankness of comment on ecclesiastical institutions and theological dogmas sometimes had an audacious sound even in the ears of rationalists. A warm, enthusiastic, praying theist, he had none of the blind horror of atheism that led him to denounce or shudder at it, but in his own little chapel could calmly listen to its argument ;—with an ardent admiration of Jesus which allowed him to lavish on his " Saviour " the most endearing and adoring epithets, he did not shrink from the scholar who denied his transcendent attributes, or went so far as to connect him with the less humane aspects of his religion ;—a believer in Christianity as the highest authentication of the moral law, he read the argument of those who regarded it as an obstacle in the way of progress ;—believing in a blessed immortality for mankind and entertaining a hope of it that breaks out in sweet words of trust at every anniversary of a dear one's death, he professed openly to be supremely interested in the concerns of the present life. He had a profound personal humility, a sense of spiritual need that was at times pathetic, a longing for interior peace and perfection that was as keen the last month of his

life as it was at the outset of his career,—and along
with it he had a confidence in his own sentiments and
moral convictions that no authority of state or church
could shake. A rare combination of child and hero, he
never failed to meet the requirements of either character, yet neither excluded or seemed to exclude the
other ; the hero never forgot to be a child, the child
was ready for any heroism. His perpetual sense of
responsibility kept him simple, humble and meek. His
perpetual feeling of duty kept him braced for action.
The conviction that he was " nothing " did not impair
the conviction that he was accountable for unusual
trusts. Nothing could be more absolutely free from
self-consciousness than his private journal. It contains
not a single morbid sentence. He was accused of egotism, perhaps justly. But the egotism is more than
justified that counteracts the disabling effects of an
unusually deep passive piety, and gives the requisite
self-assertion to a nature that without it, might easily
have lapsed into lethargy or luxury of soul.

A Methodist clergyman, who knew Mr. Smith in his
declining months, and learned thus late to know him as
something very different from the "infidel" he had
heard of—implores the writer, who had known him and
about him for twenty years, not to erect a mere " literary
monument " to his memory, but to do justice to his
spirit of loving faith. The admonition is unnecessary.
The biographer could not, if he would, build a literary
monument to one who was in no sense a literary man.
Gerrit Smith's piety of thought and feeling was too large
a part of him to be left out of account, even by a literary
artist. But it may be permitted the biographer to re-

mind his uneasy monitor that Gerrit Smith's intellect never abandoned its post, and was burly enough even at the last to deal a good blow on the side of human reason against despotism, whether enthroned in church or bible, priest or clergyman. In his old age the weapon he had wielded so stoutly, remained in its velvet sheath. But it was not rusty or dull. Nobody provoked the gracious old man to draw it, and his loving eyes greeted all comers as friends with whom it might be sweet to hold communion for an hour. The world now was an oasis to him, where he could lay by his weapons and sit on the grass beneath the palm, and share the date and the water flask with his " dearest foe."

CHAPTER IV.

HUMANITY.

ON the occasion of erecting a monument on the grave of Myron Holley, at Rochester, June 13, 1844, Mr. Smith pronounced a touching eulogy on that devoted " Friend of the Slave," which contained the following description of the true philanthropist. Mr. Smith himself cannot better be portrayed than in his own language. It came directly from the heart when he spoke of his friend ; he meant it ; he described qualities which he honored sincerely in others and tried to honor practically himself. Funereal tributes are proverbially extravagant ; but in this instance the eulogium was no more than adequate to the virtues of the deceased. Scarcely was it adequate to the qualities of the speaker himself.

" The world is in a sad condition, and will continue to be, until man, as man,—until man, for his mere manhood, shall be held in honor. So long as a man must be rich, or learned, or polished, or the subject of some other adventitious attraction, in order to be valued ; so long will the world abound in every variety and depth of wrong and wretchedness. Inasmuch as a very large proportion of the human family have but their manhood, if that shall fail to commend them, how can the prospect of a better condition ever open upon them ? So long as bare manhood is insufficient to elicit respect, the vast majority of our fellow men will be exposed to the clutches of slavery ; so long will they be regarded as fit tools for war, or, as they are contemptuously called, ' food for powder ; ' and, so long too, will deep ignorance and abject poverty be looked upon as their appropriate lot.

"Statesmen and political economists have their schemes for getting rid of the poor : but the radical and only remedy is to get rid of poverty itself ; or rather to get rid of that spirit of aristocracy and caste, which is the disease, of which poverty is but a symptom and a fruit. Most persons believe, and claim too that they have the Saviour's authority for believing it, that, to the end of time, a large portion of the human family must, necessarily, be poor. But, poverty is no more necessary than sin ; or, rather, than any other sin. I say no more necessary than any other sin ; because to the common remark : ' It is no sin to be poor,' I do not subscribe. I do not say, that the subject of poverty is always, or even generally the sinner : but, I do say, that his poverty argues the existence of a sin somewhere. When the Saviour said, that there would always be poverty, He virtually said, that there would always be sin.

England is groaning under the burden, the crushing burden, of her multitudinous poor. But, suppose her rich and proud ones were to be inspired with the love of man. Obeying the Saviour and the impulses of their changed hearts, they would, at once, welcome to their hospitalities the inmates of the alms-houses and work-houses, the ragged beggars of the streets, and the many, whom poverty has been the chief agent in driving to brothels and other dens of iniquity. What would be the effect of such a turning of the hearts of those rich and proud ones to these poor and despised ones ? What less than that the hearts of these poor and despised ones should grate-fully turn to their benefactors ? This association of the rich with the poor—of the haughty with the humble—would, indeed, be blest both to them who stooped down to it, and to them who were raised up to it. On the one hand, it would put the idle and the vicious poor on their good behavior ; would stimulate them to a career of industry and virtue ; would supply with new and efficient motives for self-improvement both the honest and dishonest poor, whose self-respect is now withered, and whose energies are now prostrated by the neglect and scorn which they suffer. On the other hand, it would teach those who had proudly and disdainfully forsaken the masses of their fellow men, how much more of true honor and happiness there is in the natural position of standing by the side of their brother, than in the unnatural position of standing upon him.

"Do for the poor what you will—' though you bestow all your goods to feed the poor, and though you give your body to be burned ' —all will be vain unless you hold out to them the honest right hand

of human brotherhood.　But that token of your love for them—
that recognition of their place in the human family and in your hearts
—would, as I have already said, bring blessings to yourselves, as
well as to them.　If, among its happy consequences, would be the
disappearance of their poverty, the giving up of your pride of riches
would be among them also.　You may multiply poor-houses—but it
will avail nothing.　The poor-house, that cruel device, will still prove
itself to be as useless, as it is cruel ; for, instead of arresting the
spread of poverty, it has the effect of increasing it, by its heart-
hardening influence on the rich, and by its chilling influence on the
self-respect, on the hope, on the entire heart, of the poor.　The
poor-house, like the American Colonization Society, takes from our
sight, and, in taking from our sight, takes from our sympathy also,
those, whose presence and association with us are vitally needed for
their and our mutual welfare—for their and our mutual nourishment
of their and our wronged and sickly manhood.　Like that society
also, it produces in us a loathing of those whom we should love ;
and whom we can no more afford to loathe, than they can to be
loathed.　Let us keep the poor with us.　' Out of sight out of mind,'
is an adage of most emphatic application, in this case.　Let us not
drive them away from us.　Let us ' hide not ourselves from our own
flesh.'　Let us not be like the statesmen of whom Wordsworth
speaks, in his Cumberland Beggar : ' who ' in their impatience of
the poor :

> " have a broom still ready in their hands
> To rid the world of nuisances."

"　The rich and the poor should dwell together.　Their intermixture
is for the profit of both.　It cannot fail to result in a similarity of
their circumstances, and in the production of a character common to
both, and far better than now belongs to either.

*　*　*　*　*　*　*

"　I would, in this connection, advert to the great radical mistake
on the subject of education.　A concern for the public safety, and,
I admit, a measure of benevolence also, are multiplying schools for
the enlightenment of what are called the lower classes.　I would not
speak disparagingly of schools.　Nevertheless, they are an inferior
agency in the work of education.　The practically admitted equality
of all men, and the free intercourse of all human minds with all
human minds, and of all human hearts with all human hearts, would
contribute to this work unspeakably more than schools can.　Besides,
whilst on the one hand, schools have utterly failed to produce this

admission of equality and this intercourse ; this admission and this intercourse would, on the other hand, prepare the way for the amplest supply of schools. This object—the enlightenment of the lower classes—cannot be effected, until the cord of caste is cut, and the lower classes are permitted to mingle freely with the higher ;— until, indeed, all classes are permitted to constitute one class. Under the present arrangements of society, the masses must, necessarily, remain in ignorance. Boston boasts much of her free schools, and of the accessibility of her fountains of knowledge to all grades and classes of her people. But, let the barriers, which aristocracy has erected in that city, be thrown down, and more would be done in five years, toward making the diffusion of knowledge 'and the blessing of education commensurate with her whole population, than can be done in five hundred years, if these barriers remain. I admit, that, even in the present state of the world—that, even in the present order, or rather disorder, of things—something is done, and more may be, to enlighten, comfort, and bless, the ignorant, the poor, and the wretched. But the pride of rank has built thick and high its division wall across the human brotherhood ; and to every attempt for the welfare of the many, it frowningly replies : " Hitherto shalt thou come, but no farther."

" And, not only is aristocracy an insuperable obstacle to the universality of education ; but the aristocrats themselves are, by the very exclusiveness of their spirit, prevented from obtaining a sound education. The legitimate end of education, or rather true education itself, is an increase of sympathy with God, come that increase from whatever sources it may. He is the best educated man, who has attained to the deepest and most abiding sympathy with his Maker. But that a man should sympathize with his Maker, and not with the human family, is an impossibility. " He that loveth not his brother, whom he hath seen, how can he love God, whom he hath not seen ? " It is, without exception, true, that he whose sympathies are too select to embrace the whole human family, is still unacquainted with the great heart and real character of God : and it is also true, without exception, that he who is the subject of this unacquaintance, is, in the view of such as rightly define knowledge and education, most emphatically ignorant and uneducated—and this too, whatever books and schools may have done for him.

*   *   *   *   *   *   *   *

This sincere love of man as man was the characteristic trait of Gerrit Smith. It was founded on respect

5

for human nature, faith in human capacity, confidence in future progress, assurance of hope in the complete destiny of the race. His humanity was not born of sentiment or natural feeling, but of religious principle. It was not the humanity of the philanthropist who makes a trade of doing good to his neighbors. It was not the humanity of the Christian who regards believers with approval and unbelievers with compassion. It was not the humanity of the patriot who loves his countryman, of the white man who loves his race, of the masculine being who loves his sex. It was love for the human creature, without regard to accidents of condition. The customary form of charity—that of giving money to the needy—was exercised by him with more discretion than is supposed, for he knew its tendency to work inhumanly, to the degradation of those it seems to help ; but it was exercised on a scale rarely equalled in extent, probably never equalled in the variety of its objects. It was an early saying of his that he meant to die poor. " God gives me money to give away," was his pithy remark at the close of his life, when common sympathy becomes cool, and ordinary purse strings become stiff. No one will ever know how much he gave away ; no record of it was made. The tide of benefaction was perpetually flowing, in large streams or in small, and must have carried away thirty, forty, fifty thousand dollars a year. The daily applications from strangers often amounted to tens of thousands of dollars. More than once they reached a hundred thousand and over. Nor was it dispensed in driblets. It is still an open question whether it be wiser charity to build an institution for the use of generations, like the Cooper Union, or the Peabody Institutes, or to make happy the multitude of living men and women, and thus prepare a present generation for better days. Gerrit Smith did both. His private benefactions were boundless. He literally gave away fortunes to relieve immediate distress. Old men and women asked for sustenance in their infirmity. To redeem farms, to buy unproductive land, to send children to school, applications were made from every part of the country. A girl wants a piano; a boy wants money to buy a watch, and encloses a photographic likeness of himself, to be returned, in case the request is declined. A woman solicits the gift of an alpaca dress, and is particular that the trimmings be sent with it. The small cheques flew about in all directions, carrying in the aggregate thousands of dollars, hundreds of which fell on sandy or gravelly soil, and produced nothing. He was reconciled to the seeming waste, for he felt that it would probably be wasted if spent otherwise; he was sure it would be wasted if spent on selfish pleasure or personal adornment, and he thought the waste of charity no worse than the waste of passion. The love was edifying if the gift was ill bestowed. He did not deliberately pour his water on the sand. But permanent institutions, too, bear witness to the solid character of his bounty. The public subscription papers of his times usually bore his name at the head, and for the largest sum. There were $5,000 to a single war fund. The English destitute received at one time $1,000, the Poles $1,000, the Greeks as much or more. The sufferers by a fire at Canastota received the next morning $1,000. The sufferers by the Irish famine were gladdened by a gift of $2,000. A thousand went to the sufferers from the grasshoppers in Kansas and Nebraska. The Cuban subscriptions took $5,000. Individuals in distress, anti-slavery men, temperance reformers, teachers, hard working ministers of whatever denomination, received sums all the way from $500 to $50. In cases where money was required to vindicate a principle—as in the Chaplin case—thousands of dollars were contributed. To keep slavery out of Kansas cost him $16,000. He helped on election expenses, maintained papers, supported editors and their families, was at perpetual charge for the maintenance of societies organized for particular reforms. The free library at Oswego, an admirable institution, comprising about six thousand wisely selected volumes, with less trash than any public collection of books we ever saw, owes its existence to his endowment of $30,000 in 1853. Judicious management, seconded by the liberality of the city, makes this library a minister to the higher intellectual culture. His own college, Hamilton, received $20,000; Oneida Institute thousands at a time; Oberlin, a pet with him on account of its freedom from race and sex prejudice, was endowed with land as well as aided by money. The central college at McGrawville appealed to him, not in vain. The Normal School at Hampton obtained in response to an appeal for help in 1874, $2,000. Reading rooms, libraries, academies of all degrees drew resources from him. Seminaries in Virginia, Tennessee, Georgia, Vermont, tasted his bounty. Gen. R. E. Lee's Washington College was as welcome as any to what he had to bestow. Berea College in Kentucky received in 1874, $4,720. Storer College at Harper's Ferry, received the same year, two donations each of a thousand dollars. Fisk University at Nashville, the Howard Univer-

sity at Washington, drew handsomely from his stores.
He at one period, shortly before the establishment of
Cornell University, projected a great university for the
State of New York, for the highest education of men
and women, white and black, and would have carried
his plan into execution but for the difficulty of procuring
the superintendent he wanted. His donation of $10,000
to the Colonization Society—because he had pledged it,
though when he paid the money he had satisfied himself
that the Society was not what he had been led to believe—was considered by many abolitionists a proceeding the chivalrous honor whereof hardly excused the
indiscreet support given to what he now regarded as a
fraud. His charges for the rescue and maintenance of
fugitives from southern slavery were very heavy; in one
year they amounted to $5,000. To meet the incessant
casual calls that were made on him, it was a custom to
have checques prepared and only requiring to be signed
and filled in with the applicant's name, for various
amounts. No call of peculiar necessity escaped his attention, and his bounty was as delicate as it was generous.
Whole households looked to him as their preserver and
constant benefactor. A unique example of his benevolence was his donation, through committees, of a generous sum of money, as much as $30,000, to destitute
old maids and widows in every county of the State.
The individual gift was not great, $50 to each, but the
total was considerable; the humanity expressed in the
idea is chiefly worth considering.

The primary source of his wealth was land. He was
one of the great landholders of the country; and yet he
was a leader in the cause of land reform. It was his

belief that the land should, no more than the air or the light, be appropriated by individuals, but that each man had a right to as much as he needed. This faith he openly professed, preached it, printed it, attended conventions held to advocate it. Unlike a living " friend of the working man," who justifies the keeping of his private property on the ground that he received it from another and therefore could not call it his own to give away,—Gerrit Smith reasoned that he had no claim to keep what he had not earned, and could not improve. His views of land reform exposed him to ridicule as a visionary, and to obloquy as a hypocrite. His land titles were disputed; the value of his gifts was questioned ; he was accused of making a reputation for philanthropy by giving away worthless tracts. A simple narration of facts will best refute these calumnies. On the 1st of August, 1846, the following letter was addressed to Rev. Theodore S. Wright, Rev. Charles B. Ray, and Dr. J. McCune Smith, as representative men of their people.

Dear Friends, — For years I have indulged the thought, that, when I had sold enough land to pay my debts, I would give away the remainder to the poor.

I am an Agrarian. I would that every man who desires a farm, might have one ; and I would, that no man were so regardless of the needs and desires of his brother men, as to covet the possession of more farms than one. Do not understand that I sympathize with lawless, violent and bloody Agrarianism. " My soul, come not thou into their secret; unto their assembly mine honor, be not thou united."

I have, with the Divine blessing, been able to make sales of land the present year, so extensive, as to inspire me with confidence, that my debts, very great as their sum still is, will be paid, in a few years. It is true, that, to make this event more certain, I must sell more land. Nevertheless, I feel it safe to make a beginning *now,* in the

work of distributing land. I have, indeed, heretofore given tracts
of land to public institutions, and a few small parcels to individuals:
but I have now to enter upon the greater and better work of making
large donations of land to the poor.

I will, at the present time give away but a part of the land, which
I intend to give away. It will, perhaps, be better not to give away
the remainder, until my debts are wholly paid. This land was accumulated principally by my father, the late Peter Smith.

I hope to be able to make, in all, some three thousand deeds—
most of them now, and the remainder within two or three years.
The deeds will generally convey from forty to sixty acres of land
each.

To whom among the poor I shall make these deeds, is a question
I did not solve hastily. I needed no time to conclude, that, inasmuch
as my home and the land are both in this State, it would be very suitable to select my beneficiaries from among the people of this State.
But, for a long time, I was at a loss to decide, whether to take my
beneficiaries from the meritorious poor generally, or from the
meritorious colored poor only.

I could not put a bounty on color. I shrank from the least appearance of doing so : and if I know my heart, it was equally com-
passionate toward such white and black men as are equal sufferers.
In the end, however, I concluded to confine my gifts to colored people. I had not come to this conclusion had the land I have to give
away been several times as much as it is. I had not come to it,
were not the colored people the poorest of the poor, and the most
deeply wronged class of our citizens. That they are so, is evident,
if only from the fact, that the cruel, killing, Heaven-defying prejudice
of which they are the victims, has closed against them the avenues
to riches and respectability—to happiness and usefulness. That
they are so, is also evident from the fact, that, whilst white men in
this State, however destitute of property, are allowed to vote for
Civil Rulers, every colored man in it, who does not own landed estate to the value of two hundred and fifty dollars, is excluded from
the exercise of this natural and indispensably protective right. I
confess, that this mean and wicked exclusion has had no little effect
in producing my preference, in this case. I confess too, that I was
influenced by the consideration, that there is great encouragement
to improve the condition of our free colored brethren, because that
every improvement in it contributes to loosen the bands of the
enslaved portion of their outraged and afflicted race.

And, now, will you permit me to tax you with no little labor—

the labor of making out a list of the colored men in certain counties, who shall receive a deed of land from me? My only restrictions upon you in making out this list, is,

1st. That upon it there be the name of no person younger than twenty-one and no person older than sixty.

2d. That there be upon it the name of no person who is in easy circumstances as to property; and no person, who is already the owner of land.

3d. That there be upon it the name of no drunkard—and I had almost added of no person who drinks intoxicating liquor—since to drink it, though ever so moderately, is to be in the way to drunkenness.

4th. That the total number of names in the list be one thousand nine hundred and eighty-five; that

127	thereof be the names of the persons residing in the county of	Suffolk.
215	" " " " " "	Queens.
197	" " " " " "	Kings.
861	" " " " " "	New York.
32	" " " " " "	Richmond.
31	" " " " " "	Rockland.
115	" " " " " "	Westchester.
150	" " " " " "	Dutchess.
5	" " " " " "	Sullivan.
106	" " " " " "	Ulster.
136	" " " " " "	Orange.
10	" " " " " "	Putnam.

I take the liberty to suggest, that the true course, in the case of each of the aforesaid counties, will be to have the names of the persons who are qualified to share in my lands, or rather to share in the chance of getting them, written on slips of paper—these slips put in a vessel—and as many drawn therefrom as there are persons in the county to receive deeds.

Could I receive the list by the first day of next month (and I most earnestly hope that I can), I should be able to put a considerable share of the deeds into your hands by the first day of the following month; and, in that case, the grantees might be put in possession of them by the middle of October. It may be a year or more, ere I can supply all with deeds—and it is possible that some may be finally unsupplied. A part of the names—that is, an incomplete list, you might perhaps be able to send me in a week or two.

Do not fail to have the names and places of residence written very legibly. Should it be so, that, from the death of some of the grantees, or from other cause or causes, you cannot deliver all the deeds, you will, in that case, promptly return me such as are undelivered, and recommend other persons as worthy of the land described in them. The deeds will come to the grantees clear of all fees for drawing them, and taking the acknowledgment of their execution.

For all this service which I ask at your hands, I can make you no other compensation than that of thanking you for helping me promote a scheme of justice and benevolence.

There is still a balance of purchase money and interest due to the State of New York, on a large proportion of the parcels of land. The aggregate is a very large sum. But I propose to begin paying it within six months, and I hope to have it all paid within two years.

There is also a great amount of taxes due on them—for which they will be sold next year, or the year after, if not previously paid. I will pay the taxes so far as to prevent such sale—and this will be in full of all taxes up to 1844 or 1845 exclusive. I should be grieved, and have abundant reason to be, should any of the grantees suffer their parcels of land to be sold for the non-payment of taxes.

Among the parcels which I give away, will doubtless be found some that are unfit for cultivation. Most of these, however, will be more or less valuable for timber. I hope that the grantees will prize their lands sufficiently to guard them against trespassers.

I have a few large tracts of land, which, because they are either very remote from settlements, or very mountainous and sterile, I prefer selling for what they will bring, to giving them away to those who need lands for agriculture.

I write to gentlemen in other parts of the State, asking of them services in respect to other counties similar to those which I ask of you.   Very respectfully
                        Your Friend,
                                GERRIT SMITH.

Peterboro, September 9, 1846.

Messrs. THEODORE S. WRIGHT, CHARLES B. RAY, J. M'CUNE SMITH.

Dear Friends — I have now made out two thousand of the three thousand deeds of land which, in my letter to you of the first of August last, I proposed to give to the colored men in this State. A large share of them have already been sent to you and the other committees charged with the distribution of them. They are all dated 1st September, 1846.

The gentleman who took my acknowledgment of the execution of the deeds, being both a judge and counsellor of the Supreme Court, it will be unnecessary to have certificates of the County Clerk attached to them. This expense, and the expense of recording such certificates, the grantees will be saved. The recording of the deed will be but little, as the form is so very brief.

When I shall make out the remaining one thousand deeds, is uncertain. Perhaps a couple of years hence. Prudence requires, that I should first pay off all, or a great part, of the large debt, (purchase money, interest and taxes) due on the land I have already given away. The prospect is now fair that, by the divine blessing on my continued toils, I shall be enabled to pay my debts, make out the thousand deeds, and have, over and above the needs of my family, a considerable sum to expend in purchasing the liberty of slaves. I wish you to understand, that there is one use of property far more delightful to my heart than giving it away to the poor. It is, expending it in the purchase of my fellow-men from under the yoke of slavery. I speak, not as a stranger to this use of property; but from oft repeated experience of its sweetness. I am utterly insensible to the force of the arguments—even though employed sometimes by abolitionists—against the duty of purchasing liberty for the slave. Were three millions of our own countrymen dying of the cholera, the first and most religious use of property would be to afford them relief. But three millions of our countrymen are in the chains of slavery; and the argument for conceding to them the first and holiest claim on our property, is as much stronger than in the former case, as slavery is more horrible than disease or death. I am aware that it is said, that we endorse the usurpation of the slaveholder, when we purchase his slave,—even though we purchase him for the sole purpose of freeing him. As well, however, may it be said that we justify the murderer when we pay him the sum which, with his dagger at the throat of his victim, he demands for the release of that victim.

I am grieved to learn, that intemperance has made such havoc among the colored people of this State. I fear that, notwithstanding all the scrutiny on this point of my committees, there will be found to be, here and there, a drunkard on the list of names they have sent me. As a matter of course, vain, and worse than vain, will be my grant of land to a drunkard. And now, my friends, may I request you to prepare, and send out a circular among the persons whose names the committees have collected? This circular will contain your best advice in respect to the habits and duties of the grantees. It will, of course, inculcate the deepest abhorrence of intoxicating drinks.

With great regard,

Your friend,

GERRIT SMITH.

The land alluded to in the above letters was in Franklin, Essex, Hamilton, Fulton, Oneida, Delaware, Madison and Ulster Counties.

This generous gift was received with gratitude. The three men to whom the letters were addressed prepared an address to their people impressing upon their minds the obligation that such an act laid upon them to justify the donor's munificence by their own conduct. They set forth in strong language the nature of the opportunity granted, reminded them of the corresponding duty to accept it in the spirit cherished by their benefactor, called on them to summon their manhood—to practice system, economy, self-reliance, mutual assistance, temperance, and hailed the promise of a new career on the continent for their oppressed and discouraged race. The assertion that the lands were worthless was indignantly repelled.

On the 1st of May, 1849, the following letter was addressed to John Cochran, Isaac T. Hopper, Daniel C. Eaton, George H. Evans, and William Kemeys:

Dear Sirs : — I still have village and city property—but on the large share of it there remains and must long remain, a very great debt. The debt due to the State of New York on my other land will, I hope, be paid within the coming year. All, or nearly all such of this land as shall then remain upon my hands, I shall wish to give away. There will perhaps be enough of it to enable me to make gifts to a thousand persons. These persons must be white inhabitants of the State of New York ; must be between the ages of twenty-one and sixty ; must be virtuous, landless and poor ; and must be entirely clear of the vice of drinking intoxicating liquors. Moreover they must, in each county, be taken from the sexes in equal numbers.

Along with each gift of land there will be a gift of ten dollars in money. Where the land is worth removing to, and where there is a disposition to remove to it, this money will help defray the expense of removal. In perhaps every case, it will be sufficient to pay the two or three years taxes now due, and also the taxes for a number of years to come.

Each county, except Madison, is to share in the proposed gifts, and each according to the amount of its population. I shall not be blamed for making this exception, by any who are aware that, in some two hundred and fifty instances, I have given to the inhabitants of the county of Madison either land, or money to enable them to buy land. Nor shall I be blamed for distributing the thousand parcels among white persons exclusively, by any who are informed that three thousand colored persons have received deeds of land from me, entirely free of all charge either for the land, or for the expense of the perfected deeds thereof. I will remark here, that the deeds of the thousand parcels will be made, acknowledged and prepared for record at my own expense.

The number of beneficiaries in each county will be as follows :

Albany	30	Hamilton	2	Rensselaer	24
Alleghany	16	Herkimer	14	Richmond	4
Broome	10	Jefferson	26	Rockland	6
Cattaraugus	12	Kings	32	Saratoga	16
Cayuga	20	Lewis	8	Schenectady	4
Chautauqua	18	Livingston	12	Schoharie	12
Chemung	8	Monroe	28	Seneca	10
Chenango	16	Montgomery	12	St. Lawrence	26
Clinton	12	New York	150	Steuben	20
Columbia	16	Niagara	14	Suffolk	12
Cortland	10	Oneida	34	Sullivan	6
Delaware	14	Onondaga	28	Tioga	8
Dutchess	22	Ontario	16	Tompkins	14
Erie	32	Orange	20	Ulster	18
Essex	10	Orleans	10	Warren	6
Franklin	8	Oswego	22	Washington	16
Fulton	6	Otsego	20	Wayne	16
Genesee	10	Putnam	4	Westchester	18
Greene	12	Queens	12	Wyoming	10
				Yates	8

Total 1000

The next thing in this letter is to say that I have a great favor to ask of you. It is that you go to the pains of selecting the beneficiaries in your county. And that you do, by the 1st of March next, let me know their names and residences.

To guard the beneficiaries of your county against disappointment. I wish you would inform them that most of the land is of inferior quality ; that it is probable that in some instances, it will prove to be unfit for farming ; in some of little or no value either for farming or timber ; and that it is possible (I trust but barely possible) that my title may fail. You will, moreover, inform them that in the event of my not having land enough to give each of the thousand a parcel, some of those chosen in your county may be left unsupplied. You are, however, authorized to say to them that whoever of the thousand shall fail to get a parcel of land from me, shall get, instead thereof, forty dollars in money,—and this too, in addition to the ten dollars. The fifty dollars will enable its possessor to buy forty acres of government land. I hope that it will be expended in some land or other ;—for one of my deepest convictions is, that every person who can, should make himself the acknowledged owner of a piece of land. His doing so would hasten the day, when the right to the soil shall be everywhere acknowledged to be as absolute, universal and equal as the right to the light and the air. May that blessed day come quickly !—for, until it does come, our world will be one of disorder, oppression, poverty, vice :—and, let me add, it never will come, until the religion and politics, the churches and governments of the world shall be so imbued with the spirit of justice and brotherly love as to call for the coming of that day.

The parcel for each beneficiary will probably vary from thirty to sixty acres. In a few instances it may exceed sixty ; and in a few, where its value may be far above the average of the parcels, it may be less than half of thirty. All the land is in the State of New York.

Respectfully your friend,

GERRIT SMITH.

On January 4th, 1850, another letter on the subject was addressed to the same men.

Gentlemen — I proposed, last spring, to make gifts to five hundred males and five hundred females, inhabitants of this State. I requested you to select from the city and county of New York seventy-five of each sex ; and I requested persons in the other counties of our State, to select the remaining four hundred and twenty-five of each sex. You kindly and promptly undertook the labor, which I presumed to assign you ; and I now have the pleasure to receive from you the one hundred and fifty names.

I have come to the conclusion that it is not best for the females to receive land from me. What land I have left, and my title to which is unquestionable, is with small exceptions, unfit for farming. My gifts to colored people took all my large tracts of farming land, save one in the county of Franklin ; and this can perhaps, hardly be called a farming tract. It is of inferior soil ; and I cannot say that it is very valuable in any respect. Notwithstanding some of the lots abound in pine, the tract is too far from market to make it very desirable for its timber. The Boston and Ogdensburgh Railroad, however, passes within some sixteen or eighteen miles of it.

This tract, which contains nearly nineteen thousand acres, and which my deceased father had his surveyor divide into farm lots, I conclude to give to the five hundred men, each of whom will, as I formerly proposed, receive ten dollars along with his deed.

The five hundred females will each receive fifty dollars. This sum is sufficient to purchase forty acres of Government land. I hope that each one who does not so expend it, will expend it in the purchase of other lands. To you, who know my heart on this subject, I need not say how deeply I feel that every person needs to be the admitted owner of a parcel of land. This every person should be, without having to pay for it. But if a free ownership be withheld, still let there be an ownership whenever it can be bought, if for no other reason than that the more who are the admitted owners of land, the sooner will that ownership be acknowledged to be a natural, universal and inalienable right. I would have every person get a parcel of land who can get it.

Alas, that good men should be so slow to see that the acknowledged right of every generation and the whole of every generation, to the use of the earth, as well as to the use of the sea, the light and the air, is necessarily preliminary to that state of universal comfort and happiness and holiness for which good men labor and pray ! So vitally important, so indispensable is this right, in my view, that no person who rejects it can get my vote to be a civil ruler or a moral instructor. How long will the people consent to be put off with bribes and toys and deceptions in the place of the acknowledgment of their right ? The governments of the earth all refuse to acknowledge the right of the people to the soil. And yet the people, stripped though they are of this greatest right, and of this only effectual security for all their rights, sustain and honor these governments ! And this they do, because their governments help them pay their parsons or their school-masters, or bribe them in some other way. Only let the governments of the earth give back to their subjects the rights of which they are robbed; and their subjects will lack neither the ability nor the disposition to take the whole care and bear the whole burden of their schools and churches.

I send you herewith seventy-five deeds of land, and seven hundred and fifty dollars for the seventy-five males you have selected, and three thousand seven hundred and fifty dollars for the seventy-five females you have selected. Should the grantees wish to make inquiries respecting the land, I hope they will make them of you. I cannot even read, much less can I answer, all the letters which I receive.

To the committees in the other counties I will send deeds and ten dollars with each as fast as I receive from them the names of the males whom they select. My gifts to the females whom they select, I shall not be able to complete in a less space of time than a year or eighteen months, as my first duty with the moneys I receive is to employ a large share of them in continuing to reduce the great amount of debt which I still owe. It is probable, however, that I shall, every month, pay the females of one or more counties.

With great regard, your friend,
Gerrit Smith.

Before taking his seat in Congress, Gerrit Smith, as if he would go unincumbered into the national arena, issued the following circular:

Peterboro, March 22d, 1853.

To ——

Dear Sir—Ere leaving home to take my seat in Congress, I should like to dispose of all my remaining lands. They are scattered through some twenty counties of the State of New York. Very few of them are in the western, and none in the south-eastern part of the State.

These lands are generally of inferior quality, and are worth more for fuel and lumber than for farming. I would sell them cheap rather than retain them. Descriptions of them can be obtained at my office.

I expect to be at home pretty constantly for the present. Such of these lands as I may not be able to sell previously, I will, should the collection of people authorize it, offer at auction at my office, Wednesday, 1st day of June next.

In case of the sale of any parcel of land whether on said 1st day of June or before, for not more than fifty dollars, all the purchase money must be paid in hand. Where the sale is for more than fifty dollars and not less than one hundred dollars, one-half must be paid in hand. Where for one hundred dollars and over, one quarter. For the balance the purchaser may have a long credit.

I have still a little property in the cities of Schenectady and Albany, and much in the city of Oswego. I should be glad to sell it all.

GERRIT SMITH.

The experiment of colonizing the blacks in northern New York was not successful. Mr. Smith candidly admitted that it was not. The failure was due in part, no doubt, to the intractability of the land and the harshness of the climate. Much of the territory given to the blacks, and to the whites as well, was unsuited to agriculture, as Mr. Smith frankly stated. He never concealed the true character of the acres he gave away; he never took or asked praise for giving away good land, when he gave away bad. The failure of the plan was in some measure owing to the infelicity of the soil. But in a greater measure it was owing to the inefficiency of those that accepted it. The disabling infirmities and vices of the black people Mr. Smith had the courage to admit. He had little hope of them as they were; on the best land they would have done nothing. They had none of the qualities that make the farmer. He knew they had not. Messrs. Wright Ray and McCune Smith knew they had not. Their stirring appeal was ineffectual. Gerrit Smith's heroic hope that opportunity and necessity would rouse the blacks to manhood was illusive. The beneficiaries could not respond to the call of the benefactor. Had the land been the richest in the State they would not have responded, for they could not; it was not in them. Is it fair to lay the blame upon him? Would it not be fairer to commend the practical wisdom that squandered low priced instead of high priced lands in a venture so uncertain? The experience of civilization proves that manliness thrives on hardship. If the hardship is shrunk from or shirked, the inference is that the elements of manhood are wanting. It does not appear that the blacks ever accused their benefactor of gaining the reputation of philanthropy at their expense; but the whites did. The candid student of the subject will probably conclude that the fault lay, not so much in the land or its donor, as in the inefficiency of the people who desired a Capua, and rebelled when they found a New England. The man who had most cause for discouragement was Gerrit Smith himself. Many men, good men too, would have abandoned all efforts at elevating the lowly of his race, after so disastrous a result of so courageous an attempt.

It is needless to say, now, that Gerrit Smith's humanity made no account of the distinctions of race. In 1836 he wrote to his wife: " I hope you will have grace to set your face like a flint against the accursed spirit of aristocracy. I hope our dear Lilly, if she has one particle of that wicked thing in her heart called prejudice against people of color, will make haste to get rid of it. This prejudice is a quarrel with God." To many he is known chiefly by his devotion to the Africans, they being, in his regard, the most inhumanly treated. His consideration of them in gifts of land and money attests the warmth of his interest. It was at his instance that Peterboro became one of the chief stations of the " underground railroad," as the arrangement was called by which escaped slaves were passed on through the northern States to Canada; and his open invitation was heard and caught at with eagerness. It was not so much a *welcome* that he gave as a *bidding*. He called the slaves to come out of their Egypt; advised them to repeat the old device of plundering their masters of the means of escape, to take what they needed, food, money, horses, that their flight might be swift and their rescue sure. "The doctrine that I am to look on every other man as my brother,—ay, as another self—is a doctrine which bids *me* peril and suffer and inflict as much for his sake, as I would have *him* peril, and suffer and inflict for it. It may not be his duty to lose life or take life in order to exempt himself from slavery. But if he is authorized to go to these extremities, it is absurd to say that I sin if I carry my help of him to the like extremities." The station at Peterboro was usually full. In times of unusual excitement, like those immediately succeeding the "Fugitive Slave Bill," it was no uncommon thing to see negroes in the street asking the way to Mr. Smith's house. The busy man left his affairs and bestowed immediate care on his guests; fed them, clothed them, gave them money for necessary expenses, sent them in his own wagon to Oswego, and saw them in safety on their way northward. He was immensely cheated, of course; but he took the cheating patiently, saying that he would rather be swindled twenty times than miss a single chance of delivering a fellow-man from slavery.

It was wonderful what pains he would be at, what trouble he would take, what risks he would incur, what money he would spend, to compass this object. Hearing that a southern slaveholder, dying, had declared his slaves, fifty in number, emancipated, on condition of their being taken to a northern state and provided for, he wrote instantly, directing that they be sent to him. Ten only reached Peterboro; the rest dropped off by the way, some tired, some disheartened, some deterred by the misstatements of ill wishers, who represented Mr. Smith's promises as deceptive. The ten strangers, who persevered to the end, being in need of no further transportation, were quartered in the old ancestral house, then unaltered and unoccupied. The descendants of these negroes still live in Peterboro. Mrs. Smith was born in Maryland, and there a favorite slave remained when the family removed to New York. The poor creature was sold and resold till the trace of her was nearly lost. By the help of a special agent she was found, purchased, brought to Peterboro, and there cared for during the remainder of her life.

Dr. Alexander Ross, of Toronto, whose remarkable exploits in "running off" slaves between 1855 and 1865, caused such consternation in the Southern States, was in communication with Gerrit Smith from first to last, was aided by him in his preparations with information and counsel, and had a close understanding with him in regard to his course of procedure. Both these men made the rescue of slaves a personal matter.

Here is an incident that shows the quality of Mr. Smith's concern. A slave called Anderson, taking the advice of the northern philanthropist, ran away from his bondage in Kentucky and escaped to Ohio. The master pursued, overtook and seized the fugitive; there was a struggle; the slave killed the master and fled to

Canada. Some months afterwards, friends of the slain
man, learning that Anderson was in Toronto, induced
the Governor of Kentucky to make a requisition on the
provincial Governor of Canada to deliver the criminal,
under the provisions of the Ashburton Treaty which
was signed at Washington, in 1842. The order was
taken to Canada, and the writ was served. Anderson
was not unknown in Toronto. He had behaved well,
and had made friends. The circumstances of his being
a fugitive from slavery interested many in his fate.
Fortunately there was telegraphic communication with
the States. A message sent to Mr. Smith was carried
by swift express to Peterboro. Smith remembered the
man and the incidents of his escape. He left his office
at once, ordered his horses and was on his way to Toronto in less than two hours from the moment of Anderson's arrest. At Canastota, nine miles from home, he
sent a message bidding the friends of the fugitive block
proceedings till he arrived. At Buffalo there was no
time to stop ; he pushed on and reached Toronto in
season for the opening of the court. There he offered
himself as counsel for Anderson. The case being presented, the unprofessional advocate, in a speech, une-
laborated and unpremeditated, except on the hurried
journey, but of great power and cogency, made his plea.
The incidental points pressed were these :—1. That Anderson, in killing his pursuer had been guilty of no murder, but at the worst of justifiable homicide. He had
obeyed the law of nature, the supreme law, in slaying
one who would have taken from him what was dearer
than life ; the alleged crime was therefore no crime,
rather it was a manly, heroic deed, entitling the man to

praise and not to punishment. 2. The deed was done in Ohio, not in Kentucky, and as Ohio had made no requisition, the proceedings even though the man could be fairly charged with murder, were void. 3. The question whether Anderson should or should not be given up was one for the English law to decide. The case must be tried by English law, which made no recognition of slavery. The main argument was, however, addressed to the point that neither the Ashburton Treaty nor the United States Constitution required the surrender of fugitive slaves, but that both demanded their freedom. Still even this argument, full and cogent as it was, owed its compelling power to the devotion to humanity which inspired the orator, making his very stature seem gigantic. The advocate gained his cause triumphantly. The speech made a prodigious impression, coming as it did from a glowing heart, a mind of great fertility, and fortified by a touching power of eloquence. It was printed, and circulated over all the United States. It was commented on in the London *Times*, which applauded the action of the provincial tribunal, declared that the law of England fully sustained the judgment, and characterized Gerrit Smith as the Robert Peel of America.

Gerrit Smith was in attendance on a convention of the Liberty Party at Syracuse, Oct. 1, 1851, when the alarm bell told the Vigilance Committee that a black man had been seized under the " Fugitive Slave Law." Rev. Samuel J. May was rising from the dinner table when the news came, and by making haste reached the court house where a crowd had already assembled to watch the proceedings. The excitement was gathering. The prisoner, Jerry McHenry, manacled and guarded,

was being put through "the summary process" peculiar
to those occasions, and his friends were hurriedly taking
counsel together for his deliverance. Suddenly the lad,
being loosely watched, slipped from his captors and ran
for his life. His pursuers were the fleeter; they overtook him, mastered him after a short but furious struggle, flung him into a wagon and drove him, pinioned to
the floor of the cart by the weight of two policemen,
back to the jail. It was now evening and the trembling
fugitive, hearing the uproar without, thought his hour
had come. And so it had,—the hour of his deliverance.
Gerrit Smith was on the field, animating and impelling.
Sturdy arms drove a battering-ram against the prison
door; it yielded; Jerry was dragged forth, put into a
light carriage drawn by a fleet span of horses; money
was thrust into his hand; a great voice bade him to
keep clear of the States, and he was before long safe in
Canada. The next morning, before the convention,
Gerrit Smith presented the following resolutions:

1. Whereas Daniel Webster, that base and infamous enemy of
the human race, did in a speech of which he delivered himself in
Syracuse last spring, exultingly and insultingly predict that fugitive
slaves would yet be taken away from Syracuse, and even from anti-
slavery conventions in Syracuse; and whereas, the attempt to fulfil
this prediction was delayed until the first day of October, 1851, when
the Liberty Party of the State of New York were holding their Annual Convention in Syracuse; and whereas, the attempt was defeated by the majestic and mighty uprising of two thousand five
hundred brave men, before whom the half dozen kidnappers were
but "as tow;"—therefore,

Resolved, That we rejoice that the city of Syracuse—the anti-
slavery city of Syracuse—the city of anti-slavery conventions—our
beloved and glorious city of Syracuse—still remains undisgraced by
the fulfilment of the satanic prediction of the satanic Daniel
Webster.

Resolved, That the gratitude of our hearts goes out to the God of the oppressed for the defeat of this attempt to replunge a poor brother into the horrors and hell of slavery ; and that although we are pleased to know that the outraged and indignant people spared the life of every one of the kidnappers, we nevertheless feel bound to declare that if any class of criminals deserve to be struck down in instant death it is kidnappers.

Resolved, That notwithstanding the enactment of the " Fugitive Slave Law," and the general acquiescence in it under the influence of the devil-prompted speeches of politicians and devil-prompted sermons of priests, give fearful evidence that this is a doomed and damned nation, we nevertheless cannot forbear to derive some little hope from the recent resistance to kidnappers in Pennsylvania, and from the resistance to them yesterday in Syracuse, that a patient and long-suffering God has not left this superlatively wicked nation to perish.

Resolved, That every fresh demonstration of the character and claims of slavery, serves to bind the principles of the Liberty Party still closer and closer to our hearts ; and to make it more manifest that we have no right to vote for any person for civil office—however high or however low may be the office—who is not an out and out abolitionist.

To those whose memory goes not back to these times of dread excitement, the spirit of these resolutions will seem fanatical, and their language intemperate. But they who lived then, and shared anything of the feeling that prevailed, will bear testimony that the sentiments expressed are no stronger than was usual with anti-slavery men, nay, hardly so strong. The abolitionists had no words to convey their detestation of the " Fugitive Slave Law," its authors, executors and apologists. In their view it was atheistic and inhuman ; it involved an utter practical disbelief in the principles of justice and kindness ; a repudiation, not of the Bible merely, not of Christianity alone, but of every form of religious duty, of every sentiment that had become native to mankind. In Mr. Smith's mind, the feeling was one not of anger, not at all of vindictiveness, but of moral abhorrence ; it was the feeling that the Christian has for the atheist, that the saint has for Satan. His faith was in the inherent virtue of man, and slavery as the suppression of this virtue, was literally a godless institution, a creation of the evil one.

The following letter, never before published, I think, requires no explanation :

Peterboro, Nov. 21, 1846.

Mr. William Lee :

Dear Sir, — Your master, Mr. M —— writes me that you are a very bad man, and that the best thing to do with you is to sell you to a severe southern master. I take pity on you as my brother man, and send Mr. M —— one hundred and sixty dollars. Ten dollars of the one hundred and sixty, I ask him to hand you to bear your expenses here. The remaining one hundred and fifty dollars are for himself. He consents to part with you for that sum.

I write Mr. M —— to direct you to my home. I shall not be here when you arrive. I hope to find you in a good family in my neighborhood when I return. . . . I do not wish you to return me a single dollar of the one hundred and sixty dollars which you cost me. You must be content with small wages in the winter, and all the smaller as you are a stranger. But if you prove yourself to be industrious, sober and good-tempered, you will soon command good wages and have money enough to buy yourself a little home.

William ! I don't believe that the best thing to do with you was to sell you to a hard master. I believe that the best thing for you was to make you a freeman, and now that you are a freeman, you will prove yourself to be a good man, an industrious man, an honest man, a kind-tempered man. Now William, show your old master what a good man a bad slave is capable of becoming when he has his freedom.

Come to see me, William, when I get home. The Lord bless and guide you, and give you a good heart.

Your friend,
Gerrit Smith.

The "evangelical" minister who permits the use of this letter pronounces it worthy to rank with Paul's letter to Philemon. And so it is. There is this notable difference however between the two epistles, that the one is written to a master, the other to a slave; the one appeals to the "christian" feeling of a slave-holder for a slave who has become a Christian; the other appeals to the spirit of humanity in a slave who has become a man.

This regard for the "bare man" was never hidden by ceremony or affectation. The anniversary of the rescue of Jerry was kept for several years, and Gerrit Smith was happy to preside so long as he felt that the observance was sincere. When, in his judgment, it became a mere ceremony, he would have nothing more to do with it. To the invitation, which came as usual, in 1859, he made reply:

"My interest in these anniversaries has greatly declined for the last two or three years; and I am now decidedly of the opinion that it is unwise to continue to repeat the farce any longer. The rescue of Jerry was a great and glorious event. Would God it had been duly improved! But those who achieved it, and I include in this number all who cheered it on, and rejoiced in every step of its progress, have, with few exceptions, proved themselves unworthy of the work of their own hands. We delivered Jerry in the face of the authority of Congress and courts; and, as most of us believed, in contempt also of a provision of the Constitution itself. We delivered him believing that there was no law and could be no law for slavery. On that occasion our humanity was up; and in vain would all the authorities on earth, even the bible itself included, have bid it down. Our humanity owned Jerry for its brother; and so did it cling to him, that all the wealth of the world would not have sufficed to buy it off, or taught it to ignore and betray him.

Oh, had the thousands, who, on that memorable night crowded the streets of Syracuse, but maintained the sublime elevation to which the spirit of that night exalted them, what a force for the over-

5

throw of slavery would they not have accumulated by this time! But they soon fell from it. They soon sunk down to the low level of their political and church parties. Jerry was forgotten; their humanity was dead. . . .

" We had better give up the celebration of the rescue of Jerry. The thing is quite too great and good for us. Earnest and honest men are alone suited to it. We Jerry rescuers are mean men and sham men."

The courage of this position will be appreciated by those who have known how much harder it is to disagree with friends than to fight enemies. He was personally no coward who rescued the slave: he was morally no coward who reproved the slave rescuers.

A humanity so completely unconscious of the distinctions of race, was, naturally, unconscious of the civil and moral distinctions of sex. That this large hearted philanthropist devoted himself less ardently to the cause of woman's emancipation than to others, was owing probably to its less conspicuous and crying importance, and to the fact that no great battle raged about it. The opposition was not organized because the evil was less manifest. The principle was, however, evident to the philanthropist's clear mind, and his enunciation of it was decided and unqualified. His complaint was directed however against women themselves,—that they were wanting in respect for their own dignity, were creatures of fashion, slothful, capricious, vain of the silken chains they wore. Their passion for dress, their persistency in wearing a dress that condemned them to a life of display, made them slow and inactive, injured their physical health and doomed them to sedentary occupations, was in his judgment, at the root of the whole evil complained of. The reform that most concerned him in connection with women was the dress reform. The first to discard the trailing skirt and put on what afterwards was unfortunately called the " Bloomer " was his own daughter. Long, printed letters to Mrs. E. C. Stanton and Miss S. B. Anthony, committed him to the most extreme doctrine on the subject of the equality of the sexes. The following letter is interesting :

Albany, Oct. 25, 1852.

MISS PELLET, Oberlin, Ohio :

Dear Friend — On my way to this city, to take part in defending the persons charged with rescuing "Jerry," you were so good as to hand me Professor Fairchild's Report, "on the joint education of the sexes." I have read it with great interest. It is eloquent and able. Nevertheless, I can find some fault with it.

Professor F. on page 27 admits the doctrine that the sexes differ in their "mental constitution." That is as I understand him, that they differ *naturally* in this respect. Now I regard this doctrine as very false and very pernicious : and I believe that the wrongs of women will never be righted until this doctrine that there is sex in mind is exploded. But, if I read the Professor rightly, he does himself virtually tell us, on pages 33 and 34, that this doctrine is not founded in truth. He there confronts it with his "experience of twelve years " in a school where "the sexes pursued the entire range of academical study in common."

On page 37 Professor F. would guard well "the feminine instincts." But why not the masculine also? What means he by "feminine instincts?" On page 38 he would have "womanhood become more beautiful, and manhood more strong." But why would he not have each become both beautiful and strong? Beauty is as desirable and attainable an element in male character as in "female character ; " and so is strength as desirable and attainable an element in "female character" as in male character. On page 30, the Professor is concerned to preserve the modesty and delicacy of woman. And why should he not be as much concerned to have man modest and delicate as woman ?

Heaven speed the day when man shall be expected to blush as quick and as deep as woman, at every degree of impurity : and when the churches and schools and public sentiment of the whole world shall demand the same mental and moral character—the same mental and moral strength, beauty and delicacy—for woman as for man—for man as for woman.　　　GERRIT SMITH.

In the same strain is the following extract from a letter to Susan B. Anthony, written in 1853 :

"I know not why it is not as much the duty of your sex as it is of mine, to establish newspapers, write books and hold public meetings for the promotion of the cause of temperance. The current idea that modesty should hold women back from such services is all resolvable into nonsense and wickedness. Female modesty ! Female delicacy ! I would that I might never again hear such phrases. There is but one standard of modesty and delicacy for both men and women ; and so long as different standards are tolerated, both sexes will be perverse and corrupt. It is my duty to be as modest and delicate as you are, and if your modesty and delicacy may excuse you from making a public speech, then may mine excuse me from making one."

In a letter addressed to Mrs. Stanton, in 1869, on the right of women to vote, the ground taken is absolute enough to satisfy any champion of that cause.

"Women have as full right as men to participate in making the laws by which, equally with men, they are governed." . . . " Men are ever defining woman's sphere—but as well might women be guilty of the like arrogance in regard to man's sphere." "Every one should be left at entire liberty to choose an individual sphere—a man to choose to knit or sew—a woman to choose to fell trees or to be a blacksmith." The title to vote is claimed for women on four grounds. 1. As a natural right. 2. As a necessity for complete representation. 3. As a help to the enlargement of woman's range of thought and action. 4. As a qualification to be a worthy helper of man in the task of promoting progress.

In the course of argument on these points, thoughts of the most radical, searching kind were thrown out. The method of forcing the issue by persistent application at the polls found favor with him.

"I wish " he wrote, " women would, everywhere, throng the polls and offer their votes, and do this from year to year, until men can no longer withstand the appeal. Such earnestness and such determination would not fail to convince men of woman's faith in her right to vote ; and this would be quickly followed by their own belief in her right to vote, and by a breast full of shame at having withheld the right from her."

To Mrs. Stanton's inquiry why, with his opinions, he had no more faith in the movement, he frankly replied :

" It is not in the proper hands ; the proper hands are not to be found. The present age, although in advance of any former age, is nevertheless very far from being sufficiently under the sway of reason to take up the cause of woman and carry it forward to success."

" Only let woman attire her person fitly for the whole battle of life—that great and often rough battle, which she is as much bound to fight as man is, and the common sense expressed in the change will put to flight all the nonsensical fancies about her inferiority to man. No more will then be heard of her being made of a finer material than man is made of : and, on the contrary, no more will then be heard of her being but the complement of man, and of its taking both a man and a woman (the woman of course but a small part of it) to make up a unit. No more will it then be said that there is sex in mind—an original sexual difference in intellect. What a pity that so many of our noblest women make this foolish admission ! It is made by the great majority of the women who plead the cause of woman."

" I am amazed that the intelligent women engaged in the ' Woman's rights movement' see not the relation between their dress and the oppressive evils which they are striving to throw off. I am amazed that they do not see that their dress is indispensable to keep in countenance the policy and purposes, out of which those evils grow. I hazard nothing in saying that the relation between the dress and the degradation of an American woman is as vital as between the cramped foot and degradation of a Chinese woman ; as vital as between the uses of the inmate of the harem, and the apparel and training provided for her."

" Women are holding their meetings ; and with great ability do they urge their claims to the rights of property and suffrage. But, as in the case of the colored man, the great needed change is in himself, so also in the case of woman the great needed change is in herself. Of what comparative avail would be her exercise of the right of suffrage if she is still to remain the victim of her present false notions of herself and of her relations to the other sex ? "

" The next ' woman's rights convention ' will, I take it for granted, differ but little from its predecessors. It will abound in righteous demands and noble sentiments, but not in the evidence that they who enunciate these demands and sentiments are prepared to put themselves in harmony with what they conceive and demand. In a word, for the lack of such preparation, and of the deep earnestness which alone can prompt to this preparation, it will be, as has been every other ' Woman's rights convention,' a failure."

That these opinions were heretical in the judgment of the advocates as well as of the opponents of the cause, was clearly apprehended. That he would be accused of breaking down social distinctions, of unsettling moral usages, of flying in the face of the Bible, and setting at naught the precepts of religion was avowed. But the penalty of all this enormity is cheerfully encountered. The claims of humanity in this regard as well as in regard to the questions of temperance and liberty are boldly preferred to the claims of church, bible and society.

The humanity of this man knew absolutely no distinction of persons. He respected humanity in the most unpromising subjects and under the most adverse circumstances. In the adjoining town of Nelson, on the Cherry Valley Turnpike, there lived, in 1856, an old man, a farmer, named John Buck. He had lived there some sixty years. On the evening of the 14th of March, Buck was found dead in his barn, which stood opposite his house, with an ugly wound in his head. His horse was loose in the barn, and it was conjectured might have kicked the old man of eighty to death. There were no blood stains of consequence anywhere in the barn or the house, or on the white snow between, or on the dead man's person. There was clearly no attempt at robbery. But there was a blood-stained axe in the house that suggested murder. The last person seen with the dead man, who lived quite alone, was George William Zecher, a young Dutchman, who lived nearly three miles from the scene of the murder in the adjacent town of Eaton. Zecher was arrested, examined and committed for trial before the grand jury, which met at Morrisville. The incident caused great excitement through the county. Mr. Smith, learning that Zecher came from the same part of Holland with his father, was poor, a stranger, friendless and unable to speak English intelligibly, went to see him in jail, talked with him, as well as he could in Dutch, became interested in him, heard his story, was persuaded of his innocence, was impressed by his " harmless, childlike spirit," " his simple, artless manner," " his beautiful and sublime steadfastness in the truth," " his straightforward account of himself;" the " many virtues " of the prisoner won his heart, and he undertook his defence. It was no easy task. He, though destined for the law, and acquainted with so much of law as concerned the management of estates, was not by profession a lawyer, and the district attorney, David J. Mitchell, was one of the able lawyers of the State. Mr. Smith was even obliged to obtain permission to practice at the New York bar in order to defend his client. At the time he was ill, as the entries in his diary show.

Dec. 1, 1856. I go this morning to court at Morrisville to defend poor Zecher. I am suffering much from sickness, and hoarseness. I return at evening.

2, I go again, much depressed by my fears that I shall not be able to speak for the poor prisoner. I return at evening.

3, I have raised a great deal of phlegm this morning. I go again
to court, hoping my voice may so improve that I can speak to the
jury. I return at evening.

4, To court again, and return at evening. I slept but half an
hour last night.

5. I go to court again. I am very sick and my head aches
much. I slept but two hours last night.

The effort was made the following day,—December
6. It was the second trial. At the first, the jury had
disagreed. Another judge was on the bench. Mr. Smith
spoke between five and six hours, in his hearty, natural,
ingenuous way, producing great effect on the crowded
assembly by his open, sincere bearing, and his cordial
conviction; at the end of the first half-hour his head became clear, his voice recovered its tone; the fullness of
his heart flooded his mind and brightened his speech.
The case went to the jury at seven o'clock. Mr. Smith,
hat in hand, approached Zecher, took his hand and said:
"I have done all I could for you. I leave you in the
hands of an intelligent jury who, I believe, will never
decide that your life shall be taken for a crime they are
not sure you ever committed. If you are cleared by the
jury, as you cannot speak our language and have no
home, come to my house at Peterboro, and I will find
you employment." Then, bowing to the court and
bar he withdrew. At eleven o'clock that night the news
came to him that Zecher was acquitted. Early the next
day, the man appeared and received such a welcome as
Gerrit Smith knew well how to give. There was family
worship of thanks and prayer, the tears streaming down
the noble man's face as he turned it heavenward.

The man remained about a year in Mr. Smith's employ. At the end of that time it was thought best to

send him back to his native land. Preparations were made : passes were secured. The diary tells the tale.

Wednesday, *Jan.* 13, 1858, 6 A. M. George William Zecher and wife with their two children, Charles or Carl, little more than two years old, and William, born last June, left us a few moments ago for Germany. His parents sent for him to come and live with them. I had Zecher and wife with me in the library this morning. I gave them my best advice ; especially full was I in regard to strong drink and tobacco. I prayed with them. I received Willie's last assurance of his entire innocence in the matter of Mr. Buck's death, and never was I so fully convinced of his innocence as when he now told me of it and looked upon me with his large and honest (childlike honest) eyes. We parted from each other with tears and kisses—and with many thoughts and deep emotions. How I toiled for his acquittal, when he lay under the charge of murder! How I carried him for nearly a year in my anxious heart, even as a tender mother carries her sick child.

Zecher departed ; on the 19th a letter was received from a kinsman in New York saying that he had reported himself and then disappeared. The surmise was natural that he had deserted, either not sailing at all, or sailing without his family. On the 23d the good man was made unhappy by reports that his *protegé* was dishonest, quarrelsome, profane ; that he chewed tobacco and drank ; that he beat his wife, and threatened to leave her. It seemed not unlikely that he was the kind of man to commit the crime of manslaughter of which he had been acquitted. If Mr. Smith thought so he kept his suspicion in his heart, and none the less went on putting his faith in human nature.

A more remarkable case than this of Zecher, as showing how completely the humanity of the philanthropist rose above considerations of merit and demerit in the individual, and comprehended the vicious as well

6*

as the suspected—was that of the mob in Peterboro. Thus he pours out his feelings in the diary.

June 22, 1842. Peterboro, dear Peterboro, is deeply perhaps indelibly disgraced ! A mob broke night before last, into the house of Henry Devan, abused his person, dragged him out, and rode him through the village on a board ; and the worst of all is that I find scarce any individual who sympathizes with me in the indignation with which this outrage inflames me. Many will say that a mob is to be condemned, but will add, in the cold breath with which they utter it, that they have no pity for Devan, that he deserved no better treatment ; thus do they virtually justify the mob. The provocation to this outrage is the charge, (I know not how well substantiated,) that Devan has recently been guilty of fornication. The late crime of E. M., and the late conversion of the Peterboro temperance house into a house of death, did much to disgrace our village. But, in this instance, not one or two individuals only, but the people themselves have disgraced it.

This is the story told in detail by himself. It is given in his own language that his whole action may be understood. It is a revelation of the spirit of the man. That the feeling manifested was no superficial or evanescent one, but deep and earnest, appears in the fact that years elapsed before the bitterness of the recollection passed away.

June 22, 1842. I learned yesterday morning, that the previous night, a mob broke into H. Devan's house—abused his person and dragged him out in the presence of his family—rode him on a board through the village—and were with difficulty restrained from putting tar and feathers upon him, and torturing him with spirits of turpentine.

This intelligence called up various emotions in my breast. I was melted with pity toward my poor outraged fellow man. I was fired with indignation toward those who had visited this outrage upon him. I was filled with grief in view of the deep, if not indelible disgrace, which was brought upon my beloved Peterboro—a village in whose mob-abhorring, and law-abiding and otherwise good character, I had taken so much pride and pleasure.

I went into the village and to my amazement, found it quiet and no one ready to sympathize with me in the feelings of my soul. It is true that my friends N. Huntington and F. Dana said that mobs were wrong and that the persons engaged in this mob deserved to be punished ; but in the same cold breath with which they made this remark, they would speak disparagingly of all sympathy with Devan. Mr. Dana repeatedly said—" I have no pity for Devan." His doctrine of course, is that if a man be wicked and vile, his brother man is under no obligation to pity him for the blows inflicted upon his body or for the insults inflicted upon his manhood. Is this a Christian doctrine ? Does not Christ pity the sufferings of the vilest man on earth ? Then must not His disciples do likewise ? Is this doctrine learnt of Him, who " maketh His sun to rise on the evil and on the good, and sendeth rain on the just and on the unjust ? "

Our county court was in session. But not a neighbor did I see, who was desirous to have a complaint made to the grand jury against the lawless ruffians. I started for Devan's house—but met him, ere I had gone far. As soon as he came up to me, he burst into tears. I felt myself honored by his tears—honored by this evidence that he calculated on my sympathy. He accompanied me to my office. I wrote the district attorney, giving him a brief account of the outrage, and expressing my earnest hope that the offenders would be brought to justice. I handed it to Devan together with a little money to bear his expenses during his stay in Morrisville.

In the afternoon of yesterday, I sat an hour in Major Curtis' store. I found him justifying the mob. Said he, to use his own words,—" There are no laws to punish Devan's crimes—and therefore we must not complain if the boys make laws for the occasion." By "boys" he meant the persons who composed the mob. Mr. Perry G. Palmer came in. He was filled with the same spirit which animated the Major. To use his precise words, he said : " *Perhaps*, they might have taken a better way to punish him." I owe it however to them to say, that before I left the store they both admitted in words, that the mob was not to be approved.

Mr. Dana, who had been at court both yesterday and to-day, informed me, this evening, that Devan's complaint to the grand jury was ineffectual. He said that he thought the district attorney was indisposed to the finding of bills in the case—and he admitted that he himself had done nothing to bring the offenders to justice, and that he knew of no person beside Devan and myself, who had lifted a finger to that end. Indeed, he went so far as to remind me, that the fact of my standing alone in this matter should lead me to question whether it is right ground on which I stand.

I have learned from Mr. Dana, Mr. Scofield and other sources, of the efforts, and very successful efforts too, which are making in this community to load me with the odium of giving countenance to Devan's vices. To identify myself with Devan in the affair of this mob is what I desire. It is my delight, as it is my duty, to put my soul in his soul's stead. I wish to have the liveliest conception—a realizing sense of the brutal wrongs that have been done him. How far I am the friend and patron of vice, my life—not my lips—must say.

I am very sensible, that, because of the stand I have taken in this matter, there is a very strong and almost universal feeling against me in this community. No man here is so odious and detested as Devan—and my neighbors will be slow to forgive me for having said openly to him, as I did yesterday : " Well, Devan, I pledge myself to you, that I will stand by you in your endeavor to bring these offenders to justice." My family are apprehensive that I shall be the victim of the next Peterboro mob : and, in my own judgment, nothing but my somewhat influential position in society saves me from being mobbed. They who can strike down the rights of the meanest and poorest man have no principle to restrain them from trampling under their feet the rights of any other man. For the mob that shall be rallied to drag me from my family I shall hold those leading citizens of Peterboro responsible, who either wink at, or openly justify, or, at least, have not the spirit to condemn the mob that dragged Devan from his family. That we may anticipate more mobs in Peterboro is reasonable from the fact, that the countenance given to the recent lawless ruffianism has emboldened persons to threaten to mob others. I am not aware that my name has been mentioned among those who are to be mobbed. Mr. Chapin's and Mrs. Brown's have been.

I am happy to find this evening, that Elder Stevens has just such views of this outrage as I should expect that eminently good man—that meek, unambitious and unworldly man—would take. Mr. Scofield also is right. In a public conversation, however, respecting the outrage, he allowed himself to speak of Devan's vices and baseness. This was inconsiderate in him. If we would feel right toward the mob—if we would duly pity Devan for his wounded body and cloven-down rights, we must guard against indulging in untimely thoughts and remarks about his demerits. The good Samaritan did not repress his indignation, and stay his ministering hand while he should inquire into the moral character of the wounded man.

Peterboro, which I have loved very greatly—too much—is no longer lovely to me. It is a deeply, perhaps an indelibly, disgraced village. But, perhaps not indelibly. It would recover all its lost beauty, if its leading citizens were to put upon this outrage the seal of their reprobation, and if, as a probable consequence of such testimony, they who composed the mob should be brought to feel their crime, to repent of it, and to humble themselves before the man whom they abused and insulted. So great a change, however, I can hardly hope for.

I am not pained about Peterboro, because I think it worse than other places—but because I find that it is no better than other places. How often I had boasted of its preëminently pure, and moral character—and especially of its mob-hating character! In 1835 Peterboro was probably the only village in this State to which the mobbed Utica Convention could have openly retreated with safety. "How is the gold become dim ! How is the most fine gold changed !"

The change in my pecuniary circumstances made it proper for me to determine to leave Peterboro. I should have left it with regret, but for this horrible outrage and the general acquiescence in it. One of the regrets which I shall now feel in leaving it is, that, *for the present*, my business will make it necessary for me to revisit it so frequently.   GERRIT SMITH.

The foregoing is Gerrit Smith's memorandum of facts connected with the atrocious outrage on Henry Devan the night of June 20, 1842—and of some of his feelings and reflections in view of that outrage.

June 24, 1842. I am happy to find that W. Loring Fowler, who at first was indifferent to the outrage, now views it in a just light.

June 25, I have had a long conversation with W. Scofield this morning. He reasons and feels on the subject, just as he should do. James C. Jackson is most heartily right. So is George ——.

Saturday, *June* 25, 1842. I wrote and put upon my office door and on one of the doors of the Presbyterian church copies of the following notice. I also handed a copy to Mr. Scofield with the request that he would read it in the church to-morrow.

"NOTICE.

" The citizens of Peterboro and its vicinity are respectfully invited to meet in the Presbyterian church in Peterboro, Saturday 2 P. M., July 2, for a friendly consultation respecting the mob by which their village has recently been disgraced, and to ascertain the duties which at this crisis, they owe to themselves, to violated law and violated religion. June 25, 1842."

July 2, 1842. I this day attended the above meeting. There were about fifty persons present—only three of them females—viz. : —— —— ——. Mr. Scofield opened with prayer. Elder —— was appointed chairman and S. Addison Dana secretary. Mr. —— N. Schofield, Mr. Boyle of Ohio, Mr. Shaw of Vermont and myself took the principal part in the discussion. The meeting was of about four hours continuance. A series of resolutions introduced by myself was unanimously adopted, with the exception of the 5th. One person, a Mr. Charles Hopkins, as I was informed, voted against that resolution, for the reason as he alleged, that Mr. Devan's "body" was not "bruised." A series of resolutions was offered by Mr. W. P. Clemens, not written, and I believe not approved by himself. They were read and discussed—but so generally if not universally, were they disapproved of by the meeting, that no one in the meeting urged that the sense of the meeting be taken on any one of them.

1. *Resolved,* That no crimes, however heinous or clearly proven, are to be punished in ways forbidden by the laws.

2. *Resolved,* That to deny legal protection to the hated and despised is to take the ground, that the laws are made for the exclusive protection of the respectable and the favorites of public opinion.

3. *Resolved,* That they who, whether through their own or others' wrongs, are deprived of that shelter from violence and outrage which public opinion affords, are the very persons who most need the protection of law, and to whom right-minded men will be especially eager to minister that protection.

4. Whereas there are some persons amongst us, who contend that it is necessary to mob fornicators ; and whereas there are persons in other parts of our country, who maintain, some, that it is necessary to mob and hang abolitionists, and others that it is necessary to mob and hang gamblers : *Resolved,* Therefore, that to admit the plea of necessity for mobbing in any one of these cases is to open the door for mobs in every case, where the lawless may think them necessary.

5. Whereas, there are some persons amongst us who, notwith-

standing their avowed indifference to the bruised body and insulted manhood and cloven down rights of the victim of the late Peterboro mob—who, notwithstanding their avowed pleasure in his suffering— do nevertheless, seek to make themselves and others believe, that they warmly disapprove of the mob itself: *Resolved,* Therefore, that the incompatibility of such disapproval with their pleasure in, or unconcern for the sufferings of the victim of the mob, is shown not only by the nature of things, but by the interest which they, who profess this warm disapproval of the mob, manifest to prevent the exposure of those who composed it.

6. *Resolved,* That the doctrine that we are not to sympathize with the wicked person who suffers wrongs and outrages, is abhorrent to humanity and religion—is a doctrine that would turn man into a monster toward his fellow man—is a doctrine that, were it in the heart of God, would " shut the gates of mercy on mankind."

7. *Resolved,* That this village whose citizens have, until the recent outrage, been conspicuous for their humane and law-abiding character, is now deeply disgraced, and that the wisest means should be immediately and earnestly employed for the recovery of its lost character.

8. *Resolved,* That it is not by subjecting to legal penalties the person conspicious in the late mob, that our village can be redeemed from its deep disgrace. Violated law might be honored in that wise. But it is only by bringing the offenders to feel and deplore and publicly confess their wrong doing, that Peterboro can be restored to the hearts of those who dearly loved her, ere the reign of mobocracy gave her a new and loathsome aspect.

9. *Resolved,* That the repentance of the offenders, especially if coupled with the acknowledgment that they merit legal punishment, would not only remove from our village its deep stains of disgrace, but would also confer more honor on the laws than would their enforcement.

10. *Resolved,* In conclusion, that we earnestly and affectionately invite all who were concerned in the mob, to make both to the public and to Henry Devan, a frank and full acknowledgment of their error, that so great an outrage, which doubtless had its origin in an inconsiderate and sportive state of mind, rather than in a malignant and cruel spirit, may be forgiven and forgotten.

But Gerrit Smith did not limit his kindness to strangers. He was not one of the " infidels " who neglect their own flesh and blood. While he respected, honored and blessed the humanity outside of his circle, those inside enjoyed a perpetual flow of good will. His affections were as constant and considerate as they were ardent. Words and acts of endearment fell from his mouth, dropped from his hands, exhaled from his person. His devotion to wife, children, grandchildren, great grandchildren was proverbial. His diary makes tender mention of his " dear Martha " and his little children, dead, ten, twenty, thirty, forty years after they had passed away. The wound seems never to heal. He follows the apostolic injunction, and owes no debts but those of love.

On the death of his father, in 1837, he paid to the eight children of his brother and sister twenty thousand dollars each, for their share of the property, that being at the time its supposed value. Thus he became possessor of the entire estate, and stood acquitted legally of all responsibility to the other heirs. But in 1860, the property meanwhile having greatly increased in worth, he made an apportionment of one hundred and twenty thousand dollars to his nieces and nephews. In 1862 a second sum of equal amount was given. In 1864 a further gratuity of eighty thousand dollars, in all constituting three hundred and twenty thousand dollars, completed this exhibition of remarkable conscientiousness. The six nieces received, each, thirty thousand dollars. The two nephews, children of his elder brother, seventy thousand dollars. The papers conveying these sums are so unostentatious in form that they fail to impart an idea of the transaction to one unfamiliar with the preceding events. The performance was set down sim-

GERRIT SMITH'S HOUSE AT PETERBORO

THE STUDY

ply to the account of equity. It was his conscience, not his heart that prompted the deed. The man's sentiment of justice demanded more of him than most men's sentiment of love.

A rhymed diary recorded in snatches of verse, humorous, sentimental, pathetic, the various occurrences of the household, arrivals and departures, birthdays, festivities, events for congratulation, accidents and pranks of the young people, jests of the elders, pet whimsies, family jokes and traditions, the vein of pleasantry running through the volume, for a volume there is, and a large one,—attesting the unfailing cheeriness of the man. In the morning, the light step of the early riser crept down the stairs, and soon the melodious voice was heard humming little songs, for the delight of the singer. At table his talk was varied and playful ; he told a good story ; was lively at repartee ; was happy in proposing and responding to sentiments. In the evening, before going to bed, it was his custom to talk over the events of the day with the family circle, closing the hours with friendly chat, as he had opened them with worship. He was fond of singing and talking, as people endowed with sympathetic voices usually are. At home and in church he joined in and led the music, if occasion required. His taste was simple, hence his demands were not exorbitant.

The house he lived in was a large square mansion, of wood, which stood about twenty-five yards from the village street on a domain of some thirty acres. It was built by his father in 1799, and altered in 1855. A wide hall ran through it from front to back. On one side was the general parlor, out of which opened a small conser-

vatory; on the opposite side was the library, a room of
twenty feet square, occupied on two sides with plain
shelves containing between fifteen hundred and two
thousand volumes. The dining-room adjoined the
library; the kitchen was behind. The brick office where
the business was done stands a few yards distant from
the house. The sleeping accommodation was abundant
and elastic. As many as twenty-two guests found shelter, on occasion, beneath the roof. All the rooms were
furnished with extreme simplicity. There were no mir-
rors, no heavy draperies, costly carpets, luxurious lounges
or chairs. The host would have nothing too fine for the
humblest visitor. A few common prints relieved the
bareness of the walls; two or three family portraits hung
in the more private rooms; an old Dutch cattle piece
was the only oil painting that all could see, and that few
would stop to look at. The stately portico in front of
the house suggested a grandeur which the interior, comfortable and pleasant as it was, did not carry out. The
place was a village by itself. Some thirty buildings
stood on the domain. The farm, garden, stables, shop,
employed a considerable force of men in several capacities, for the estate was kept in excellent condition,
though without ostentation, the desire to employ work-
men being quite as constraining on the proprietor as the
necessity for having the work done.

The village was remote from the centres of busy life,
retired among the hills, too high above the valley level
for approach by railway. The opening of the railroad
through Canastota, nine miles distant, depleted Peterboro by carrying travellers further on, and making it
easier to get away. Previous to that, the village was

thriving; intelligent, active minded people lived there; it was a nucleus of popular spirit; there were several churches, there was an academy, a well-patronized hotel; public meetings were frequent and alive. Judge Smith drew and kept about him men of affairs; Gerrit Smith brought people of prominence in political life, and freshened the soul of the place with discussions on matters of general concern. At present, Peterboro is a quiet, inert, dull village. It has no hotel, no activity, no interest for traveller or sojourner. To play croquet on the long common seems to tax the energies of the middle aged; to sit and gossip before the three or four inefficient shops on the street is the occupation of the elders. The inhabitants are chiefly retired farmers whose wants are of the fewest and whose resources are about equal to the satisfaction of their wants. A few families of blacks subsist in humble dwellings. The meeting houses have been abandoned, or have changed their use. The Methodists alone exhibit vitality. The Baptist meeting house is dilapidated. The Presbyterian was bought by Mr. Smith and converted into an academy; the upper part is transformed into a public hall. The Independent chapel opens its doors now and then to a preacher who relies on the neighboring villages for a congregation. Mr. Greene Smith, Gerrit's only son, maintains open house during the summer, does what he can to preserve alive the traditions of hospitality, and keeps up there the spacious and attractive bird-house, for the preservation of the specimens he had procured on his shooting expeditions in all parts of the country. The family still make free with the mansion and grounds, but the tide of strangers comes no more. How they ever came to the remote village, how the tide ever ran so high above the plain is a mystery, or would be a mystery, did we not know what attractive power there is in a warm heart. Gerrit Smith was Peterboro, and would have been found out had he dwelt among Alpine snows. His door was always open; his greeting was always warm. The guest, bidden or unbidden, friend or stranger, was taken in. Hospitality was not irksome to him. His wife, warm-hearted and affectionate, sympathetic with all his sentiments, ideas and purposes, a moral and spiritual coöperator, delicate of constitution and poetic in temperament, devolved upon a housekeeper the administration of the large establishment, and, as her part, diffused an air of cheerful serenity over the household. " Heaven has broke loose ! " the husband would exclaim when the wife came into the breakfast room. The younger members helped the elders in the discharge of the day's hospitable tasks.

The diary of Gerrit Smith is a record of arrivals and departures.

" A man calling himself George Brown, of Corning, comes here to-night with a very heavy pack on his back. He is accompanied by his wife and child. The child is deaf."

" Mrs. Crampton, a beggar woman, spent last night with us. Charles Johnson, a fugitive slave from Hagerstown, took tea at our house last evening and breakfasted with us this morning."

" Mr. William Corning, a wandering pilgrim, as he styles himself, dines with us. He is peddling his own printed productions."

" Peter Johnson, a colored, illiterate man, calling himself a missionary, arrives this afternoon. He has been among the colored people in Canada, and is going to Hayti."

" Mrs. Phiak of Port Byron, a poor old Dutch woman, arrives. She leaves after breakfast. A begging blind man, and a begging woman and her son from Cazenovia breakfast at our house."

" Poor Graham, the insane literary colored man, has been with us a day or two."

"William Henry Douglass, of Paterson, New Jersey, son of Aaron Douglass, comes to our house this morning. Says he is nineteen years old, and ran away from his home a week ago last Saturday. Has been to Buffalo, repents of his folly, and is on his return home. He has no money. I gave him three dollars and some bread and cheese. He breakfasts with us, and starts for home."

"Elder Cook and William Haines of Oneida depot arrive this evening. Mr. H. is a 'medium,' and speaks in unknown tongues."

"Dr. Winmer of Washington City, with five deaf mutes and a blind child take supper and spend the evening with us."

"We find Brother Swift and wife and daughter at our house, where they will remain until they get lodgings. There come this evening an old black man, a young one and his wife and infant. They say that they are fugitives from North Carolina."

"A man from —— brings his mother, six children and her half sister, all fugitives from Virginia."

"An Indian and a fugitive slave spent last night with us. The Indian has gone on, but Tommy McElligott (very drunk) has come to fill his place."

The family recollect the arrival one night—when the house was dark, of a woman whose trunk burst open as it was flung upon the steps. Mr. Smith rose and answered the bell, courteously welcomed the stranger who announced herself as a claimant on his hospitality, and she stayed until she was ready to go. A friend tells of the arrival simultaneously with himself of a trance medium, who, after the usual "grace" by the host, lifted up her voice in oracular discourse. Mr. Smith listened courteously till the outbreak had spent itself, then proceeded with the meal. The family did not profess admiration or partiality for this tavernous mode of social life and would occasionally object to the master's practice of retiring to his library or office and leaving to them the entertainment of unbidden guests. But the law of hospitality must be respected. The visitor was never directly told to go. Occasions are recorded in which

the dismissal was indirectly conveyed. In one instance
when the claims of the wanderer had been overworked,
and the household, failing after due lapse of time to
discover the angel in the stranger who came unawares,
begged the good man to speed the parting guest, the
morning prayer contained a special petition that the
friend *who was about to leave them on that day* might be
brought safely on his way. The petition was heard, and
the circle was diminished by one, ere evening.

The dinner-table often presented a motley sight.
The bidding of the New Testament was fulfilled. The
highways and the byways were represented at the feast.
High and low, great and small, wise and simple, black
and white, senators, politicians, farmers, sat down together. If any objected to promiscuous association, a
side table was provided ; but few went into the exile.
Says one who knew him well :

> " I have seen eating in peace, at one time, at dinner, in his house
> —all welcome guests—an Irish Catholic priest, a Hicksite Quakeress
> minister, a Calvinistic Presbyterian deacon of the Jonathan Edwards
> school, two abolition lecturers, a seventh-day Baptist, a shouting
> Methodist, a Whig pro-slavery member of Congress, a Democratic
> official of the ' Sam Young school,' a southern ex-slave holder and
> a runaway slave, Lewis Washington by name, also his wife, one or
> more relatives, and ' Aunt Betsy ' Kelty. And he managed them all.
> Not one was neglected. He did the honors of his table, carving his
> meats like a gentleman bred, and to the manner born ; conversing
> with each in such a sweet way as to disarm all criticism, and making
> everyone feel that, if he could be other than himself, he would rather
> be Gerrit Smith than any other living man."

The dining-room being of moderate size, it was often
necessary to spread an additional table in the long hall.
The host knew no distinction of persons. The board
was abundantly but simply spread. The guest, however

accustomed to the daily sherry must dispense with wine at Gerrit Smith's table. Of that best of vintage, a cordial welcome and cheery conversation, there was never lack, and they who once had the privilege of sitting there wished they might often repeat it. To enjoy it once was a thing to be long remembered. It was a lesson in practical humanity that could be admired by those who could not imitate it. Many a reformer there learned how simple was the problem which his philosophy could not solve; and many a philanthropist discovered the distinction between love and the *doctrine* of love. Not to have visited Gerrit Smith at home, not to have received his hearty greeting at the door, not to have seen him glowing and beaming at his porch, not to have heard his copious table-talk is to have missed one of the satisfactions of life.

CHAPTER V.

TEMPERANCE.

GERRIT SMITH was, as has been said, in the full sense of the word, a philanthropist; not a philanthropist by profession, but a hearty lover of his fellowmen; a practical lover; one who had in view certain ends to be promoted by all the means at his command. These ends were before him continually, from first to last. Hence his life had little outward variety; it does not divide into sections or episodes; dates are only of incidental moment. The story is the story of a character, and is best told in a way to exhibit the character.

At the beginning of his career, Gerrit Smith, as we know, had an unbounded popularity in his neighborhood. Handsome, engaging, frank, impulsive, an attractive speaker, public spirited, rich, and of recognized ability, any career he might choose was open to him. He was not without personal ambition; used to approbation, admiration and applause, he loved it. His sense of self-approval was keen; his desire of foreign approbation was strong. He enjoyed the feeling that he lived in the world's eye. This appears in an address to the electors of the county of Madison, written in the winter of 1823–'24 by " Juvenis." This, which he characterized later as a puerile effort, was in fact an earnest, and able plea in favor of direct elections by the people—a plea for popular government. He argues that the existing party names are meaningless, that the party issues are obsolete, that the machinery of caucus nominations and political conventions should be disused, that candidates should place themselves on their merits, and be accepted on their claims. Demagogues and office-seekers are his detestation. Corruption and bribery in his judgment, arise from the system in practice and threaten republican institutions with overthrow. The remedy he proposes, "self-nomination" is the best then suggested. The end sought is the redemption of politics from partisanship and fraud, the election to office of the best men. Hardly was he established as a responsible citizen in Peterboro before he was solicited to stand for public office. At that time—in 1826-'7—the anti-masonic fury was sweeping through the State. He, with others, caught the excitement, and allowed himself to be placed in the front rank of a party, as candidate for State senator. The step was premature. Whether, as some think, this experience disgusted him, or whether, as is more likely, he was led to see that the career of the politician was not that for which he was best fitted, certain it is that from that time he was averse to holding office, or joining any of the organized parties. He used politics as an instrument of reform, but would never be fettered by them, and never would permit party measures to be primary in his regard. His hostility to Masonry, and to secret societies of all kinds, was active to the end of his life, on the ground that they were inconsistent with the genius of republican institutions. Mr. Smith did indeed actively engage in politics as will be told in the appropriate place : he accepted nominations for office, served a short

7

term in Congress, ran the course for governor; but on every occasion his conduct showed that he was entirely destitute of political ambition. They who accuse him of that, accuse him also of the extreme of folly, for the course he pursued was the one course that was certain to be unpopular.

He was a reformer: how single-hearted a reformer will appear as the story goes on. The omnipresent, obnoxious evil of his time and neighborhood was intemperance. So habitual a vice was this, that none but a very sensitive conscience felt it at all. He himself in the thoughtless days of his youth looked on it without reproof, and, once or twice in college is said to have tasted its fascinations. But from the first hour of his responsible manhood till the end of his life he stood committed in the most clear and resolute way to the war against it. His action was of every sort, personal and political, private and public, domestic and civil. He used all the means at his command to discourage the evil and diminish it; he withdrew support of every kind from those who gave it countenance or maintenance. A total abstainer himself, he carried the presence and the power of a total abstainer wherever he went. The strength of his feeling on this subject comes out in numerous letters published and unpublished, in speeches at conventions, efforts in public meetings, remonstrances with church members, endeavors, early and late and strenuously pushed, to commit the authorities, religious and social, to the suppression of the traffic in intoxicating drinks. This would seem, from the large place it held in his activities, to have been the cause dearest to his heart. He spoke and wrote more on it than on any other.

His interest in it first suggested doubts in regard to the universal and permanent validity of all the allowances and prohibitions of Scripture.

" If it should be proven to me most clearly," he wrote to Edward C. Delavan, in 1834, " that God intended that ' strong drink ' and fermented liquors should be drunk by his rational creatures ; and that the inhabitants of Canaan and of many other parts of the world had and still have a perfect right to drink them, I would still deny that we have a right to drink them. I would say that we have so abused these mercies by our inordinate indulgence, and our rioting in them —so abused our bodies and our souls with them—that it has become necessary for us to be deprived of them altogether. As the high fed horse is turned out to winter at the stack, that he may recover his natural soundness, and as the diseased glutton is compelled to submit to a regimen which the poorest man would despise ; so this dram-drinking and drunken nation, if indeed it shall be allowed in any future age, the beverages which I have supposed it to be possible that other nations may innocently indulge in, must first be deprived of them for a season, until it may get back to the healthy state from which it has so greatly degenerated. If it shall ever be lawful for the people of the United States to take up the wine cup again, they must previously have become sober,—they must previously have rid themselves of the plague spots and madness of intemperance through long abstinence from the cause of them,—they must previously have recovered from the deep debasement to which their vile sensuality has reduced them ; and this work will take at least as long as the present generation will last. So I see no prospect, my friend, if you and I shall live to be sixty years old, that we shall have the liberty of drinking each other's health in a glass of wine or even of cider. Now, if my speculation in this paragraph is not unsound, and if these beverages are really blessings, we see that our intemperance, unfitting us for the safe use of them, even in moderate quantities, draws after it, in this respect, no small punishment,—a punishment of which we can find abundant illustrations in those sufferings and privations of manhood which are induced by the excesses of youth.

" The advocates of wine drinking very often refer us to the temperance of wine drinking countries. I believe there is less drunkenness in those countries than amongst us. There is however, enough of it in them. The opinion is spreading, I know not how justly, that even in France, so proverbial for its temperance, wine drinking produces as great an amount of injury to the mind and body, as is produced by the drinking of ardent spirits here. But even if wine countries are comparatively temperate, that should not encourage us to endeavor to become a wine country. If the objections on the score of climate and soil were not fatal to our country becoming such, there are other objections that are. Wine, to become the common beverage of all classes in this country, must be afforded at nearly or quite as low a price as cider.—Now, if we had a soil and climate as favorable for the grape as France has, we could not make wine anything like as low priced a drink, without first parting with our free institutions, which dignify and elevate our laboring classes, and to which institutions, more than to all other causes, they are indebted for their high wages and the ample rewards for the products of their toil. Before this can become a wine country like France, the labor of a man must be reduced to a shilling or two a day, and the wheels of civilization must revolve backwards, until our wives and daughters are turned into cultivators of the soil.—Where is the New England farmer, who would be pleased to see his wife and daughters laboring for their subsistence under a burning sky, and by the side of the hardier sex ; and contracting all that masculine coarseness which characterizes the women of the laboring classes in France? But, if all these objections were surmounted, who but some romantic wine bibber, would be glad to see as in France, large portions of our land covered with the vine ; and the food and clothing of our grain and cotton fields diminished in order to make room for the production of a drink that never yet warmed a man's back or kept him from starving — the virtues of which, unless perhaps when used as a medicine, are imaginary—the evils of which are incalculable—a drink, in short, which the world—at least in its present circumstances—would be indescribably better without, than it is with? France, Italy, Spain and Portugal are the great wine countries ; and no other nations in christendom are half so low as they are upon the scale of morals."

Mr. Smith was ready at all times to meet argument with argument, and facts with facts ; but the moral aspects of the subject interest him most.

" I have observed with pain," he writes to John Tappan, of Boston, " that in some parts of the country, and even in some temperance papers, the doctrine is inculcated that intemperance is a 'misfortune,' rather than a 'crime' and a 'sin.' The tendency of such a doctrine to multiply cases of superficial and transient reformation from drunkenness, and to spread contempt for divine truth is obvious. I scarcely need add that this doctrine finds no favor in this neighborhood ; and that here the advocates of moral reforms would think it infinitely more absurd to attempt to carry on a moral reformation and leave God out of it, than to attempt to enact the play of Othello,—and leave out the part of Othello."

To describe in detail, Mr. Smith's action in the temperance cause would take more space than is warranted, and would be unimportant. His efforts began as early as 1828, and continued to the end of his life. The Madison County temperance society was organized, on the total abstinence principle, in 1833. The same year, on May 7th, he delivered an address to the same effect at a convention of the American temperance society, held in New York. The same year, he wrote a pamphlet giving an account of thirty-eight reformed drunkards in the village of Peterboro. In 1837, he complains to Edward C. Delavan of a decline of interest in the cause of temperance, which he ascribes mainly to laxity of doctrine on the part of its friends. The cause will never, in his judgment prevail, till the use of ardent spirits as a beverage shall be declared *immoral*, public opinion, church usage, and bible countenance to the contrary notwithstanding. The precise date of his excepting malt liquors and wine from his bill of proscription is not on record.

Gerrit Smith's main reliance in this as in other movements for the reformation of society, was on moral influence. His faith was in the spiritual affections quickened by divine grace acting through religious belief and practice. All regenerating force was, in his opinion, latent in the moral sentiments, and the capacity of these, when aroused, was simply inexhaustible. So long as he believed in the vitality of the Calvinistic system of dogma and observance as a means for bringing the divine power to bear, he held to it and used it. But the moment he saw that the Calvinistic system no longer possessed the virtue he had imputed to it ; the moment he perceived that it did not quicken the souls of unreformed men, he sought elsewhere the communicating link between human nature and the sources of life. The necessity of that communication he kept in mind, always. The immediateness of it he cherished. The evidence of it he was willing to see in all men, whatever their mode of belief; but such evidence he required before he would give sympathy or confidence.

Hence naturally his ultimate faith was in " moral suasion." This is a specimen of his style of talking in 1843.

" Great honor is accorded to our town for having led the way, ten years ago in the reformation of drunkards by the simple and sole means of kind moral influence. Let us trust to this influence for reforming the dram-seller also. I admit that we have already tried it on him. But we have not tried it to the extent of its power ; and we have combined legal force with it. Let us now drop the force, and confine our efforts within the limits of persuasion.

" Shall we succeed if we adopt the proposed change ? The answer to this question turns on the answer to the question whether we shall prove ourselves to be well indoctrinated and hearty in the cause of temperance. If our concern for this cause is not enough to induce us to plead earnestly and frequently with the dram-seller to relinquish an occupation which beggars families and breaks hearts, and kills bodies and kills souls—he will be likely to continue in the occupation of blood-red guiltiness. And frequent and seemingly earnest as may seem these pleadings, if they are not sustained by a corresponding life, they will fail of a good effect. Let no man flatter himself that he is contributing to breaking up dram-shops, if he spends his leisure hours in them ; or if indeed he give to them the sanction of his unnecessary presence for a single moment. Let no man think that his influence is against the continuance of dram-shops if he cannot respond to the remark of the celebrated Judge Daggett of Connecticut, that they deserved to be classed with 'the depositories of stolen goods,' and to have inscribed in great capitals over their doors : 'The way to hell going down to the chambers of death.' Let no man think that he is exerting an influence against dram-shops if his temperance feeling be so shallow as to be offended by the memorable prediction of our Chancellor Walworth that 'the time will come when reflecting men will no more think of making and vending ardent spirits, than they would now think of poisoning a well from which a neighbor obtains water for his family, or of arming a maniac to destroy his own life or the lives of those around him.' Let me add, that if the farmers of Smithfield would make the evidences of their heartfelt temperance irresistible to the dram-seller, —as irresistible as the rays of a summer's sun to the ice on which they fall—let them, as not only their duty but their interest dictates, separate themselves, wholly and forever, from the manufacture of the body and soul destroying poison."

Madison county felt Gerrit Smith's influence in this matter, all through. Peterboro was a small village, with a population of between three and four hundred, but through his influence it became "a city set on a hill," visible afar off by people who imagined it a large, conspicuous and wealthy town. The name of Peterboro' called up sentiments that filled and expanded the mind. Had its noble-hearted inhabitant been a shrewd tactician he would have carried more schemes, but he would have failed to make so large an impression. His whole souled confidence in fine principles, and in the essential right-mindedness of his fellow men, made him the victim of sharpers ; but that same simple heartfulness was an inspiration to good people. The childlikeness that stood in the way of his occasional success, was the source of his influence. The worldlings, it must be admitted, enjoyed frequent chuckles at his expense.

To give an instance.   For many years, the only
tavern in the village stood at the upper end of it, and
received the patronage of the drovers, teamsters, business and other travellers who passed through the place.
The "Old Osgood House" as it was called, was not conducted on temperance principles; on the contrary, the
greatest source of income was the bar; the whiskey,
which then cost but twenty cents a gallon, flowed incessantly, and the least pecunious could afford to be generously tipsy.   The noise and disorder so shocked Mr.
Smith that he built at the other end of the village, near
his own residence, a commodious hotel, supplied it with
the requisite barns, sheds, and out-door conveniences,
furnished it comfortably throughout, put a Bible in every
room, set up in the office, instead of the line of decan-
ters, a motto, "Temperance and the Bible," gave the
use of it all to one David Ambler, of Augusta, on condition that no intoxicating liquors should be sold, and inaugurated the first temperance hotel of which there is
mention.   Though the new inn was in every respect superior to the old tavern, it did not prove a successful, or
even a dangerous rival.   The people who loved liquor,
as nearly all did, then, put up at the old place.   The
temperance people, on the groundless pretext that
board was dearer at the temperance house, but really
because they liked the gay society, or did not wish to be
peculiar, or were too lazy to leave the beaten road, did
the same.   At the end of two years, Mr. Ambler became discouraged and withdrew.   His successors fared
no better.   In spite of all the attractions of cleanliness,
quiet, good food, courteous treatment, the travelling

public passed by the door. Finally a " General " M ——
whom Mr. Smith " knew " and had employed, made an
offer for the property which was accepted. The " General " bought the old hotel property, shut up the
house, transferred the keeper to the new inn, took out a
liquor license, and Gerrit Smith's experiment defeated
itself. Instead of crushing the monster, he had given
him fresh vitality; had brought him to his very door,
within a few feet of his private office! The well-appointed
tavern became the most popular resort for tipplers and
vagabonds in the whole county. The discomfited philanthropist, driven to the last extremity, could only deliver himself from his persecutors by buying back, of
course at a high price, the property he had already
staked so much on. He did so; the hotel was again
conducted for a time, on the temperance plan, still without encouragement. The travelling public patronized
the bar-rooms of other villages; Peterboro lost its former
visitors; larger and more thriving places took the custom; the buildings were removed; the foundations were
destroyed; and the site was adopted into the owner's
private grounds. Thus ends the story of Gerrit Smith's
Temperance Hotel.

Thus, however, did not end the design to expel intemperance from Peterboro. A temperance hotel, near
by the first, continued in existence till the time of his
death. He presented it rent free to the lessee—sustained there a free reading-room and gave it his patronage; but it never succeeded—though the keeper sold
liquor privately, and there was no other hotel in the village. Temperance hotels, for natural reasons, do not
thrive in competition with inns where the exhilarations

7*

and excitements of alcohol can be enjoyed. Temperance is associated still with a low condition of animal spirits. Even in Oswego, where Mr. Smith established a hotel on temperance principles, the property yielded nothing. No charm of situation, no excellence of accommodations, no influence from the proprietor's name made amends for the absence of nervous stimulus.

The prohibitory law known as the " Maine Law " was passed in 1851, and was, for several years, the model for imitation by those who were of opinion that the government should interfere to forbid the manufacture and sale of ardent spirits. Gerrit Smith was one of these, and interested himself much in the adoption of the measure by his native State. His industry as writer and speaker was, as it always was when his heart was engaged, active and incessant. His efforts to create public sentiment, and control legislation at Albany, were unremitting, as the entries in his diary and the clippings in the scrap-book testify. His heart was full of the subject, and his whole nature followed his heart. Not blindly however; he was no impulsive enthusiast; a strong practical common sense saved him at last from a confusion of ideas into which social reformers are so often betrayed. But he had no hesitation about calling on the legal authority when it was likely to reinforce the dictates of conscience. His theory of the province of law was simple. Not to open at present his whole doctrine of government duty—his view on this point may be stated briefly and tersely in his own language in 1851. Such language is familiar to all who have read his writings, or heard his speech. The substance of it came over and over like the points in an orthodox sermon. Government, he called "a huge bull dog," guarding the house against thieves.

"Perhaps it will be asked if the duty of abolishing the traffic in intoxicating drinks would not be outside of the province of government. I answer that it would not. I ask government to abolish this traffic, not because I would have government enact sumptuary laws—for I would not. Nay, I go so far as to say, that if the drinkers of intoxicating liquors would do no more than kill themselves, I would not have government interfere with their indulgence. It is murder, not suicide, that I would have government concern itself with. Nor do I ask government to abolish this traffic because I hold that government is charged with the care of the public morals. As I have already shown you, I hold to no such thing. Why I ask government to abolish this traffic is because it is fraught directly, immensely, necessarily, with wide and awful peril to person and property. Neither property nor life is safe from the presumption, the blindness and the fury of the drunken maniac. The drunken driver upsets the stage. The drunken engineer blows up the steamboat. It is a drunkard who has ravished our wife or daughter or sister. It is a drunkard who has burned our dwelling. It is a drunkard who has murdered our family. What is a crime then, if the traffic in intoxicating drinks is not one? And what crime is there, from which government should be more prompt to shelter the persons and possessions of its subjects."

This argument applies only to the drink that maddens ; it does not touch the drink which, however harmful in other respects, is not an active source of danger to the community. If the Frenchman can show that his light wines are not responsible for the riotous spirit that disturbs the peace ; if the German can show that his beer is not responsible for the midnight violence or the crowded jail ;—then wine and beer are exempted from the application of the statute. The objection to sumptuary laws is impertinent.

" I had always understood that the temperance societies forbid the drinking, not of all liquors in which there is alcohol, but of those only which actually intoxicate. It is true that small beer contains a little alcohol. So does new bread. But neither intoxicates ; and therefore neither falls under the proscription of the temperance so-cieties. But even if the temperance societies were to forbid the drinking of all alcoholic liquors, as well those that do not as those that do intoxicate, most unreasonable would it be nevertheless to call on government to prohibit the traffic in liquors which do not intoxi-cate the drinker."

This was written to a prohibitionist journal in 1858. Again, writing to a severe prohibitionist clergyman, the same year, he says :

"Let me here say that I do not hold that the sale of all kinds of beer and wine is to be proscribed by government—though I would that all possessed the clear proof that I do, (after an experience of thirty years) that good water is the only good drink. What I do hold is that the government should prohibit the sale for a drink of all those liquors which make madmen, and which therefore put in constant peril life and property ; and fill the newspaper columns with accounts of murdered wives and murdered children, wrecked ships and wrecked cars, burnt stores and burnt dwellings. It is a deep delusion where it is not a wicked pretext, which classes such prohibition with sumptuary laws. What if there were brought into the markets of the world a newly discovered fruit, the maddening ef-fects of which should be in kind and degree like those of the liquors in question ? Would not all reasonable men be in favor of the imme-diate governmental prohibition of the sale of it ? Certainly :—and none would have the face to call the prohibition a sumptuary law. Why then should the prohibition in the case of liquors fall under that odious name ? The force of habit accounts for all this glaring inconsistency."

Writing, in 1852, after a defeat in the legislature of the " Maine Law," he says to Edward C. Delavan, his correspondent, one of the patriarchs of temperance :

" How could you, my dear friend, bring yourself to help defeat a law which the world is in such perishing need of ? The answer is at hand. In common with almost all men—good men as well as bad—you will have it that Civil Government is not of God. It would seem as if this were the last delusion which Christians are willing to have torn from them. I have done many things which make me odious to Christians. But nothing has had this effect so much as my endeavors to have Civil Government regarded—both theoretically and practically—as of God. To have it thus regarded was the object of those discourses, which, when I was much younger and stronger than I am now, I was in the practice of delivering before large assemblies in groves and on Sunday. Christians did not thank me for these discourses. So far from it, they made them the occasion for stigmatizing me with 'preaching politics,' and with being a Sabbath breaker! an infidel!! and a demagogue!!! Indeed, my bad reputation, at this day, is owing far less to all other causes put together than to those out-of-door Sunday discourses in behalf of the position that Civil Government is of God."

The "Anti-Dram-Shop Party" was formed at Smithfield, February 21, 1842, at Gerrit Smith's call. His whole heart was in it. For a time his private letters were enclosed in envelopes bearing a hideous picture of the interior of a dram shop. His lecturing tours extended to every county in the State. On winter nights he came and went, braving cold and tempest, wading through deep snows where the road was impassable to horse and wagon. His published correspondence on the matter, at this period, as the scrap books bear witness, was voluminous. The emphasis, at this time, was laid on the duty of bringing the force of moral sentiment to bear through the officers of the law. In 1843, persuaded of the extreme difficulty of this task, he returns to the reliance on moral earnestness, and exhorts the lovers of their fellow-men to increased fidelity in the work of saving souls from this death. But in 1871 the Anti-dram-Shop Party was alive.

Thus, once more, Gerrit Smith was a pioneer in radical reform. The movement to plant religion upon purely

spiritual foundations, detaching it from external authority whether of church, dogma or book, separating it from
the State and from the sect, the movement known
now as Free Religion, was positively inaugurated by
him, and illustrated in his chapel at Peterboro. The
practical attitude of the temperance reform, which is
peculiar in its freedom from fanaticism, which aimed
at the suppression of tangible mischiefs by the
force of public opinion expressed in law, an attitude in these later days assumed as a novelty and
with some show of bravery, was taken by him
twenty-five years ago, argued, defended, enforced with
a clearness of statement that left little to be added
and with a determination of purpose that knew no
wavering.

That the man was greatly indebted in this to the
prestige of wealth and of social position, is conceded.
But neither wealth nor social position would have carried him through or kept him up, if he had not been a
man of great intellectual and moral power, of strong
convictions and indomitable will, single-hearted and simple. For in the stand he took he was often alone, and
not *alone* merely but *lonely ;* friends on whose judgment
and courage he in most things relied—the only friends
he had who were entitled to be called his peers and
brothers in arms, disapproved his course, privately condemned and even publicly assailed him ; friends whom
he acknowledged to be his superiors in intellect and
character withdrew from his side. Still he remained firm
to his conviction, firm and at the same time cheerful
and gentle, forbearing and loving. They may call it

egotism who will. Such egotism when exhibited on the popular side is usually called saintliness. He submitted his will to what with him was nothing less than the will of the Supreme. The seat of that Supreme will was his private heart.

CHAPTER VI.

SLAVERY.

GERRIT SMITH was born two years before the Act of Emancipation was passed by the legislature of New York, by which all children born after the year 1799 were free,—the males on reaching the age of twenty-eight, the females on reaching the age of twenty-five. During his youth, therefore, and past the date of his second marriage, he was the son of a slave holder. The slavery he grew up with was of mild type, but on that account the better calculated to reveal the common humanity of the white and black races. The northern farmer was not, as a rule, aristocratic, overbearing, labor hating or sumptuous. He did not pass a life of idleness, or of devotion to politics as the southern " gentleman " did. He was a practical director, if not an actual sharer of the labor on his farm. His slaves were brought into close daily contact with him and were more or less assimilated to him by the association. There was little actually revolting in the relation between owner and serf under these circumstances. At the same time, and for this very reason, the relation itself appeared an unnatural one, and the occasional abuses of it by exacting, violent or careless masters, revealed the possibility of evil in it. The degradation of the slave was not sufficient to make him contemptible, and the injustice was sufficient to exasperate a sensitive mind. Young Smith early disclosed his sympathy with the subject race, his sense of the wrong done them by their social condition, his faith in their capacities, and his determination to do what he could for their elevation. Naturally, his views were moderate, his feelings quiet. The first wave of moral indignation, started in Kentucky, Tennessee, North Carolina, Maryland, by Benjamin Lundy, soon reinforced by William Lloyd Garrison, did not reach his quiet village home.

On the 10th day of June 1828, Mr. Smith attended the State Convention, held to nominate a President and Vice President of the United States. This was his second participation in general politics, the first being on occasion of the State Convention at Utica, Sept. 21, 1824, to nominate De Witt Clinton to the office of governor. The exciting subjects at this time were matters of State improvement, the development of the canals in particular, which Clinton strongly favored. In 1828, national issues were presented, and some allusion to slavery,—if not some declaration about it, at least some indication of feeling,—might have been expected. The two opposing candidates for the presidency were John Quincy Adams and Andrew Jackson. Yet, in the masterly, comprehensive, patriotic, even splendidly brilliant address, prepared by Gerrit Smith, and unanimously accepted by the delegates in convention,—an address preferred by the committee to the productions of Ambrose Spencer and Edmund H. Pendleton, intellectual magnates of the State—scarcely a passing mention is made of slavery,—and not even a passing mention is made of it as a source of national danger. Mr. Adams is warmly commended for moderate, enlightened views of statesmanship; Mr. Clay is eulogized in glowing terms, for his unselfish patriotism, his "holy zeal for the rights of man," his devotion in the cause of suffering Greece, and his share in "the merciful efforts that are making to colonize our emancipated blacks on the coasts of Africa, and to kindle up there those fires of civil and religious liberty, which are soon to blaze over that benighted land;" and Mr. Jackson is condemned as the incarnation of the violent, military, usurping spirit so radically inconsistent with republican institutions. Dangers are hinted at, such dangers as a young republic might be exposed to from despotism at home and abroad, but no peril is apprehended from the institution of slavery.

At this period of his life the Colonization Society, the suggestion of Charles Fenton Mercer in 1816, a creation of "Virginia Principles," whereof Henry Clay was president, had Mr. Smith's entire confidence. The Tappans, Arthur and Lewis, had begun to distrust it: Daniel Webster, in 1825, had retired from a meeting held in Boston for the purpose of organizing an auxiliary society, with the remark: "Gentlemen, I will have nothing more to do with the meeting; for I am satisfied it is merely a plan of the slaveholders to get rid of the free negroes." * The intelligent blacks saw through it. Honest men of the south, like John Randolph and Henry A. Wise, made no secret of its character. Its founders in plain language avowed the contempt for the free blacks on which the society was based, Mr. Clay and Bushrod Washington showing, the former by words, the

* Wilson's "Rise and Fall of the Slave Power." I. p. 219.

latter by deeds, a cordial agreement with Gen. Mercer
on this cardinal point. But piety outran prudence. Orthodox ministers and laymen in the most enlightened
States, fascinated by the prospect of planting the gospel
in Africa, overlooked the ugly features of the plan. Dr.
Leonard Bacon, the eminent divine of New Haven,
accepted office in the society, and commended it as " a
society for the establishment of a colony on the coast of
Africa," admitting in the same breath, that it was not a
society for the abolition of slavery, nor a society for the
improvement of the blacks, nor a society for the suppression of the slave trade.* Even William Lloyd Garrison delivered an address before the Colonization Society in 1829, which contained no criticism on its purposes and methods, though the feeling with which he
spoke of the wrongs and woes of the slaves foreshadowed
the exposure that soon followed. Gerrit Smith, a fervent
" evangelical," a devout believer in the Calvinistic system, and a zealous promoter of the cause of " Gospel
Truth," was detained longer than others were, in the
deftly woven snares of the slaveholders.

Signs of an impending change of view appear in the
Diary, in 1834.

July 8. "Elder John Loyd, a native of the West Indies, drinks
tea with us. He this evening presents in our church the claims of
Africa. Upwards of ten dollars are contributed. Elder Loyd, his
wife and their four children, are to go to Africa this season. He is
sent by the Methodist church as a missionary."

July 12. "I attended this evening the meeting in which our town
Anti-slavery Society was organized. The constitution is good.
Nevertheless I did not join the Society. I think I cannot join the
Anti-slavery Society as long as the war is kept up between it and

* Wilson, I. p. 215.

the American Colonization Society—a war, however, for which the Colonization Society is as much to blame as the other Society."

September 2, 1835. "We returned to Utica in time to attend a great anti-abolition meeting. My friend J. A. S—— made a good speech in it—in the main very good. The proceedings, aside from this speech, were not agreeable to my feelings. Christian morality did not characterize them."

August 29, 1835. "Every mail of late brings accounts of the lawless, riotous, murderous spirit which is prevailing over the land. . . . Defend, oh Lord, the cause of the oppressed. The friends of the righteous doctrine of immediate emancipation are sorely pressed at this time. Surround my dear friend Birney with the arms of thy love and protection, and shelter beneath the wings of thy mercy, that precious child of God, Charles Stuart."

The storm had been rising for several years. In the fall of 1831 a meeting of the friends of the slave was called at the Baptist church on West Genesee Street, Syracuse. At the hour named, fifteen or twenty persons, among them Gerrit Smith, were seen wending their way to the place. Suddenly the little band of reformers were assailed by a select mob, and pitilessly pelted with eggs in that melancholy condition of decay that best qualifies them to express derision. The unexpectedness and fury of the attack rendered a retreat advisable; Mr. Smith and his companions repaired in disarray to the neighboring village of Fayetteville. There they held their meeting, passed their resolutions, denounced in plain terms the outrage that had been put upon them, and pledged themselves to new fidelity to the black man's cause. No public man condemned the assault; the press of Syracuse on the whole applauded the deed. The popular feeling was on the side of the mob.

On the 21st October, 1835, the State Anti-slavery Convention was held at Utica. Mr. and Mrs. Smith had left home in the morning, purposing to attend the meet-

ing and then go on to Schenectady to visit his father.
Scarcely had the meeting been called to order when dis-
turbances began; the mob crowded in, interrupted the
proceedings with yells and abuse, threatened violence
if the speakers went on, and utterly defeated their purpose. Mr. Smith, who was there merely as a spectator,
sprang to his feet, protested against the interruption,
declared that he was no "abolitionist" but that he
loved fair play, and, failing to allay the tumult or prevent
the dispersion of the assembly, invited the convention
to adjourn to Peterboro where they should hold an undisturbed meeting the next day; then he turned back
instead of going on as he had purposed. At about
ten o'clock the peaceful household were roused by
the master and mistress, (who had driven nearly all the
way in the rain), and were set to making active preparations for the entertainment of an indefinite number of
guests. The night was spent in mixing bread, grinding
coffee, paring apples for pies, baking rolls and providing
the other necessaries of hospitality. At about three
o'clock in the morning, Mr. Smith appeared in the
kitchen, with pen, ink and paper, asked for a stand and
an extra candle, and poured his hot soul into the resolutions to be presented and the speech that was to support them. In the morning the guests straggled in.
About thirty arrived in season for breakfast. They were
in a sorry plight from the mud and rain, the hard journey, and the persecutions of the enemy who pursued
them as far as they could. The younger men turned the
matter into sport; but the elders found the experience
a hard one. The day was beautiful; the convention was
well attended by three or four hundred delegates; Gerrit

Smith entertained seventy or eighty at dinner, a hundred or more at tea, and with the help of sofas, lounges and softened boards gave rest at night to some' forty tired bodies. His was the great speech of the day, his were the thrilling resolutions, and he was the convert of the occasion; not the only one probably, for a flood of enthusiasm took the village off its feet, but the chief one in the whole State. From this hour his stand was taken with the Anti-slavery Society.

October 25, *Sabbath.* "The Lord carry much instruction to my mind and heart from the scenes of the past week, and may He teach me, and enable me to rely on Himself for protection in all the perils that surround and threaten me. The Lord inspire my heart with holy courage. The Lord make me His humble, confiding, holy little child, and profit greatly my dear wife by the instructive providences through which we are passing."

How great was the change through which Mr. Smith suddenly passed will be perceived from the following letter addressed to the secretary of the American Colonization Society in November, one month after the scene just described. It is a model of frankness, courtesy and magnanimity.

Peterboro, November 24, 1835.

REV. R. R. GURLEY, *Secretary of American Colonization Society.*

My Dear Friend,—Great as the pleasure would be to me of meeting, at the approaching Anniversary of the American Colonization Society, with my beloved fellow laborers in the cause of African Colonization, I must not, for this alone, make a journey to Washington. Could I connect with the anticipation of this pleasure the prospect of gaining over the Society to the views which I have so long, but in vain, pressed upon its adoption, the journey would then be made most cheerfully; but the present circumstances and complexion of the Society afford anything but such a prospect.

You well know, my dear sir, how faithfully I labored, at the Anniversary of the Society in January, 1834, and for a year before; and how much I have written to that end since, to bring back the Society to its constitutional and neutral ground, respecting the subject of slavery. The ineffectualness of these efforts is manifest in the fact, that the Society is now, and has been for some time, far more interested in the question of slavery than in the work of colonization—in the demolition of the Anti-slavery Society, than in the building up of its colony. I need not go beyond the matter and spirit of the last few numbers of its periodical for the justification of this remark. Were a stranger to form his opinion by these numbers, it would be, that the Society issuing them was quite as much an anti-abolition, as colonization society: and this would be his opinion of a society, which has not legitimately anything to do with slavery, either as its opponent or advocate—of a society of which I said in my speech before it, in January 1834, and justly, I believe, that "such is, or rather such should be its neutrality, on the subject of slavery, that its members may be free, on the one hand, to be slaveholders; and on the other to join the Anti-slavery Society." It has come to this, however, that a member of the Colonization Society cannot advocate the deliverance of his enslaved fellow-men, without subjecting himself to such charges of inconsistency, as the public prints abundantly cast on me, for being at the same time a member of that Society and an abolitionist.

It was not until some six or eight months since, that I began to despair of seeing the Colonization Society cease, within any short period, if ever, from its interference with the subject of slavery. No more than a year ago, and I was still confident that the Society would retrace its errors, and be again simply a Colonization Society: and then how soon a harmonious, successful and glorious Society!

I still owe a considerable sum on my subscriptions to the funds of the Colonization Society. It is true that the conditions on which these subscriptions were made, have not been fulfilled, and that it is now too late to fulfill them. It is further true, that most of the sum I still owe has some years to run before it is due. But I sympathize with the Society in its embarrassments, and herewith enclose you my check for the whole balance—viz., three thousand dollars. It is my wish, though I would not insist on its taking this direction against the judgment of your much esteemed board — that the whole sum be applied towards the cancelment of the debts of the Society.

At some future period, and under happier auspices, the American Colonization Society may possibly cease to meddle with slavery; and to claim that it is the remedy, and the only remedy for that evil. It may then confine its operations to their constitutional sphere, and employ all its means in the benevolent and delightful work of aiding the free people of color in our country to escape from the un-relenting prejudice and persecution under which they suffer, and to obtain in a foreign land the honorable and happy home which is cruelly and wickedly denied to them in their own. I may then have it in my heart and in my power to contribute again to your treasury. In the mean time, I cannot conscientiously do so,—nor, indeed, do anything else from which my approbation of the Society could be justly inferred.

It is proper for me to say, that I am brought to this determina-tion earlier than I expected to be, by the recent increase of my interest in the American Anti-Slavery Society. From its organiza-tion to the present time, I have looked to that society as, under God, the best hope of the slave and of my country. Since the late alarm-ing attacks, in the persons of its members, on the right of discussion, (and astonishing as it is, some of the suggestions for invading this right are impliedly countenanced in the African Repository) I have looked to it, as being also the rallying point of the friends of this right. To that society yours is hostile, I will not say without cause —without even as much as the certainly very great cause which it has for being the enemy of yours. However that may be, it is enough for my present purpose and to justify me in standing aloof from your society, to know that the Anti-Slavery Society has now become iden-tified with this threatened right ; and that if it fall, as your society is diligently striving that it shall, this great and sacred right of man will fall and perish with it.

With great regard, your friend.

GERRIT SMITH.

It will be seen from this letter that Mr. Smith did not take issue with the Colonization Society, as Mr. Garrison did, on the ground of its original purpose, but on the opposite ground that it had *abandoned* its original purpose. The original purpose is still commended as praiseworthy, and Mr. Smith hopes once more to be a fellow-worker with the society in promoting it. He was offended by the attempt to thwart and crush another purpose which he dearly cherished, and which he did not see was inconsistent with its own. At this time, in 1831, when he spoke in glowing language of the true aims of the Colonization Society, he could contemplate with enthusiastic hope the scheme of planting christian civilization in Africa, of suppressing the foreign slave trade, of improving the lot of the native tribes and the future of the free colored race at home. But he could not say now as he said in 1831, of the blacks : " They are incapable of freedom on our soil. They cannot rise in our esteem above the level of the moral state of the land of their origin, which is their appropriate, their only home. It is of first importance as regards our character abroad, that we should hasten to clear our land of our black population." The urgent question now was the freedom of this very population, *on our own soil ;* and it was because the Colonization Society angrily resisted the only efforts made to this end,—efforts that he himself had but recently characterized as in a large measure " ill-judged, rash, uncharitable and slanderous,"—that he withdrew from it his sympathy and support. He deserted the society because it deserted its principles. But he paid in full the dues he had pledged, requesting that the money might be used in payment of the society's *debts*, not in furtherance of the society's *operations*— that is, might be employed in the interest of its *past fidelity* to its ideas, not in the interest of its *present infidelity* to them.

Three years later, in 1838, he took stronger ground. Then he wrote to President Schmucker, of the theological seminary in Gettysburg, Pennsylvania :

" If the Colonization Society had not come out against the doctrine of immediate emancipation, and inferentially against the doc-

8

trine of the sinfulness of slavery, I should, in all probability, have continued a member of it down to the present time. But for its opposition to those doctrines, I might very probably have continued to think that it was producing a measure at least, of the good influences and effects which you ascribe to it. It is however, but proper to say that my confidence in the usefulness of the colonization of our colored brethren, or any portion of them on the coast of Africa or any where else,—and even though such colonization were conducted with great benevolence and with no unfriendliness to the great doctrines of the anti-slavery societies,—has undergone a great, exceedingly great diminution. It is not however on the ground of diminution, that I avow myself an anti-colonizationist. It is because it has, to use your own language, taken the " position that the colored race cannot with any propriety be emancipated on the soil,—that expatriation and emancipation must go together." . . . I would not deny that there are members of the Colonization Society who favor the doctrine of immediate and unconditional emancipation ;—though Judge Jay, in his book on colonization, speaks of me as the only one. But certain it is that they are rare ; and as certain it is that the society ridicules, denounces and abhors the doctrine. . . In view of the exceedingly wicked and abhorrent sentiments of Rev. R. J. Breckinridge, which I have cited, I cannot but think how grateful you and I should feel that God has led us to quit forever a society which generates and fosters such sentiments. Had we remained in it we might have been left to imbibe those sentiments, to adopt all its cruel and murderous policy and to keep pace with its fast increasing wickedness."

His part having been chosen, Gerrit Smith threw himself into it with the full force of his natural ardor. His labors were, in simple fact, immense. Letters were ceaselessly flowing from his pen ; speeches poured steadily from his lips ; money streamed in full current from his purse. William Goodell, most unwearied of abolitionists, wrote that the meetings in Madison County came so fast that no reports could be made of them. All the time that could possibly be spared from the demands of an exacting business was freely given. His whole mental and moral power, stimulated by the drafts on it, and fed by the sources of his religious faith, were exerted to the utmost. One man was determined to discharge the full measure of his responsibility so far as thoughtfulness and aspiration revealed it to his mind.

His genius was practical. He fixed his eye on a definite object to be attained, and he welcomed all allies to the work of attaining it, made no more foes than were necessary, put the best construction on doubtful men and measures, waived incidental and subordinate issues, encouraged rather than discouraged, and generally used the method of the enthusiast where others plied the policy of the fanatic. His object was the *abolition of slavery and the creation of a public sentiment that would demand its abolition.* Boundless was his faith in moral powers. He believed that true principles, if adhered to, honored and diffused by two or three hundred thousand people, would overmatch the falsities of millions; that truth had an inherent advantage over falsehood, right an essential superiority over wrong. The moral principle he could feel sure of; the method of policy must vary with circumstances. Hence he was at no pains to vindicate his consistency to expedients or to preserve it. On the contrary, the adherence to old methods in the face of new facts or considerations was, in his regard, a weakness. His views on even important questions had changed greatly; they were continually changing; he hoped they would change still more, all the time, as they changed, deepening his trust in the principle and increasing his wisdom to support it. He lacked the absolute quality of mind that makes the man of theory. His intellectual resources were immense, but his intellectual fibre was loose. His force was a flood, pouring on in a

wide but not sharply defined channel. Men like Beriah
Green and William Goodell were forever quarelling with
his logical vagaries, and forever exulting in his rush of
moral force. The one quality he demanded was earnestness in radical anti-slavery work.

For half-way reformers, men of one idea, he had no
respect. At an anti-sectarian convention held in Peterboro, in 1849, he presented a resolution, " that they, and
they only are Christians, who love God and man; and
that they and they only are to be recognized as Christians, who, in the fruits of their lives, evidence that they
love God and man." The resolution was sharply con-
tested. " He is an unjust man," he said in an address
to the Liberty Party of the State of New York, " who
will espouse but one good cause; and hence his fidelity
to that is not to be relied on. He is an unjust man, who
is a one-idea man; and hence he may prove traitorous to
his favorite idea." To love God was not, in his view,
to love a *definition* of God; to love man was a good
deal more than loving a particular " brand " of humanity.

Gerrit Smith's cardinal doctrine, copiously stated
and argued, was this: that slavery, being an outrage on
the first principles of humanity, was a violation of the
very idea of law; that law could neither establish it nor
protect it; that no State or national code, no constitution could give it guarantee; that the law which justified
it stultified itself in so doing, and thereby forfeited its
title to the name of law; that slavery was always and
everywhere, under all forms, and in spite of all sanctions,
an outlaw and should be an outcast. The distinction
between higher law and lower he refused to recognize.
The law, all law, had its seat in the bosom of God; all

law was high; if low things, policies, expediencies, devices, utilities took the name of law, they usurped it, and must justify their claim to use it by their acquiescence in the decrees of the moral sense.

Could slavery find shelter behind the Constitution of the United States? This was the agitated question. "Yes," replied the abolitionist; "therefore away with the Constitution." "Yes," replied the anti-abolitionist; "therefore let slavery alone." "No," said the anti-slavery Whigs, "for the Constitution is not a pro-slavery instrument." "No," said Gerrit Smith, "for slavery, in the nature of the case, cannot find shelter behind anything that bears the name of law; the Constitution that offered shelter to slavery would have no validity. The question whether or no slavery finds shelter behind the Constitution, is wanting in pertinency: there is no such question." Not without much expense of argument was this position maintained. To others it did not seem as self-evident as it did to him. The angry letters of correspondents, published and unpublished—some of them from personal friends whom he revered and loved—testify to the cost at which he held an opinion so distasteful not to the extremists alone, on both sides, but to moderate men as well. Gentle speech was not common in those times; men were consigned to purgatory and worse for the lightest offences against the party standards; and Mr. Smith's idea of the Calvinistic hereafter must have been clarified by the descriptions of the doom from which nothing short of special grace could deliver him.

His discussions of the constitutional question were as temperate in tone as they were affluent, luminous and massive in treatment. The same ground precisely that he took in regard to the Bible, that he might have the benefit of the popular reverence for the book on the side of temperance and freedom, he took in regard to the Constitution, in order that the universal veneration for the instrument, enhanced by association with the moral and religious sentiments, might assist the work of reform. Like Sumner, he contended for the anti-slavery construction of the organic law of the Republic, reinforcing the usual arguments with ingenious considerations of his own. He would not allow a shadow of suspicion to lie either on the intent or the letter of the document, but claimed that it needed no amendment; herein going beyond Mr. Sumner, who cast an implied reproach on the Constitution as it stood, by asking that it might be improved. To Mr. Smith's mind, it was good enough; it contained all that the most exacting republican could desire. His views were tersely expressed in a letter to John G. Whittier, dated July 18, 1844, and published under the title : " Gerrit Smith's Constitutional Argument." It contended that the faithful application of the principles of the Constitution would result in the speedy abolition of the whole system of American slavery ; that its framers and acceptors " believed and joyfully believed, that American slavery was to endure but a few years ;" that the omission of the words " slave " and " slavery " is a clear confession that the Constitution did not mean to recognize the legal existence of either ; that the " apportionment clause," allowing a three-fifths representation to slaves, " is a bounty on liberty, and presents a strong inducement to every State to raise its inhabitants to the rank of freemen," the " reduction of

a man to the fraction of a man " being of the nature of
an indignity which, but for the existence of slavery, would
never have been inflicted ; and that the provision to return fugitives, even if applied to slaves, was limited,
naturally, to the original thirteen States, and in them is
" null and void " because " it is contrary to the Divine
Law." The letter ends with this characteristic passage :

"The constitution is an anti-slavery instrument, and needs but
to be administered in consistency with its principles to 'effectuate the
speedy overthrow of the whole system of American slavery. It is a
power in the hands of the people which they cannot fling away, without making themselves guilty of ingratitude to God and treason to
the slave ;—for God has given it to them ; and the slave vitally needs
their righteous use of it. It may cost them much toil and self-denial
and vexation of spirit to recover that power from the perversions by
which it has upheld and extended the dominion of slavery ;—but to
all this they must submit ; and the more readily, because they have
shared, and largely too, in the guilt of those perversions. This shield
which God has given us to put over the head of the slave we have
traitorously made the protection of the slaveholder. This weapon,
which God has given us for fighting the battles of the oppressed, we
have murderously wielded on the side of the oppressor. It will be
a poor fruit of repentance, or, rather, a fruit of poor repentance, if
now, when our hearts are smitten with a sense of our wrong use of
this shield and weapon, we shall, from our study of ease and quiet,
from our desire to promote a favorite theory, or from any other cause,
throw them away, instead of manfully, courageously, perseveringly,
and therefore successfully, putting them to a right use."

In 1850, Mr. Smith made a speech in Albany, on the
relation of slavery to the Constitution, which he introduced by reading the following petition, framed by himself and numerously signed, which had been presented
to the State legislature.

To the Senate and Assembly of the State of New York :
What a wonder, what a shame, what a crime, that in the midst
of the light and progress of the middle of the nineteenth century,

such an abomination and outrage as slavery should be acknowledged to be a legal institution ! Who that reverences law, and would
have it bless the world, can consent that its sanction and support,
its honor and holiness be given to such a compound of robbery and
meanness and murder, as is slavery?

Your petitioners pray that your Honorable Bodies request the
representatives and instruct the senators of this State in Congress to
treat the legalization of slavery as an impossibility ; and moreover,
to insist that the Federal Constitution shall, like all other laws, be
subjected to the strict rules of legal interpretation, to the end that
its anti-slavery character be thereby seen and established, and all
imputations upon that character forever excluded.

The slave-holder will be strong so long as he can plead law for
his matchless crime. But take from him that plea, and he will be
too weak to continue his grasp upon his victims. It is unreasonable
to look for the peaceful termination of slavery while the North, and
especially while abolitionists of the North, sustain the claim of the
South to its constitutionality. But let the North, and especially the
abolitionists of the North, resist, and expose the absurdity of this
claim—and slavery, denied thereafter all countenance and nourishment from the constitution, will quickly perish.

Your petitioners will esteem it a great favor if your Honorable
Bodies will consent to hear one or more of them in behalf of the
prayers of their Petition.   January 22, 1850.

The argument that followed was pitched to this key.
We need not quote from its impassioned pages. They
who are at all acquainted with the course of reasoning
pursued by Lysander Spooner in the volume which Mr.
Smith warmly commended, or by the orators of the Free
Soil Party, have only to imagine them pressed with the
fervor and force of Mr. Smith's swelling heart. They to
whom the discussion is unfamiliar, must go to other
sources for information. It was Mr. Smith's endeavor
to place the Constitution *actively* on the side of humanity, as the broad manifesto of democratic institutions.
Nothing less than this contented him. When the question of amending the Constitution in the interest of

freedom was up, in 1864, Mr. Smith wrote to Charles Sumner a letter of which the following is an extract:

"An amendment implying that without it, the constitution would authorize or even tolerate slavery, would do great injustice to those who adopted the constitution. It would be wickedly blotting their memory. So much stress has been laid on the history of the constitution, it may well be said that there are two constitutions, the one the historical, and the other the literal. The former is that which has ruled the country. Terrible, all the way, has been its rule. The cry of many millions to an avenging God has come of it. The soaking of our land with blood has also come of it. That the history of the constitution has so cursed us is because it is so almost universally held to be a pro-slavery history. In other words, that this historical constitution has so cursed us is because of the ever urged and almost universally accepted claim that the literal constitution was made in the interest of slavery. Alas for the people to whom the angel of the Apocalypse cried 'woe, woe, woe,' if they suffered more than America has suffered from this historical constitution! That there is much for slavery in the history of the constitution I admit. But that there is also much in it against slavery I affirm. Pro-slavery interests however have succeeded in keeping the latter out of sight. The rejection in the convention, which framed the constitution, of the motion to require 'fugitive slaves' to be delivered up, and the unanimous adoption the next day of the motion to deliver up, no 'fugitive slaves,' but persons from whom labor or service is *due*, is a historical fact against slavery. So too is Mr. Madison's unopposed declaration in the convention, that it would be 'wrong to admit in the constitution the idea that there could be property in man.' And so also is that convention's unanimous substitution of the word 'service' for 'servitude' for the avowed reason that servitude expresses the condition of slaves and service that of freemen. Nothing however of all this did I need to say. What this thing is, which is called the history of the constitution—what is this historical constitution as I have termed that history—is really of no moment. What it is in the light of the records of the convention referred to, or of the records of the 'Virginia Convention' or any other convention, or what it is on the pages of the 'Federalist,' or of any other book, or of any newspaper, should not be made the least account of. The aggregate of all those whose words contributed to make up this historical constitution, is but a comparative handful. The one question is—What is the literal

8*

constitution? For it is that and that only, which the people adopted,
and which is therefore the constitution. They did not adopt the
discussions of the convention which framed it. These were secret.
They did not adopt what the newspapers said of the constitution.
Newspapers in that day were emphatically 'few and far between.'
But even had they been familiar with the newspapers and with the
discussions, their one duty would nevertheless have been to pass
upon the simple letter of the constitution. As Judge Story so well
says : ' Nothing but the text itself was adopted by the people.' And
I add that what the people intended by the constitution is to be
gathered solely from its text ; and that what the people intended by
it and not what its framers or the commentators upon it intended,
is the constitution. So we will take up the text of the constitution
to learn what and what alone is the constitution. Its very preamble
tells us that it is made to ' secure the blessings of liberty.' Thus,
even in the porch of her temple doth Liberty deign to meet us.
Strange indeed would it be were she to desert us in its apartments !
She does not. In our progress through the constitution we find it
pleading the power of the whole nation to maintain in every State
' a republican form of government.' Pro-slavery men tell us that
this was no more than a republican government of the aristocratic
Greek and Roman type ; and that therefore men can consistently be
bought and sold under it. But when the fathers gave us the constitution the political heavens were all ablaze with a new light—the
light of the truth ' that all men are created equal,' and that the great
end of government is to maintain that equality. Ere we get through
the constitution—ere Liberty has led us all the way through her
temple—we meet with the slavery-forbidding declaration that : ' No
person shall be deprived of life, liberty or property without due
process of law ! ' "

    *   *   *   *   *   *   *   *

What an argument it is in favor of the anti-slavery character of
the constitution, that not so much as one line, no, nor one word of it,
need be changed in order to bring it into perfect harmony with the
most radical and sweeping anti-slavery amendment. And how
strongly is this character argued from the fact, that were constitutional phrases, as innocent and inapplicable as these which are relied on to rob the noblest black man of his liberty, to be made the
ground for robbing the meanest white man of his, or even the meanest white man of his meanest dog, such use of them would be instantly and indignantly scouted by all ! And how strongly is it also
argued from the fact, that a stranger to America and to her practice

of making church and State and all things minister to slavery, could
see absolutely nothing, could suspect absolutely nothing in the constitution, which might be seized on to turn that also to the foul and
diabolical service?

But why should we stop with an anti-slavery amendment? Immeasurably more needed is an amendment to the effect that race or
origin shall not work a forfeiture of any civil or political rights.
Even an anti-slavery amendment may not be permanent. A race,
whilst deprived of rights which other races enjoy, can have no reasonable assurance that it will be protected against even slavery. But
make it equal with them, in rights, and it will be able to protect itself.

Gerrit Smith's views of government corresponded to
his views of the Federal Constitution—and was, in a similar sense, his own. There are two general theories of
the province of government; the theory that would have
government *do everything*—the "paternal" theory,—
which regards government as a providence, whose care
may properly be extended over the interests of religion,
education, charity, social and personal morals, and even
the processes of material development;—and the theory
that government should *do nothing*, a theory commonly
called "*Laissez faire*," which regards government as a
hindrance, and would abolish it altogether, or reduce it
to the function of guarding individual freedom against
the pressure of society. The first theory, if pushed to
an extreme, would dispense with personal activity, and
virtually, if not literally, annihilate private liberty. The
second, if pushed to an extreme, would leave individuals
to meet their own wants, in their own way, by single or
combined effort. The first may be called the theory of
the old world, the second the theory of the new world.
Mr. Smith was satisfied with neither. The first was
the mark of his keenest criticism, as being altogether inconsistent with the genius of institutions which rested

on individual intelligence and self-reliance. The second made inadequate provision for the protection of the moral interests, against bestiality and inhumanity. Here his strong practical instinct and his impetuous enthusiasm for reform revealed to his eye distinctions where the philosophical mind could see none. First of all he is a Christian, a believer in the bible, a man relying on the gospel, and accepting the New Testament ideas of the perfect society; it could not be expected of him therefore, that he should reason like a " philosopher " or a disciple of the later school of social science. " Bible Civil Government " is his motto; what that is, in his estimation, we are left in no doubt of. But while some of his contemporaries accepted the Old Testament theocratic idea, and advocated a spiritual rule in the name of " Him that sate upon the throne," he interpreted the bible doctrine to mean pure humanity. " We cannot," he says, " mistake the Bible apprehension of civil government when it tells us that ' rulers are not a terror to good works, but to the evil ; ' nor when it says that the ruler ' is minister of God,' or in other words, acts on and acts out the principles of God. And who can mistake it, or fail to be touched and melted by it, when he reads the injunction upon civil government : ' Take counsel, execute judgment, make thy shadow as the night in the midst of the noon-day, hide the outcasts, bewray not him that wandereth ; let mine outcasts dwell with thee ; be thou a covert to them from the face of the spoiler.' Or who can misapprehend it, or not be moved by it when he reads : ' Thou shalt not deliver unto his master the servant which is escaped from his master unto thee. He shall dwell with thee, even among you, in that place which he shall choose, in one of thy gates where it liketh him best. Thou shalt not oppress him.'

. . . Civil government is, in the eye of reason, the collective people caring for each of the people—the combination of all for the protection of each one. Such is it in spirit and scope on the pages of the Bible. We there see it to be, next to God Himself the great Protector; and as is reasonable, the special Protector of the innocent, and helpless poor." Thus the humane soul of the philanthropist adopted, accepted so far, the " paternal" idea. The independence of the American, however, saved the philanthropist from the extreme consequences of it. The working reformer is always at odds with the social philosopher. Hot feeling and cool logic are never quite in accord. Very seldom, we venture to think, do they approach so nearly as in the case of Gerrit Smith. Had his concern for other social interests been as deep and intense as his concern for temperance and emancipation, they might have touched at fewer points still. As it was, the line between what government could and could not do, was drawn with reasonable clearness. His views on this subject were so little modified in the course of many years, that in quoting them, dates are of no consequence. The simplest statement of them is found in an address on " The True Office of Civil Government," delivered at Troy, April 14th, 1851. It begins thus :

" The legitimate action of civil government is very simple. Its legitimate range is very narrow. Government owes nothing to its subjects but protection. And this is a protection, not from competition, but from crimes. It owes them no protection from the foreign farmer, or foreign manufacturer, or foreign navigator. As it owes them no other protection from each other than from the crimes of each other, so it owes them no other protection against foreigners than from the crimes of foreigners. Nor is it from all crimes that government is bound to protect its subjects. It is from such only as are committed against their persons and possessions. Ingratitude is a crime; but as it is not of this class of crimes, government is not to be cognizant of it.

"No protection does government owe to the morals of its subjects. Still less is it bound to study to promote their morals. To call on government to increase the wealth of its subjects, or to help the progress of religion among them, or, in short, to promote any of their interests, is to call on it to do that which it has no right to do, and which, it is safe to add, it has no power to do. Were government to aim to secure to its subjects the free and inviolable control of their persons and property—of life and of the means of sustaining life—it would aim at all that it should aim at. And its subjects, if they get this security, should feel that they need nothing more at the hands of government to enable them to work their way well through the world. Government, in a word is to say to its subjects: 'You must do for yourselves. My only part is to defend your right to do for yourselves. You must do your own work. I will but protect you in that work.'"

He continues:

"Whenever the work of the people is taken out of their hands by the government—or, since the people are quite as ready to shirk their work as the government is to usurp it—I might as well say whenever the people devolve it on government, it is, of course, badly done. This is true, because every work to be well done must be done by its appropriate agent. Whenever government builds railroads and canals it builds them injudiciously and wastefully. So too, whenever government meddles with schools, it proves that it is out of its place by the pernicious influence it exerts upon them. And to whatever extent churches are controlled by government, to that extent they are corrupted by it. . . . Government has naught to do but to protect its subjects from crimes. The crimes however, which it permits against them—and still more, the crimes which it authorizes and even perpetrates against them—show how extensively it fails of its duty.

"*Slavery is a crime;* nevertheless, government not only permits its subjects to be enslaved, but it actually enacts laws for their enslavement.

"*Land Monopoly is a crime;* government positively and expressly permits it. Still worse, it does itself practice it. Government is itself the great land monopolist.

"*The compelling of one generation to pay the debts of another is a crime.* Government not only suffers its subjects to be robbed of their earnings, in order to pay the debts of former generations, but it actually compels them to submit to such robbery.

"*To deny woman's right to control her property, to deny woman her right to participate in the choice of civil rulers is a crime.* But government, so far from defending these rights, does itself rob her of them.

"*The violation of the right to buy and sell freely, whenever and wherever we please is a crime.* Government does, by its tariffs, annihilate this right."

Having made these specifications, the speaker further enforces them in the most unqualified manner—still taking his standard of right and wrong from his own scripture-taught conscience.

"*Do I mean that government shall invariably and absolutely forbid slavery?* Yes—as invariably and absolutely as it forbids murder.

"*Do I mean that men have an equal right to the soil?* Yes ;— as equal as to the light and the air ; and government should without delay, prescribe the maximum quantity of land that each family may possess.

"*Do I mean that a people may repudiate their national debt?* I do. No generation is bound to enter on the race of life, incumbered with the dead weights of debt which former generations have entailed on it. Wars which the people who are carrying them on believe to be just, they are willing to pay for ; and therefore, every generation may reasonably be expected and required to pay for its own wars. Each generation must be left free to choose what wars it will engage in, and also what canals and roads it will build ; with the proviso in the one case as in the other, that it shall pay as it goes—or to say the least, that if it makes debts, it shall pay them. If no single generation can build and pay for an Erie Canal, then let one generation build it as far west as Utica ; and the next extend it to Rochester ; and the next to Buffalo.

"*Do I mean to be understood as condemning all tariffs?* I do. I would not have a custom house on the face of the earth. Whatever may be the effect on its wealth, every nation is to cultivate the freest, fullest, friendliest intercourse with every other nation. The nations of the earth constitute, and should feel that they constitute, a brotherhood.

"*Do I mean that government shall have nothing to do with schools?* I do. A popular argument for government or district schools is that they are a cheap police. I admit that good schools are. And so are good churches. And since good family-government is also a cheap police, and a thousand fold more important to this end than either schools or churches, or both put together, why should not government take under its supervision our family affairs also?

"It is asked—what will the poor do to get their children educated in case government aid is withdrawn? We answer, let them do anything rather than hang upon government for an education—for an education which, because it is governmental, is emasculated of all positive, earnest, hearty religion—for an education in which, because it is governmental, the substance of morality is exchanged for the show of morality—and in which what is honest and uncompromising and robust and manly in character is made to give place to pusillanimity, effeminacy, calculation, baseness.

"It is justice and not charity which the people need at the hands of government. Let government restore to them their land, and what other rights they have been robbed of, and they will then be able to pay for themselves—to pay their schoolmasters as well as their parsons.

"Perhaps it will be asked, whether government, under my definition of its province, would be at liberty to carry the mail; build asylums; improve harbors; and build lighthouses? I answer that nothing of all this is, necessarily, the work of government. The mail can be carried as well without as with the help of government. Some of the best and most extensive asylums in our country are those with which government has nothing to do. And the interest and humanity of individuals and communities might be relied on to improve harbors and build lighthouses, as well as to keep bridges and roads in repair. The work of civil government is not so much to take care of its subjects as to leave them in circumstances in which they may take care of themselves;—and not so much to govern its subjects as to leave them free to govern themselves."

There remains then so much room for political action, as will allow the reformer to use the powers of government for the protection of persons and property against such crimes as endanger them; notably against the manufacture and sale of liquors that infuriate men to riotous misconduct, and reduce them to pauperism,—and against slavery which is all crimes of fraud and violence in one. While honoring cordially those who withdraw from politics, and employ moral action alone, he felt, for himself, entire liberty to call in the aid of government to do what could not be done otherwise, and he worked hard to induce all who felt as he did, to organize for the purpose of carrying their views into effect.

A politician however, in the usual sense of the word, —a man that is, who adopts party measures, pursues party ends, compromises or qualifies his principle to secure immediate advantage, accepts candidates according to eligibility, and narrows his line of action to the width of a single idea, or a single aspect of an idea,—he could not be. His philosophy and his conscience alike forbade. He would join no party whose standard was not the highest, broadest, holiest. He would vote for no candidate to any office whatever, who was not sound on all moral issues, for to be unsound on any one, was to be less than sound on every one. He would vote for no slave-holder, or apologist for slavery, no dram-seller or distiller, no land-monopolist, or man otherwise careless of human rights,—be the office granted or sought for what it might be ; he would not put a pro-slavery man into the place of town surveyor,—or a dram-seller on the board of education. Every candidate for every office must be, at the root, a man of principle. The sole function of government being the protection of persons and property, it would be clearly inconsistent to entrust its authority to those who were, in any way, implicated in crime. The early Puritans of New England were of opinion that the powers of government should be in the hands of church-members alone, they best answering to the description of the "saints" that were to rule the world. Gerrit Smith gave a wider interpretation to the term "saints," defining it by no creed, profession, or evangelical test. Who the saints were, indeed, he would not undertake to say. But he would undertake to say who they were *not ;* they were not distillers or tipplers of rum ; they were not half-and-half abolitionists ; they were not defrauders, defaulters, or time servers ; they were not at heart indifferent to the common weal ; they were not men of war ; they were not land monopolists ; they were not hangers on of government, custom house politicians, members of secret societies, holders of trusts with a side view to their own interests.

Such a man, it is clear, had no place among party politicians. There was no love to spare between them and him. In their eyes he was an intractable visionary, in his eyes they were shufflers, worshippers of expediency. His experience in 1831, when he was defeated as candidate for the State Senate, made him sick of political manœuvring, and thereafter he " fought for his own hand."

The " Liberty Party " was formed, under his lead, in Jan. 29, 1840, at a convention held at Arcade, Wyoming County, New York. The object of the party, as understood by him was universal political reform ; as understood by others, it was simply the overthrow of slavery. It sprung out of the conviction that neither of the great political parties was to be trusted to deal with slavery, leaving other issues aside ; that the interrogation of their candidates was never satisfactory ; that the pledges given were either loose or dishonest ; and that nothing short of pure moral principles, independent of political arts and machinations, would answer the purpose of reform. In connection with William Jay, he had, eighteen months before,—Sept. 1838—written to W. H. Seward and Luther Bradish, candidates for Governor and Lieut.-Governor, asking their views on the slavery question, and had not felt that the trouble was altogether well bestowed. The absence of solid, hearty conviction even in right minded, well meaning men, and the difficulty which even such men found in resisting the wiles or putting by the sophistries of caucus leaders was to him wholly discouraging. The motto of the Liberty Party, devised by Mr. Smith himself, was "vote for no slaveholder for civil office—nor for any one who thinks a slaveholder fit for it."

The full idea and spirit of the party is expressed in a series of resolutions presented by Mr. Smith at a State Liberty Party Convention, held at Cazenovia, July 3, 1849. The importance of the subject justifies a full copy of them. They convey the whole mind of their framer :

1. *Resolved,* That we recognize the broadest principles of democracy and the right, irrespective of sex, or color, or character, to participate in the selection of civil rulers.

Passed unanimously.

2. *Resolved,* That when we admit that our hope of the establishment of righteous civil governments on the earth is in the prevalence of Christianity, we, of course, do not mean that spurious, or that mistaken Christianity, which upholds unrighteous civil governments, and which votes civil offices into the hands of anti-abolitionists, and land-monopolists, and other enemies of human rights.

Passed unanimously.

3. *Resolved,* That by our love of righteous civil government, of God and of man, we are bound to frown upon the public missionary associations of the world ;—nearly all their politically voting members voting on the side of the diabolical conspiracies which have, in

all nations, usurped the place and name of civil government—and such conspiracies being the preëminent hindrance to the establishment of righteous civil government, and to the spread of human salvation and blessedness.

Passed with but one dissenting voice.

4. *Resolved,* That the government which will not, or cannot, protect the lives and property of its subjects from the traffic in intoxicating drinks, is utterly unworthy of the name of civil government.

Passed unanimously.

5. *Resolved,* That it may be better to resort to revolution, than to submit to a government which compels its subjects to pay the debts of their ancestors.

Passed unanimously.

6. *Resolved,* That while we allow government to draw on posterity for the expense of wars, it is idle to hope that there will not be wars.

Passed unanimously.

7. *Resolved,* That no just nation need lay its account with being ever involved in war ; and, hence, that no just nation can have any excuse or plea, whatever, for wasting the earnings of its subjects upon fortifications and standing armies and navies.

Passed unanimously.

8. *Resolved,* That the Federal Constitution clearly requires the abolition of every part of American slavery ; and that the Phillipses, and Quinceys, and Garrisons, and Douglasses, who throw away this staff of anti-slavery accomplishment, and chime in with the popular cry, that the constitution is pro-slavery, do, thereby, notwithstanding their anti-slavery hearts, make themselves practically and effectively pro-slavery.

Passed unanimously.

9. *Resolved,* That law is for the *protection,* not for the *destruction* of rights ; and that slavery, therefore, inasmuch as it is the preëminent destroyer of right, is (constitutions, statutes, and judicial decisions to the contrary notwithstanding) utterly incapable of legalization.

10. *Resolved,* That whether men cry "no political union with slaveholders," or "no political union with gamblers," or "no political union with drunkards," they do, in each case, proceed upon the absurd supposition, that, instead of being necessarily identified with the whole body politic in which their lot is cast, they are at liberty to choose their partners in it, and to dissolve their national or state

tie with this slaveholder in Massachusetts, or that gambler in Pennsylvania, or that drunkard in Virginia.

Passed unanimously.

11. *Resolved*, That land-monopoly is to be warred against, not only because it is the most wide-spread of all oppressions, but because it is preëminently fruitful of other forms of oppression.

Passed unanimously.

12. *Resolved*, That the governments which deny to their subjects the liberty to buy and sell freely in all the markets of the world, are guilty of invading a natural and a precious right.

Passed unanimously.

13. *Resolved*, That government will never be administered honestly and economically, until its expenses are defrayed by direct taxes ; and that said taxes, to be justly assessed, must be assessed according to the ability of the payers, rather than according to their property.

Passed unanimously.

14. *Resolved*, That not only is it true, that the member of a pro-slavery church is untrusty on the subject of slavery, but that, (considering how, with rare exceptions, sectarians yield to their strong temptations to sacrifice truth and humanity on the altar of sect) it is also true, that the member of a sectarian church is not to be fully relied on for unswerving fidelity to the cause of righteousness.

Passed unanimously.

15. *Resolved*, That the genius both of Republicanism and Christianity forbids concealment, and that secret societies, therefore, do not only not promote either, but do hinder and endanger both.

Passed unanimously.

16. *Resolved*, That our only hope of the Whig and Democratic parties—parties so long wedded to slavery and other stupendous wrongs—is in their breaking up and ruin.

Passed unanimously.

17. *Resolved*, That, whilst we rejoice in the faithful testimonies and efficient labors of the Free Soil Party, against the extension of slavery, it must, nevertheless, be a poor, unnatural, absurd, inhuman, anti-republican, unchristian party, until it array itself against the *existence* as well as against the *extension* of slavery.

Passed unanimously.

18. *Resolved*, That the Liberty Party, though reduced in numbers, is not reduced in principles or usefulness—nor in the confidence, that its honest and earnest endeavors for a righteous civil government, will yet be crowned with triumph.

Passed unanimously.

19. *Resolved.* That, whilst we respect the motives of those who propose to supply the slaves with the Bible, we, nevertheless, can have no sympathy with an undertaking which, inasmuch as it implies the pernicious falsehood that the slave enjoys the right of property and the right to read, goes to relieve slavery, in the public mind, of more than half its horrors and more than half its odium.

Passed, but not unanimously.

20. *Resolved,* That, instead of sending Bibles among the slaves, we had infinitely better adopt the suggestion in the memorable Liberty-Party Address to the slaves, and supply them with pocket-compasses, and, moreover, if individual or private self-defence be ever justifiable, and on their part ever expedient, with pocket-pistols also—to the end, that, by such helps, they may reach a land where they can both own the Bible and learn to read it.

Passed, but not unanimously.

21. *Resolved,* That we welcome the appearance of the book, entitled, " The Democracy of Christianity ;" and that we should rejoice to see every member of the Liberty Party supplying himself with a copy of it.

Whereas, Lysander Spooner, of Massachusetts, that man of honest heart and acute and profound intellect, has published a perfectly conclusive legal argument against the constitutionality of slavery :

22. *Resolved,* therefore, that we warmly recommend to the friends of freedom, in this and other States, to supply, within the coming six months, each lawyer in their respective counties with a copy of said argument.

Passed unanimously.

23. *Resolved,* That we recommend that a National Liberty Party Convention be held in the city of Syracuse, on the 3d and 4th days of July, 1850, for the purpose of nominating candidates for President and Vice President, and of adopting other measures in behalf of the cause of righteous civil government.

Passed unanimously.

24. *Resolved,* That a State Liberty Party Convention be held in the village of Cortland, on the first Wednesday of next September, for nominating State officers, and for other business.

Passed unanimously.

25. *Resolved,* That, not only with our Irish brother and our Italian brother, under their heavy and galling loads of civil and ecclesiastical despotism, do we sympathize, but, also, with our fellow-men everywhere—for, everywhere, in our priest, and demagogue,

and despot ridden world, are our fellow-men suffering under civil or ecclesiastical despotism, or both ; and nowhere in it is enjoyed the priceless and two-fold blessing of Christian democracy in the State, and Democratic Christianity in the Church.

Passed unanimously.

26. *Resolved,* That unwillingness to use the products of slave labor is a beautiful and effective testimony against slavery.

Passed unanimously.

Whereas, we rejoice to see the first number of the "Liberty Party Paper"—a paper which, we doubt not, will faithfully represent, and ably inculcate the principles of the Liberty Party :

27. *Resolved,* therefore, that we call on all the members of the Liberty Party to regard it as their first duty to that party, to subscribe for, and endeavor to induce others to subscribe for, this paper.

Passed unanimously.

28. *Resolved,* That we hear with profound sorrow, of the very severe, if not indeed entirely hopeless, sickness of our honored and beloved James G. Birney—a man who, for his wisdom, integrity, high and heroic bearing, deserves a distinguished place in the regards of his fellow-men.

Passed by a unanimous standing vote.

29. *Resolved,* That we honor the memory of Alvan Stewart, who, for so many years employed his remarkably original and vigorous powers in promoting the cause of liberty and the cause of temperance.

Passed unanimously by a standing vote.

SAMUEL WELLS, Pres.

A. KINGSBURY, } V. Pres.
J. C. HARRINGTON, }

S. R. Ward, } Sec's.
W. W. Chapman, }

That a party based on principles so radical and so abstract should hold together long, or achieve definite political results, could not be expected. In fact, it did neither. At the very first general election after the party was organized, many of its enrolled members voted for Harrison and Tyler, Whig candidates, neither of them anti-slavery men, and the first a soldier. Four years afterwards, when Henry Clay was the Whig candidate, so many voted for him as to threaten the very existence of the Liberty Party. In New Hampshire Liberty Party men elected a Whig Governor, to the deep disgust of Mr. Smith, who preferred to be beaten *with* his candidate than *by* him, thinking defeat through fidelity to principles better than victory through their betrayal. In the same state Liberty Party men helped the Whigs elect General Wilson to Congress. In Massachusetts they preferred John G. Palfrey, whom Mr. Smith characterized as " an unrepentant voter for Henry Clay," to James G. Carter, " that accomplished, tried and able friend of the slave." Mr. Smith complained that Liberty Party men by hundreds and thousands, voted pro-slavery tickets that they might aid the cause of temperance ; that the vast majority of them were eager to entrust the Whigs with the task of framing the fundamental law of the State, and that he himself had been stigmatized by the Liberty Party press as a calumniator because he held the party to its highest responsibilities. For years the burden of the leader's speeches and letters was reproach against the party for its infidelities and backslidings ; but he would not desert it. In 1847, William Goodell pronounced the Liberty Party dead and buried, with a solemn verdict of suicide, and adjured Mr. Smith to let it rest, and to help in forming another party on a better basis. But his friend would not consent. In 1848, at Buffalo, he reiterated the original doctrines of the party, declared that it was popular not local, national not sectional, permanent not temporary, comprehensive not partisan; that it simply enunciated the principles of the founders of the government, and though sadly demoralized, was not irretrievably ruined. In 1849, though the vote in the town of Smithfield had been reduced from one hundred and eighty to forty, and of the forty all were not faithful to the "whole gospel" of the party, some being members of churches which bore no open testimony against slavery, and others engaged in the business of supplying grain for the distilleries,—still the loyal few met and chose local officers. In 1851, at a convention held by the Liberty Party in Buffalo, he was nominated as President of the United States, as he had been in 1848. In 1860 the party was still alive, and he wrote a sympathizing, encouraging letter to the convention held at Syracuse in August of that year ; but it had no vitality. In fact it was never a power in the country. It demanded too much of its constituency, and stretched itself along a too extended line. Its controlling spirits were enthusiasts, fanatics in two or three instances, who could neither follow leaders nor lead followers. Mr. Smith, the largest of them, was no manager, tactician or diplomatist, but a warm-hearted, strong-souled agitator who held moral interests to be supreme, and despised above all things the arts of the politician. In the dispute on the question whether one should stand by pure principle at the imminent risk of losing a partial advantage, or should secure the partial advantage at the risk of compromising the pure principle, he placed himself unhesitatingly with the devotees of principle, though men whom he revered chose the other side. Theodore Parker, in 1848, voted for Martin Van Buren in the hope of achieving a partial triumph for the "Free Soil" party ; Gerrit Smith, in 1844, refused to support Henry Clay and thereby pre-

9

vented an election from which men like W. H. Seward
anticipated the best results to the anti-slavery cause.

The " Industrial Congress " at Philadelphia, nominated him for president in 1848; the Land Reformers
nominated him in 1856.   Both invitations were declined
on the plea of disinclination to public life, and the pressure of private affairs.   The anti-slavery State Convention at Syracuse, in 1840, put him in nomination for
Governor against his will.   But when the State mass
convention, at Syracuse, nominated him in 1858, he accepted it with a " hopeful and courageous heart," in face
of the fact that not a single paper in the State, daily or
weekly, advocated the running of an " abolition or prohibitory " ticket.   He accepted it on principle, and because the circumstances were desperate ; accepted it in
the faith that frank, bold, persuasive speech backed by
moral truth would be more than a match for the whole
power of the press.   And, in accepting the nomination
he accepted the suggestion that the candidate shall
" canvass the State, and meet the masses of the people
in their several counties, to discuss before them, and
with whomsoever shall question him, the principles, measures and policy which should characterize the administration of the government of the great State of New
York."

It was hard work, but he girded himself manfully for
it.   He began his task on the 15th of August, and ended
it on the 2d of November, having attended fifty-three
meetings, travelled some four thousand miles, and spent
between four and five thousand dollars, paying of course
all expenses from his private purse.   The meetings were
long, exciting and exhausting, for his heart was in the

work, and he answered all questions on all subjects, with
that absolute candor which was characteristic of him.
He begged, as on his knees, for votes. Yet the result
was a complete overthrow. In some counties not a single man voted his ticket. Old friends and fellow-laborers in the causes of abolition and temperance turned
the cold shoulder on him, and even reproached him for
obstructing the measures he was hoping to advocate.
On the day of election, the Republican candidate received two hundred and forty-seven thousand eight hundred
and sixty-eight votes ; the Democratic candidate received
two hundred and thirty thousand three hundred and
twenty-nine votes ; the " American " candidate received
sixty-one thousand one hundred and thirty-seven ; the
" Independent " candidate, Mr. Smith, received five
thousand four hundred and forty-six.

All the parties were against him ; not alone the great
parties Democratic and Whig, but the Free Soilers, and
the Abolitionists who did not vote at all. In fact, as
family quarrels are proverbially the bitterest, so the an-
imosity was particularly cordial between these diverse
champions of a common cause. The following letters,
one addressed to an eminent abolitionist, the other to a
conspicuous Free Soiler, disclose the state of feeling
that existed when they were written. Such was the
way in which honorable men wrote to and about one
another. The letters are long, but they represent both
sides of the controversy, one by implication, the other
by direct language. No one will be surprised at their
tone who recalls the political condition of the country
when they were written ; the years immediately preceding the hour of most imminent peril.

Peterboro, October 23, 1846.

Hon. STEPHEN C. PHILLIPS, of Salem, Mass.:

Dear Sir — This day's mail brings me the speech which you delivered at the meeting recently assembled at Faneuil Hall to consider the outrage of kidnapping a man in the streets of Boston.

I am not insensible to the ability, eloquence, beauty, of this speech:—and yet it fails of pleasing me. The meeting, after I saw its proceedings, was no longer an object of my pleasant contemplations. Indeed, Massachusetts herself has ceased to be such an object. There was a time, when, among all commonwealths, she was my *beau ideal.* Her wisdom, integrity, bravery—in short, her whole history, from her bud in the Mayflower to the blossoms and fruits with which a ripe civilization has adorned and enriched her—made her the object of my warm and unmeasured admiration. But, a change has come over her. Alas, how great and sad a one! She has sunk her ancient worth and glory in her base devotion to Mammon and Party.

When, in the year 1835, one of her sons—that son to whom she, not to say this whole nation, owes more than to any other person, was, for his honest, just, and fearless assaults on slavery, driven by infuriate thousands through the streets of her metropolis with a halter round his neck, Massachusetts looked on, applauding. So far was she from disclaiming the mob that she boasted, that her "gentlemen of property and standing" composed it. Indeed, one of her first acts after the mob, was to choose for her governor the man who promptly rewarded her for this choice by his official recommendation to treat abolitionists as criminals.

Massachusetts was not, however, lost to shame. It was not in vain that the finger of scorn was pointed at her for this mob and for other demonstrations of her pro-slavery. For very decency's sake, she began to adjust her dress, and put on better appearances. Indeed, anti-slavery sentiment became the order of the day with her: and, from her chief statesman down to her lowest demagogue, all tried their skill in uttering big words against slavery. But, the hollowest sentiment and the merest prating constituted the whole warp and woof of this pretended and unsubstantial opposition to slavery. Massachusetts still remained the slave of Party and Mammon. She would still vote for slaveholders, rather than break up the national parties to which she was wedded. She would still make every concession to the slave power to induce it to spare her manufactures.

A fine occasion was afforded Massachusetts, a few years ago, to talk her anti-slavery words, and display her anti-slavery sentiment; and right well did she improve it. I refer to the casting of the fugitive slave George Latimer into one of her jails. Instantly did she show anti-slavery colors. She was anti-slavery all over, and to the very core also, as a stranger to her ways would have thought. But beneath all her manifestations of generous regard for the oppressed, she continued to be none the less bound up in avarice— none the less servile to the South. The first opportunity she had to do so, she again voted for slaveholders.

Then came the project to annex Texas. The slaveholders demanded more territory to soak with the sweat and tears and blood of the poor African. This was another occasion for Massachusetts to make another anti-slavery bluster. She made it :—*and then voted for Clay*—for the very man who had done unspeakably more than any other man to extend and perpetuate the dominion of American slavery. As a specimen of her heartlessness, in this instance of her anti-slavery parade, her present Whig Governor, who was among the foremost and loudest to condemn this scheme of annexation, is now calling, in the name of patriotism, on his fellow-citizens to consummate it by murdering the unoffending Mexicans.

Next came the expulsion of her commissioners from Charleston and New Orleans. Again she blustered for a moment. She denounced slavery and the South. She boasted of herself, as if she still were what she had been ; as if " modern degeneracy had not reached " her. But, the sequel proved her hypocrisy and baseness. After a little time, she quietly pocketed the insult, and was as ready as ever to vote for slaveholders.

I will refer to but one more of the many opportunities which Massachusetts has had to prove herself worthy of her former history. It is that which called out your present speech. This was emphatically an opportunity for Massachusetts to show herself to be an anti-slavery State. But she had not a heart to improve it. Her own citizens in the very streets of her own gloried-in city, had chased down a man, and bound him, and plunged him into the pit of perpetual slavery. The voice of such a deed, sufficient to rend her rocks, and move her mountains, could not startle the dead soul of her people. They are the fast bound slaves of Mammon and Party. True, a very great meeting was gathered in Faneuil Hall. Eloquent speeches were made ; and a committee of vigilance was appointed. But nothing was done to redeem herself from her degeneracy : nothing to recall to her loathsome carcass the great and glorious spirit which had departed from it ; nothing was done for the slave. When the year 1848 shall come round, Massachusetts, if still impenitent, will be as ready to vote for the slaveholders whom the South shall then bid her vote for, as she was to do so in 1844.

Your great meeting was a farce ;—and will you pardon me, if I cite your own speech to prove it? That speech, which denounces your fellow-citizen for stealing *one man,* was delivered by a gentleman, who (risum teneatis ?) contends, that a person who steals *hundreds of men* is fit to be President of the United States ! It is ludicrous, beyond all parallel, that he, who would crown with the highest honors the very prince of kidnappers, should, with a grave face, hold up to the public abhorrence the poor man, who has only just begun to try his hand at kidnapping. Then, your *contemptuous bearing* towards Captain Hannum and his employers !—how affected ! If you shall not be utterly insensible to the claims of consistency, who, when you shall have Henry Clay to dine with you, will you allow to be better entitled than this same Captain Hannum and his employers to seats at your table? Cease, my dear sir, from your outrages on consistency. You glory in Mr. Clay. How can you then despise and reproach those who, with however much of the awkwardness of beginners, are, nevertheless, doing their best to step forward in the tracks of their " illustrious predecessor ? "

It would be very absurd—would it not?—for you to denounce the stealing of a single sheep, at the same time that you are counting as worthy of all honor the man who steals a whole flock of sheep. But, I put it to your candor, whether it would be a whit more absurd than is your deep loathing and unutterable contempt of Captain Hannum and his employers for a crime, which, though incessantly repeated and infinitely aggravated in the case of Mr. Clay, does not disqualify him, in your esteem, to be the chief ruler of this nation— to be, what the civil ruler is required to be—" the minister of God."

You intimate, that the State Prison is the proper place for Captain Hannum and his employers. And do you not think it the proper place for Henry Clay also? Out upon partiality, if, because he is your candidate for the presidency, you would not have this old and practical man-thief punished, as well as those who are but in their first lessons of his horrid piracy !

To be serious, Mr. Phillips—*you* are not the man to have to do with Captain Hannum and his employers, unless it is to set them an example of repentance. It becomes you not to look down upon them —but to take your seat by their side, and to bow your head as low as shame and sorrow should bow theirs. No—if Captain Hannum and his employers should steal a man every remaining day of their lives, they could not do as much to sanction and perpetuate the crime of man-stealing, as the honored and influential Stephen C. Phillips has done by laboring to elect to the highest civil office the very man stealer, who has contributed far more than any other living person to make man-stealing reputable, and to widen the theatre of its horrors.

Alas, what a pity to lose such an occasion for good as was afforded by this instance of kidnapping. That was the occasion for you and other distinguished voters for slaveholders to employ the power of your own repentance in bringing other pro-slavery voters to repentance. That was the occasion for your eyes to stream with contrite sorrow, and your lips to exclaim : " We have sinned :— we have sinned against God and the slave :—we have not sought to have Civil Government look after the poor, and weak, and oppressed, and crushed :—but we have perverted and degraded it from this high, and holy, and heaven-intended use, to the low purposes of money-making and to the furtherance of the selfish schemes of ambition : we have not chosen for rulers men who, in their civil office, as Josiah in his, ʻjudged the cause of the poor and needyʼ—men who, in their civil office, could say, as did Job in his, ʻI was a father to the poorʼ—ʻI brake the jaws of the wicked and plucked the spoil out of his teethʼ—but we have chosen our Clays and our Polks— pirates, who rob, and buy and sell, the poor—monsters, who, with their sharks' teeth devour the poor." Deny, doubt, evade it, as you will—you may, nevertheless, my dear sir, depend upon it, that it is for your repentance and the repentance of all the voters for slave-holders, that God calls. He calls, also, for the repentance of the American ministry, that so wickedly and basely refuses to preach Bible politics, and to insist on the true and heaven-impressed character of Civil Government. Depend upon it, my dear sir, that your disease and theirs is one which can be cured by no medicine short of the medicine of repentance. I am not unaware that this is a most offensive and humbling medicine—especially to persons in the higher walks of life ;—nevertheless, you and they must take it or remain uncured. No clamor against Captain Hannum and his employers— no attempt to make scape-goats of them—will avail to cure you.

Alas, what a pity that a mere farce should have taken the place of the great and solemn measure which was due from your meeting ! Had your meeting felt, that the time for trifling on the subject of slavery is gone by; and had it passed, honestly and heartily, the Resolution : " *No voting for slaveholders, nor for those who are in*

political fellowship with slaveholders," it would have had the honor
of giving the death-blow to American slavery.   This resolution,
passed by such a meeting, would have electrified the whole nation.
Within all its limits every true heart would have responded to it, and
every false one been filled with shame.

When the glorious Missionary, William Knibb, had seen the
slaveholders tear down and burn a large share of the chapels in
Jamaica, he set sail for Great Britain.   Scarcely had he landed, ere
he began the cry, "*Slavery is incompatible with Christianity.*"   He
went over his native land, uttering this cry.   A mighty cry it was.
The walls of British slavery felt its power as certainly as did the
walls of Jericho the shout by which it was prostrated.

The power of the cry: "*No voting for slaveholders, nor for
those who are in political fellowship with slaveholders,*" would,
were it to proceed from the right lips, be as effective against the
walls of *American* slavery, as was the cry of William Knibb against
the walls of *British* slavery.   You, and Charles Sumner, (I know
and love him,) and Charles Francis Adams, and John G. Palfrey,
are the men to utter this cry.   Go, without delay, over the whole
length and breadth of your State, pouring these talismanic words
into the ears of the thousands and tens of thousands who shall flock
to hear you ; and Massachusetts will, even at the approaching election, reject all her pro-slavery candidates.   Such is the power of
truth, when proceeding from honored and welcome lips !

Be in earnest, ye Phillipses and Sumners and Adamses and Pal-
freys—be entirely in earnest, in your endeavors to overthrow slavery.
You desire its overthrow, and are doing something to promote it.
But you lack the deep and indispensable earnestness ; and, therefore, do you shrink from employing the bold and revolutionary
means which the case demands.   No inferior means however, will
accomplish the object.   As well set your babies to catch Leviathans
with pin-hooks, as attempt to overthrow American slavery by means
which fall below the stern and steadfast purpose: "*Not to vote for
slaveholders, nor for those who are in political fellowship with
slaveholders.*"   But, only press the hearts of your fellow-men with
this, the solemn and immovable purpose of your own hearts—and
fallen Massachusetts rises again—and American slavery dies—and
your names are written in everduring letters among the names of
the saviors of your country.

Very respectfully yours,

GERRIT SMITH.

Peterboro, Nov. 23, 1846.

EDMUND QUINCY, Esq., of Massachusetts :

Dear Sir, — I have this evening, read your letter to me, in the last Liberator. I am so busy in making preparations to leave home for a month or two, that my reply must be brief. A reply I must make —for you might construe my silence into discourtesy and unfriendliness.

From your remark, that you have not seen my " recent writings and speeches," I infer, that you do not deign to cast a look upon the newspapers of the Liberty Party. Your proud and disdainful state of mind toward this party accounts for some of the mistakes in your letter. For instance, were you a reader of its newspapers, you would not charge me with " irreverently " using the term " Bible politics." You evidently suppose that I identify the federal constitution and the Liberty Party with the politics of the Bible. But, in my discourses on " Bible politics," which, to no small extent, are made up directly from the pages of the Bible, I seek but to show what are the Heaven-intended uses of civil government, and what are the necessary qualifications of those who administer it. So far are these discourses from commending the constitution, or the Liberty Party, that they do not so much as allude either to the one or to the other. Again, were you a reader of the newspapers of this party, you would know its name. You would in that case know, that " Liberty Party " is the name, which, from the first, it has chosen for itself ; and that " Third Party " is only a nickname, which low-minded persons have given to it. You well know, that there are low-minded persons, who, seeing nothing in the good man who is the object of their hatred, for that hatred to seize upon, will try to harm him by nicknaming him. It is such as these, whose malice toward the Liberty Party has, for want of argument against that truth-espousing and self-sacrificing party, vented itself in a nickname. Be assured, my dear sir, that I have no hard feelings toward you for misnaming my party. You are a gentleman ; and your error is, therefore, purely unintentional. Upon your innocent ignorance—too easy and credulous in this instance, I admit—the base creatures who coined this nickname, have palmed it as the real name of the Liberty Party. You are a gentleman ; and hence, as certainly as your good breeding accords to every party, however little and despised, the privilege of naming itself, so certainly, when you are awake to this deception which has been practiced upon your credulity, you will be deeply indignant at it. I see, from his late speech in Faneuil Hall, that even Mr. Webster has fallen into the mistake of taking " Third Party "

9*

to be the name of the Liberty Party. The columns of the Liberator have, most probably, led him into it. Being set right on this point yourself, you will of course, take pleasure in setting him right. He will thank you for doing so ; for when he comes to know, that " Third Party " is but a nickname, and the invention of blackguards, he will shrink from the vulgarity and meanness of repeating it. Again, were you a reader of the newspapers of the Liberty Party, you would not feel yourself authorized to take it for granted, that to hold an office under the constitution is to be guilty of swearing to uphold slavery. On the contrary, you would be convinced, that nine-tenths of the abolitionists of the country—nine-tenths, too, of the wisest and worthiest of them—believe, that an oath to abide by the constitution is an oath to labor for the overthrow of slavery. Were you a reader of the newspapers of the Liberty Party, you would know, that this position of these nine-tenths of the abolitionists of the country is fortified by arguments of William Goodell and Lysander Spooner, which there has been no attempt to answer, and that, too, for the most probable reason, that they are unanswerable. I am not sure, that you have ever heard of these gentlemen. Theirs are perhaps, unmentioned names in the line of your reading and associations. Nevertheless I strongly desire that you may read their arguments. Your reading of them will, I hope, moderate the super latively arrogant and dogmatic style in which you, in common with the abolitionists of your school, talk and write on this subject. If this or aught else, shall have the effect to relax that extreme, turkey-cock tension of pride, with which you and your fellows strut up and down the arena of this controversy, the friends of modesty and good manners will have occasion to rejoice.

I have not taken up my pen to write another argument for the constitution. Two or three years ago, I presumed to write one : and the way in which it was treated, is a caution to me not to repeat the presumption. I shall not soon forget the fury with which the Mr. Wendell Phillips, whom you so highly praise in the letter before me, pounced upon it. Nothing short of declaring me to be a thief and a liar could relieve his swollen spirit, or give adequate vent to his foaming wrath. He would, probably, have come to be ashamed of himself, had not his review of me been endorsed by Mr. Garrison, and also by one, who it is said, is even greater than Mr. Garrison— " the power behind the throne."

I do not doubt, my dear sir, that you and your associates have sincerely adopted your conclusions respecting the constitution. That you should be thoroughly convinced by your own arguments

is a natural and almost necessary consequence of the self-complacency, which uniformly characterizes persons who regard themselves
as *ne plus ultra* reformers. I wish you could find it in your hearts
to reciprocate our liberality, in acknowledging your sincerity, and to
admit, that we, who differ from you, are also sincere. No longer
then would you suppose us, as you do in your present letter, to be
guilty of "jesuitical evasions," or to be capable of being, to use your
own capitals "PERJURED LIARS." No longer then would you
and the gentlemen of your school speak of us as a pack of office-
seekers, hypocrites, and scoundrels. But you would then treat us
—your equal brethren, as honestly and ardently desirous as yourselves to advance the dear cause to which you are devoted—with
decency and kindness, instead of contempt and brutality. I honor
you and your associates, as true-hearted friends of the slave ; and
nor man, nor devil, shall ever extort from my lips or pen a word of
injustice against any of you. I honor you also for the sincerity of
your beliefs, that they, who dissent from your expositions of the constitution, are in the wrong. But I am deeply grieved at your super-
ciliousness and intolerance toward those, whose desire to know and
do their duty is no less strong nor pure than your own. Far am I
from intimating that the blame of the internal dissensions of the
Abolitionists belongs wholly to yourselves. No very small share of
it should be appropriated by such of them as have indulged a bad
spirit, in speaking uncandidly and unkindly of yourselves. All classes
of Abolitionists have need to humble themselves before God for having retarded the cause of the slave by these guilty dissensions.

I would that I could inspire you with some distrust of your infal-
libility. I should, thereby, be rendering good service to yourself
and to the cause of truth. Will you bear to have me point out some
of the blunders in the letter to which I am now replying? And,
when you shall have seen them, will you suffer your wonder to abate,
that the great body of Abolitionists do not more promptly and im-
plicitly bow to the *ipse dixits* of yourself and your fellow infallibles?
Casting myself on your indulgence, and at the risk of ruffling your
self-complacency, I proceed to point out to you some of these
blunders.

Blunder No. 1. You charge me with holding, that the clause of
the constitution relating to the slave-trade, provides for its abolition.
What I do hold to, however, is, that the part of the constitution
which entrusts Congress with the power to regulate commerce, provides for the abolition of this trade. That Congress would use the
power to abolish this trade, was deemed certain by the whole con-

vention which framed the constitution. Hence a portion of its members would not consent to grant this power, unless modified by the clause concerning the slave-trade, and unless, too, this clause were made irrepealable. When the life-time of this modification had expired, Congress, doing just what the anti-slavery spirit of the constitution and the universal expectation of the nation demanded, prohibited our participation in the African slave-trade. I readily admit, that the clause in question is, considered by itself, pro-slavery. But it is to be viewed as a part of the anti-slavery bargain for suppressing the African slave-trade—and as a part, without which, the anti-slavery bargain could not have been made. Did I not infer from your own words, that you cannot possibly bring yourself to condescend to read the "writings or speeches" of Liberty-party men, I would ask you to read what I wrote to John G. Whittier and Adin Ballou on that part of the constitution now under consideration.

Blunder No. 2. But what pro-slavery act can that part of the constitution which respects the African slave-trade, require at the hands of one who should *now* swear to support the constitution? None. No more than if the thing, now entirely obsolete, had never been. What a blunder then to speak of this part of the constitution, as an obstacle in the way of swearing to support those parts of it which still remain operative!

Blunder No. 3. In your letter before me, as well as in your approval of an article in the Liberator of 30th last month, you take the position, that the pro-slavery interpretations of the constitution, at the hands of courts and lawmakers, are conclusive that the instrument is pro-slavery. But you will yourself go so far as to admit, that all slavery under the national flag, and in the District of Columbia, and indeed everywhere, save in the old thirteen States, is unconstitutional. Nevertheless all such parts of unconstitutional slavery have repeatedly been approved by courts and law-makers. You say, that the constitution is what its expounders interpret it to be; and that, inasmuch as they interpret it to be pro-slavery, you are bound to reject it. But the dignified and authoritative expounders of the Bible interpret *it* to be pro-slavery. Why, then, according to your own rules, should you not reject the Bible, also? Talleyrand, you know, thought a blunder worse than a crime. You and I do not agree with him. But we certainly cannot fail to agree with each other, that your blunder No. 3, is a very bad blunder.

Blunder No. 4. You declare, that because the constitution is as you allege, pro-slavery, it is inconsistent and unfair to reject a slaveholder from holding office under it. Extend the application if you will, that you may see its absurdity. The constitution of my State makes a dark skin a disqualification for voting. Hence, in choosing officers under it—even revisers of the constitution itself—I am not at liberty, according to your rule, to exclude a man from the range of my selection, on the ground that he is in favor of such disqualification. Nay, more, I must regard his agreement with the constitution on this point, as an argument in favor of his claim to my vote. Again—to conform to your rule, a wicked community should, because it is wicked, choose a wicked preacher—or because it is ignorant, choose an ignorant schoolmaster. Yours is a rule that refuses to yield to the law of progress, and that shuts the door against all human improvement. You would, for the sake of their consistency, have an individual—have a people—remain as wicked as they are— and vote for drunkards and slaveholders, because they have always done so. The provision of the constitution for its own amendment, is of itself, enough to silence your doctrine, that the agreement of a man's character and views with the constitution, is necessarily an argument for, and can never be an argument against, his holding office under it. This provision opens the door for choosing to office under the constitution, those who disagree with it. This provision implies, that in the progress of things, a man's agreement with the constitution may be a conclusive objection to clothing him with official power under it.

But I will stop my enumeration of your blunders, and put you a few questions.

1. Do you not believe, that it was settled by the decision in the year 1772 of the highest court of England, that there was not any legal slavery in our American Colonies?

2. Do you not believe, that there was no legal slavery in any of the States of this nation, at the time the constitution was adopted?

3. Do you not believe, that the constitution created no slavery; and that it is not to be held as even *recognizing* slavery, provided there was, at the time of its adoption, no legal slavery in any of the States?

4. Do you not believe, that had the American people adhered to the letter and spirit of the constitution, chattel slavery would ere this, have ceased to exist in the nation?

You will of course, be constrained to answer all these questions in the affirmative. And I wish that, when you shall have answered them, you would also answer one more—and that is the question whether, since you are hotly eager for the overthrow of all civil government (they are not governments whose laws, if laws they may be called, are without the sanctions of force) you ought not to guard yourself most carefully from seeking unjust occasions against them, and from satisfying your hatred of them, at the expense of candor and truth ? An atheist at heart is not unfrequently known to publish his grief over what he (afflicted soul !) is pained to be obliged to admit are blemishes upon the Bible. His words are, as if this blessed book were inexpressibly dear to him. Nevertheless, his inward and deep desire is, that with or without the blemishes he imputes to it, the Bible may perish. Our Non-resistants throw themselves into an agony before the public eye, on account of the pro-slavery which they allege taints the constitution. But, *aside* and in their confidential circles, their language is : " Be the constitution pro-slavery or anti-slavery, let it perish." Were the constitution unexceptionable to you on the score of slavery, you would, being a Non-resistant, still hate it with unappeasable hatred. Now I put it to you, my dear sir, whether the Non-resistants, when they ask us to listen to their *disinterested* arguments against the anti-slavery character of the constitution, do not show themselves to be somewhat brazen-faced ! I say naught against your Non-resistance. That I am not a Non-resistant myself—that I still linger around the bloody and life-taking doctrines in which I was educated—is perhaps, only because I have less humanity and piety than yourself. Often have I tried to throw off this part of my education ; and that the Bible would not let me, was, perhaps, only my foolish and wicked fancy.

You ask me to join you in abandoning the constitution. My whole heart—my whole sense of duty to God and man—forbids my doing so. In my own judgment of the case, I could not do so without being guilty of the most cowardly and cruel treachery toward my enslaved countrymen. The constitution has put weapons into the hands of the American people entirely sufficient for slaying the monster within whose bloody and crushing grasp are the three millions of American slaves. I have not failed to calculate the toil and self-denial and peril of using those weapons manfully and bravely—and yet for one, I have determined, God helping me, thus to use them—and not, self-indulgently and basely, to cast them away. If the people of the north should refuse to avail themselves of their constitutional power to effectuate the overthrow of American slavery, on them must rest the guilty responsibility, and not in that power—for it is ample. To give up the constitution is to give up the slave. His hope of a peaceful deliverance is, under God, in the application of the anti-slavery principles of the constitution.

No—I cannot join you in abandoning the constitution and over-throwing the government. I cannot join you, notwithstanding you tell me that to do so is " the only political action in which a man of honor and self-respect can engage in this country." Your telling me so is but another proof of your intolerance and insolence—but another proof of the unhappy change wrought in your temper and manners by the associations and pursuits of your latter years. Your telling me so carries no conviction to my mind of the truth of what you tell me. It is a mere assertion ;—and has surely, none the more likeness to an argument by reason of the exceedingly offensive terms in which it is couched.

Since I began this letter, I have received one from a couple of colored men of the city of Alexandria. Never did I read a more eloquent, or heart-melting letter. You remember that Congress, at its last session, left it to the vote of the whites in that part of the District of Columbia south of the Potomac, whether that part of the District should be set back to Virginia, and colored people be sub-jected to the murderous and diabolical laws which that State has enacted against colored people, the free as well as the bond. The letter which I have received, describes the feelings of our poor colored brethren, as they saw themselves passing from under the laws of the nation into the bloody grasp of the laws of a slave State. I will give you an extract :

" I know that, could you but see the poor colored people of this city, who are the poorest of God's poor, your benevolent heart would melt at such an exhibition. Fancy, but for a moment, you could have seen them on the day of election, when the act of Congress, retroceding them to Virginia, should be rejected or confirmed. Whilst the *citizens* of this city and county were voting, God's hum-ble poor were standing in rows, on either side of the Court House, and, as the votes were announced every quarter of an hour, the suppressed wailings and lamentations of the people of color were constantly ascending to God for help and succor, in this the hour of their need. And whilst their cries and lamentations were going up to the Lord of Sabaoth, the curses and shouts of the people, and the sounds of the wide-mouthed artillery, which made both the heavens and the earth shake, admonished us that on the side of the op-pressor there was great *power*. Oh sir, there never was such a time here before ! We have been permitted heretofore to meet to-gether in God's sanctuary, which we have erected for the purpose of religious worship, but whether we shall have this privilege when the Virginia laws are extended *over* us, we know not. We expect that our schools will all be broken up, and our privileges, which we have enjoyed for so many years, will all be taken away. The laws of Virginia can hardly be borne by those colored people that have been brought up in a state of ignorance and the deepest subjection: but oh sir how is it with us, who have enjoyed comparative liberty? We trust that we have the sympathies of the good and the virtuous. We know that we have yours and your associates in benevolence and love. Dear friend, can you and yours extend to our poor a helping hand, in this the time of our need? Remember, as soon as the legislature of Virginia meets, which is in December, they will extend their laws over us: and in the spring forty or fifty colored families would be glad to leave for some free State, where they can educate their children, and worship God without molestation. But, dear sir, whither shall we go? Say, Christian brother, and witness heaven and earth, whither shall we go? Do we hear a voice from you saying: 'Come here?' Or, are we mistaken? Say, brother, say, are we not greater objects of pity than our more highly favored and fortunate brethren of the North—(Heaven bless and preserve them!")

If such, my friend, is the woe, when but a few hundred colored persons (and part of them free) find themselves deserted by the National Power, what will it not be, when, in the bosoms of three millions of slaves, all hope of the interposition of that Power shall die? That Power I would labor to turn into the channel of deliverance to these millions. That Power you would destroy. Alas, were it this day destroyed, what a long, black night would settle down upon those millions! Vengeance might, indeed, succeed to despair; and its superhuman arm deliver the enslaved. But, such a deliverance would be through blood, reaching, in Apocalyptic language, "even to the horses' bridles:" and to such a deliverance neither you nor I would knowingly contribute.

But I am extending my letter to double the length I intended to give it—and must stop.

With great regard, your friend,

GERRIT SMITH.

The period between 1850 and 1860 was crowded with excitement. In those years the slave power made its desperate effort to get control of the government, and in the attempt exasperated to fury the people of the north. Anti-slavery men of every complexion were put

to their mettle. The "agitators" went up and down ;
the preachers thundered ; the politicians worked their
wires in frenzy ; vigilance committees were unsleeping ;
the "underground railroad" laid tracks on the surface
and opened new connections. A man like Gerrit Smith
could not restrain himself. In January, 1850, Mason's
bill to provide for the more faithful execution of the
clause in the Constitution requiring the return of fugitive
slaves was introduced. It was referred to the Judiciary
committee ; reported with amendments ; laid on the
table ; brought up on the 19th of August ; fiercely deba-
ted, and finally carried on the 16th of September. The
intervening months were spent by the negroes and their
friends in preparing for the worst. The worst came
soon. William L. Chaplin, general agent of the New
York Anti-Slavery Society, a publisher of tracts, books
and other "revolutionary" documents, editor of the Albany Patriot, a man of remarkable intelligence, ability,
and nobleness of character, personally intimate with
William Goodell, Beriah Green and their fellow-workers,
being in Washington, whither he had gone against Mr.
Smith's advice, was arrested for aiding the escape of two
young men, slaves of Robert Toombs and Alex. H.
Stephens, thrown into prison, and after five months of
incarceration, released on giving bail for twenty-five
thousand dollars. As the offence was punishable with
imprisonment, years, if not life long, and as conviction was
certain, his friends decided that the bail should be forfeited. There were lawyers' fees and incidental expenses
amounting to several thousands of dollars. To indemnify
the bail in Maryland cost nineteen thousand dollars ;
six thousand were required for the bail in Washington.

Even Gerrit Smith, prodigal as he was, winced under the imposition. " I am robbed of these twelve thousand dollars ; I have been robbed of a great deal from time to time, in the sums which I have felt myself morally compelled to pay in the purchase of the liberty of slaves. I greatly needed all this money to expend in other directions."

His state of mind on the passage of the Fugitive Slave Bill is indicated in the resolutions which he offered at different meetings called at this period. The law is called " the foulest of all blots upon civilization ; the greatest of all outrages upon religion and humanity; the heaviest of all reproaches upon republicanism."—It is a " diabolical law," which receives " the full measure of our contempt and hate and execration, and which we pledge ourselves to resist actively as well as passively, and by all such means as shall, in our esteem, promise the most effectual resistance." " If Christianity teaches anything, it teaches that the crime of dragging Hamlet, and Long, and Boulding and Harrison from this State into slavery was the crime of dragging Jesus Christ into slavery. They who dragged the poor naked and bleeding Jerry through the streets of Syracuse for the purpose of replunging him into the horrors of slavery, would have dragged Jesus Christ to the Cross." " Were we not a nation of atheists we would as soon think of enacting a law to enslave God Himself, as of enacting a law to enslave the beings whom He has made in His image ; as soon think of having kidnappers chase Him through His universe, as of having them chase the beings whose rights He holds as sacred as His own." " I glory in law. With the great Apostle I count it ' holy and just and good.' With the Psalmist I can say, ' it is my delight.' When the immortal Hooker so beautifully and sublimely says that ' law has her seat in the bosom of God, and her voice is the harmony of the world,' he thrills my whole soul. I will obey law. But I will not obey the dictates of devilism, which impudently install themselves in the place of law." " When poor Jerry the fugitive slave of Syracuse, whispered in my ear : ' I will never go back into slavery—I will have every bone in my body broken first,' I did not infer that he intended violence to any. He may have meant nothing more than that he would let his oppressors kill him sooner than he would consent to be reduced to a condition which he dreaded more than death. It is only the *principle* of resistance—without saying whether it should be active or passive—whether with the will merely, or with weapons also—which I have recommended." " It is our duty to peril life, liberty and property in behalf of the fugitive slave to as great an extent as we would peril them in behalf of ourselves." " It may not be the slave's duty to lose life or take life in order to exempt himself from slavery. But, if he is authorized to go to these extremities, it is absurd to say that I sin, if I carry my help to him to the same extremities." Such announcements as these show how he worked.

PREACHING POLITICS.

The citizens of the County of Madison are invited to attend a meeting in Peterboro, *Sunday, Nov.* 3, 1850.

It is expected that GERRIT SMITH will on that occasion, present the Bible view of Civil Government, and examine the late diabolical law for reducing the poor to slavery.

The exercises are to begin at 10 A. M., and, if the weather be pleasant, are to be in the open air. Good singers are especially invited to attend.

October 26, 1850.

FIVE THOUSAND MEN AND WOMEN WANTED.

To attend the Meetings in
CANASTOTA, Wednesday, Oct. 23d, 10 A. M.
CAZENOVIA, Friday, Oct. 25th, 10 A. M.
HAMILTON, Wednesday, Oct. 30th, 10 A. M.
PETERBORO, Friday. Nov. 1st, 10 A. M.

None but *real* men and women are wanted. The *sham* men and women who can stick to the Whig and Democratic parties are not wanted. These parties made the accursed law under which oppressors and kidnappers are now chasing down the poor among us, to make slaves of them. Hence there is no hope of good from persons who can stick to these Devil-prompted parties.

We want such men and women to attend these meetings as would rather suffer imprisonment and death than tolerate the execution of this man-stealing law. We want such as would be glad to see William L. Chaplin, now lying in a Maryland prison on account of his merciful feelings to the enslaved, made Governor of the State of New York. We want, in a word, such noble men and women as used to gather under the banners of the good old Liberty Party.

Let us then, get together again, to speak the truth, and to sing the truth. Those were good times when we came together to hear warm-hearted speeches for the slave, and to hear Otis Simmons' daughters, and Rhoda Klinck, and Miss Cook, etc., etc., sing

"*Come join the Abolitionists.*"
"What mean ye that ye bruise and bind ? "
"*The Yankee Girl.*"
"There's a good time coming, boys."
October 10, 1850.

In the midst of this excitement, while the North was ringing with cries of terror and shouts of defiance, and the anti-slavery feeling was glowing at fever-heat, Mr. Smith was elected to Congress by a plurality of votes;—the Whig candidate receiving 5,620; the Democratic 6,206; the " Independent " 8,049. He was sitting at table, it is said, when the news was brought. His were not the only hands that were raised in astonishment—for the spectacle had not been seen before. Here was a simple-hearted bible-Christian going where Christianity was a worldly institution, and the bible a sealed book; an independent going where the party politician alone was regarded; a believer in the Laws of Nature going where such things were not so much as heard of; a servant and friend of his kind going to the one place in America where everybody was supposed to have his price, and the arts of deception, invented in contempt and practiced with heartless cruelty, were prized above all others. He never drank, and he was to be the associate of men who tippled at all hours of day and night. He never smoked or chewed tobacco, and he was about to live among people who thought the air unfit to breathe until it was thick with the fumes of cigars, and in whose opinion the indispensable article of furniture was the spittoon. He went to bed with the chickens and rose with the birds, and he was to pass months in a city where day began in the afternoon, and reached the meridian at midnight. The man of prayer is sent down to the metropolis of profanity; the free soul to the stronghold of slavery; the child of the Spirit to the arena of gladiators. The people wondered; editors smiled good-naturedly or sarcastically; the politicians derided; the high-minded rejoiced. The " New York Times " scouted the nomination:

" It seems to us mere wantonness—idle nonsense—to send such a man to Congress, to take part in practical legislation upon practical subjects. Those who elected him doubtless did it quite as much on account of his character or from a desire to see what *could* be done as with an expectation that he would prove influential or useful, in his new position.

Mr. Greeley, in the " Tribune," wrote:

" We are heartily glad that Gerrit Smith is going to Washington. He is an honest, brave, kind-hearted Christian philanthropist, whose religion is not put aside with his Sunday cloak, but lasts him clear through the week. We think him very wrong in some of his notions of political economy, and quite mistaken in his ideas that the constitution is inimical to slavery, and that injustice cannot be legalized : but we heartily wish more such great, pure, loving souls could find their way into Congress. He will find his seat anything but comfortable, but his presence there will do good, and the country will know him better and esteem him more highly than it has yet done."

His friend, William Jay, hailed his election in a triumphant strain :

Bedford, November 9, 1852.

My Dear Sir—Rarely have I been so delightfully astonished as by the intelligence of your election. What a rebuke of the vile pledge given by the Baltimore convention to resist all anti-slavery discussions in Congress or out of it, wherever, whenever, however, and under whatever shape or color it may be attempted ! What a scorn is it on the atrocious effort of Fillmore and his Cabinet to convict of the capital crime of levying war against the United States, a peaceful, conscientious man, merely because he refused to aid in the villainy of catching slaves, that *you*, an undoubted *traitor* according to Webster's exposition of the constitution, should be sent, not to the gallows, but to Congress !

How must our Cotton Parsons mourn over the irreligion of Madison and Oswego, represented in the councils of the nation by a man who openly avows a higher law than the constitution, and who preaches that obedience to an accursed Act of Congress is rebellion against God !

You and I, my dear sir, very honestly differ in opinion on some points, but we cordially agree as to the diabolism of American slavery and the fugitive slave act ; and most sincerely do I rejoice in your election.

May the blessings of the Almighty rest upon you, and may He give you wisdom from on high, to direct you in the discharge of your new duties ; and may he deliver you from that fear of man which is at once the snare and the curse of almost all our public men.

Your friend,

WILLIAM JAY.

William H. Seward wrote cordially thus :

Auburn, Nov. 10, 1852.

My Dear Sir, — I thank you for your circular. I cannot congratulate you on your election over the candidate of my own party. But I may say that it is full of instruction which I think the two parties needed, and that I look to its effect with confidence, as I do to your action in the house as full of hope and promise for the cause of Liberty and Humanity.

Faithfully your friend,

WILLIAM H. SEWARD.

The closing prayer in Mr. Jay's letter was answered : that all were forced to admit, whatever may be thought of the one that preceded it. Whether or no there was wisdom, there surely was no fear of man. Mr. Smith went to Washington on no false pretences, as is testified by the address he issued.

To the voters of the Counties of Oswego and Madison.—You nominated me for a seat in Congress, notwithstanding I besought you not to do so. In vain was my resistance to your persevering and unrelenting purpose.

I had reached old age. I had never held office. Nothing was more foreign to my expectations, and nothing was more foreign to my wishes, than the holding of office. My multiplied and extensive affairs gave me full employment. My habits, all formed in private life, all shrank from public life. My plans of usefulness and happiness could be carried out only in the seclusion in which my years had been spent.

My nomination, as I supposed it would, has resulted in my election,—and that too, by a very large majority. And now, I wish that I could resign the office which your partiality has accorded to me. But I must not—I cannot. To resign it would be a most ungrateful and offensive requital of the rare generosity, which broke through your strong attachments of party, and bestowed your votes on one the peculiarities of whose political creed leave him without a party. Very rare, indeed, is the generosity, which was not to be repelled by a political creed, among the peculiarities of which are :

1. *That it acknowledges no law and knows no law for slavery ;*

that not only is slavery not in the federal constitution, but that, by no possibility could it be brought either into the federal or into a State constitution.

2. *That the right to the soil is as natural, absolute and equal as the right to the light and air.*

3. *That political rights are not conventional but natural,—inhering in all persons, the black as well as the white, the female as well as the male.*

4. *That the doctrine of free trade is the necessary outgrowth of the doctrine of the human brotherhood ; and that to impose restrictions on commerce is to build up unnatural and sinful barriers across that brotherhood.*

5. *That national wars are as brutal, barbarous and unnecessary as are the violence and bloodshed to which misguided and frenzied individuals are prompted ; and that our country should, by her own Heaven-trusting and beautiful example, hasten the day when the nations of the earth " shall beat their swords into ploughshares and their spears into pruning hooks ; nation shall not lift up sword against nation, neither shall they learn war any more."*

6. *That the province of government is but to protect—to protect persons and property ; and that the building of railroads and canals and the care of schools and churches fall entirely outside of its limits, and exclusively within the range of " the voluntary principle." Narrow however as are those limits, every duty within them is to be promptly, faithfully, fully performed :—as well, for instance, the duty on the part of the federal government to put an end to the dram-shop manufacture of paupers and madmen in the city of Washington, as the duty on the part of the State government to put an end to it in the State.*

7. *That as far as practicable, every officer, from the highest to the lowest, including especially the President and Postmaster, should be elected directly by the people.*

I need not extend any further the enumerations of the features of my peculiar political creed ; and I need not enlarge upon the reason which I gave why I must not and cannot resign the office which you have conferred upon me. I will only add that I accept it ; that my whole heart is moved to gratitude by your bestowment of it ; and that, God helping me, I will so discharge its duties as neither to dishonor myself nor you.

GERRIT SMITH.

Peterboro, November 5, 1852.

What the man wrote he meant. These were convictions not opinions with him; his daily life was founded
upon them; he was, in fact, their incarnation. To betray
or to compromise or to qualify them was morally impossible. At this time he was out of health. For six or
seven weeks his head had been " filled with horrors ;"
now " swimming," now " unbalanced and toppling, now
bursting with fullness, and now as heavy as lead." The
journey to Washington was made by slow stages. He
reached the city on the 1st of December; the session
began on the 5th, but it was the 12th before he was in
condition to take his seat. Yet, in this state, so ailing
and distressed, he had, before leaving Peterboro, made
ninety-two visits on friends and neighbors, and arranged
his affairs as if he never expected to return.

The necessities of his own and his wife's health, aside
from his habitual demand for space, made it wise for
him to hire a house and to keep up an establishment.
The hospitality of his nature, which rendered it a necessity with him to keep open doors, filled his mansion
with guests; his friendliness and courtesy and unaffected
humanity which knew no distinction of persons, drew
all kinds to him ; his wonderful resources of conversation, his invariable pleasantry, his sincere respect for
other men's opinions, and his utter freedom from dislike
to people of views entirely opposed to his own, his uni-
form dignity, urbanity and sweetness, made his frequent
entertainments peculiarly attractive. The hospitalities
of Peterboro were revived in Washington. He gave two
dinners each week, and invited every member of the
House. At his table men of all parties and all conditions met and sat down together. The southerners, in

10

especial, were fascinated by the open-handed, wide-hearted welcome the man extended. Aristocratic though they were, they enjoyed the atmosphere of this genuine Democrat whose humanity embraced all extremes with an equal ease; slaveholders and slave propagandists though they were, they felt no rancor towards the man whose spirit was animated by a love so entire. His pleasant association with slaveholders exposed him to suspicion and criticism, as similar associations with Pharisees and women who were "sinners" exposed one who was greater than he; in these cases the fault-finder fails to discern the nobleness which exalts the human nature above the conventional classifications of State and Church. His father having been a slaveholder until he had reached manhood, and formed his habits of social intercourse—his wife having come from a slaveholding community—several of his friends and relatives being slaveholders—he could appreciate the personal and social qualities of men whose ideas he detested, whose policy he opposed with all his might. But to their opinions and habits he made no concession. There was no wine on his table; he offered no cigars; he countenanced no rudeness or indelicacy. His guests took him as he was, and were glad to, for his originality was his charm. They could not fear him, and they could not suspect him; for his complete separation from party organizations made him incapable of political harm, and his perfect frankness disarmed mistrust. They dreaded him about as much as they dreaded the abstractions of the New Testament. He, on his part, was guileless as a saint. There is not the least reason to believe that he courted popularity or sought influence, or did anything but act out his nature. The weakest as well as wickedest accusation that was made against him was that of trying to outwit politicians by giving them cold water dinners! Even he was not simple enough to think that the reward promised to the proverbial cup offered in the name of discipleship, covered cases of *that* nature. The weakness of the insinuation that his head was turned by popularity in Washington and his simplicity of nature spoiled, is exposed by a single incident that occurred there. There was discord in the kitchen, and a dispute on the question of milking the cow. He settled it, not by dismissing the servants, but by going into the yard and milking the cow himself. There was plenty of fresh milk after that.

Had he been sycophantic he would have disguised somewhat his opinions in the speeches he made before Congress. Or, perhaps his outspokenness there covered the same deep design that lurked at the bottom of the goblet! The speeches were frank enough to justify suspicions of only the deepest wile. The longest plummet line would come short of the bottom of such deceit. They must be astute critics who can detect the diplomatic intent in this little sentence, which occurs in his maiden speech on the reference of the President's Message : " What a disgusting spectacle does the administration present, in its deliberate corruption of the bible, for the guilty purpose of sparing so abominable and vile a thing as slavery ! "

This first speech was made on December 20, 1853, eight days only after he took his seat. The speech on War, called out by the bill making appropriation for the support of the Military Academy for the year ending June

30, 1855, was delivered January 18, 1854; the speech on
the Homestead Bill followed, February 21; the speech
on government aid in constructing a railroad through
the Territory of Minnesota came next, March 7; the
speech on the Nebraska Bill was made, April 6; the
speech on the Pacific Railroad scheme, May 30, improved the opportunity for declaring further his views
on the limits of government; the speech for the Abolition of the Postal System was delivered June 15; the
speech on the Mexican Treaty and " Monroe Doctrine "
was pronounced, June 27; the speech in favor of pro-
hibiting all traffic in intoxicating drinks in the city of
Washington preceded by only three days the speech
against providing intoxicating drinks for the navy, July
25. Eight or nine shorter speeches were thrown in,
making altogether a full record of work for a man past
middle age and impaired in health.

To analyze these speeches would take more space
than is warranted, for they are at once comprehensive
and discursive.* It is sufficient to say that they fully
declared his mind on all the points presented in his
manifesto, and which have been already explained. His
ideas of government, war, slavery, temperance, finance,
are stated with his usual clearness, fearlessness and
force. No peculiarity or eccentricity is concealed or
qualified. Their style is simple, direct, unrhetorical.
They are earnest talks, without close arrangement, or
literary finish; massive, exuberant, flowing, delivered
with an air of confidence wholly unlike the studied manner of this class of productions. Impressive they must
have been, and interesting; but were probably not con-

* Gerrit Smith in Congress. New York, 1855.

vincing to the listening politicians, who had never learned the force of the pure reason. His general ideas they smiled at as visionary ; harmless because impracticable. Some of his particular notions, such for instance as that of a national police, composed of men strong in intelligence and character, who should represent the power of the country in place of the army, stamped him, in their regard, as a crazy enthusiast. It is pretty clear that to all but his enemies, Mr. Smith's career in Congress was a disappointment. The *Chicago Tribune* expressed a common sentiment when it described him as a wrong headed fanatic, wilful and intractable, conceited and wayward, whose intellect ran to paradox, whose wisdom was akin to folly, and who injured his own side more than the opposition. His constituency were indignant because he resigned at the end of a single session the place he had accepted unwillingly, at great inconvenience and sacrifice, and had filled as well as he could, and as long as he thought himself useful, and would have held longer had not a better man, as he thought, Henry C. Goodwin, stood ready to take it.

" What member of Congress,." he said, " ever worked harder than I did ? What one ever made so many speeches and on so great a variety of subjects, in a single session ? Remember that you put me in nomination against my will. I had entertained no more thought of going to Congress than to the moon. I went there, leaving my large private affairs unsettled, and plans unfinished, which, in at least my own view, were plans of usefulness to my fellow-men. The Congress of which I was a member was in session eleven months. Perhaps no member was more constantly in his seat for the first eight months. I then resigned, and left my constituents, without putting them to the pains and expense of a special election, to supply my place for the remaining three months. They did supply it with a man of talents, and an earnest friend of the slave. Surely, in the light of these facts, I ought not to be censured for my resignation."

Criticism on the Congressional career bore upon three points. 1. His vote against the " Homestead Bill," which he had advocated in one of his most eloquent speeches. 2. His refusal to become a party to the Republican plan to prevent the taking of a vote on the Nebraska Bill. 3. His plea for the annexation of Cuba to the United States. The first he justified easily, and with the full approval of leading abolitionists,—Judge Jay enthusiastically applauding,—on the ground that the bill, *as voted on*, was altered so as to confine the homestead privilege to *white* people, thus excluding the blacks from the land, and virtually denying their right, as human beings, to the unrestricted gifts of Providence. His action in the second case was explained on the idea that it was an infringement on the democratic principle for a minority, by party tactics, to thwart or obstruct the will of the majority. From this position nothing could move him ; neither the supplications of the abolitionists, nor the remonstrances of the Republicans ; neither the persuasions of his friends, nor the taunts of his enemies. The principle he acted on, when, instead of sitting all night in the house that he might count one, he went as usual to his quiet bed, was one he had meditated on for years, and had worked into the very texture of his mind ; and he could not, in an hour of feverish excitement, desert it. In vain the abolition press abused him ; 'in vain the New York Tribune poured upon him its sarcasm, its argument steeped in gall ; in vain some taunted him with cowardice, others scolded at him for wrong-headedness, and others again jeered at his incurable propensity to go to bed at sundown, though Fate was knocking at the door ; he never saw the impropriety

of his action, and consequently never was sorry for it
The acrid criticism of Horace Greeley did provoke him
to a reply which called out counter replies, and led to a
sharp controversy in which he met the fate that always
befals the assailant of a powerful newspaper, but in which
he did succeed in putting the real facts of the case before
the country. His final vote against the bill, taken at
eleven o'clock at night, amid the fumes of tobacco and
whiskey, the hissing of spittoons, and the unseemly
clamor of half drunken representatives, was a sufficient
vindication of his earnestness, and a sufficient answer
to the foolish taunt that he consulted his personal ease
more than the cause he was sent to serve.

The annexation of Cuba was a side question; consequently the position he took in regard to it puzzled
more than it enraged. He defended his position, not
as others did, on geographical, commercial or any kindred considerations; certainly not as the slaveholder did,
who urged annexation because it would extend the area
of his darling institution; but because, as an abolitionist,
he wished for the overthrow of slavery and believed
that the annexation of Cuba would help to bring it about.
His reasoning was original, and may have been fanciful,
but it was honest. He argued that, Cuban slavery
being better in theory than the American, though worse
in practice, each would tend to modify and destroy
the other; the American practice ameliorating the condition of the blacks in Cuba, the Cuban theory mitigating
the cruelty of the American slave laws, while both were
brought under the action of republican ideas. Again,
he argued that the annexation of Cuba would put a stop
legally to the African slave trade, and would make Spain

an anti-slavery nation. The withdrawal of Spanish troops from Cuba, and therefore of military support of the institution, would follow as a thing of course, and the system would take its chance in a population too nearly allied by temperament, blood, habits and social condition to the blacks to keep them long in bondage. The slaveholders would be too few to maintain it, and it would disappear. For the project of replacing Spanish troops by American could not for a moment be entertained, even if American troops could be relied on to enforce the stricter laws of our slavery in an island where, for ages, a milder system had prevailed. The attempt would provoke a bloody insurrection which the whole force of the United States would be unable to quell. These are abstract considerations, resting upon conjecture merely, and carried no weight against the popular instinct, which, on the one side, made the slaveholders a unit in favor of annexation, and leagued the abolitionists as one man in opposition to it. The reasoning may have been good, nevertheless ; at all events its originality does not convict it of folly ; still less does it convict the reasoner of baseness.

Gerrit Smith, in Congress, was precisely what he was out of it, what he had always been, what those at all acquainted with him, might have known he always would be. He was himself.

The following notes indicate Mr. Sumner's feeling:

Washington, 9th Aug., '54.

My Dear Friend — Your speech on temperance has made a convert in *Francis Markoe, Esq.*, of the State Department, occupying an important bureau there, who expresses an admiration of it without stint. He wishes some twenty-five copies to circulate among friends. Will you send them to him with your frank ?

I leave to-morrow for the North, regretting much not to see you again before I go—regretting more that you forbid me to hope to see you next winter when I return to renew our struggle.

You *ought not* to desert!

Ever yours,

CHARLES SUMNER.

Boston, 16th Oct., '55.

My Dear Gerrit Smith — Pardon me; but I do not see on what ground you can be excused from a public lecture here in Boston and also in New York. Here is an opportunity to do much good. Your presence would give character and weight to our cause. It cannot afford to miss you.

You excuse yourself on account of your many engagements at home. I understand these; but we have a right to expect you to make the necessary sacrifice. *You are rich, and can afford it.* Let your great fortune miss for a short time your watchful eye, and come to us in Boston and New York. One lecture will do for both places.

Here also is an opportunity to commend your views by argument, and personal presence, which you should not abandon.

I do long to have our great controversy, which is so much discredited in the large cities, upheld by your voice. Come among us. Let us have those rich tones, and that generous heart, and that unmitigable hatred of slavery to leaven our masses. Come. Do.

Ever sincerely yours,

CHARLES SUMNER.

Honorable Gerrit Smith.

Washington, 18th March, '56.

My Dear Gerrit Smith — I have your volume, "Gerrit Smith in Congress," and am glad to possess it.

I am happy also that it owes its origin in any degree to a hint from me.

Of this I am sure. It will remain a monument of your constant, able and devoted labors during a brief term in Congress, and will be recognized as an arsenal of truth, whence others will draw bright weapons.

Douglas has appeared at last on the scene, and with him that vulgar swagger which ushered in the Nebraska debate. Truly—truly—this is a godless place. Read that report, also the President's

10*

messages, and see how completely the plainest rights of the people of Kansas are ignored. My heart is sick.

And yet I am confident that Kansas will be a free State. But we have before us a long season of excitement, and ribald debate, in which truth will be mocked and reviled.

Remember me kindly to your family, and believe me,

My dear friend,

Sincerely yours,

CHARLES SUMNER.

Mr. Smith's powerful speech against the Nebraska Bill, the motto whereof was " No slavery in Nebraska; no slavery in the nation; slavery an outlaw," was delivered on the 6th of April, 1854; the bill passed the house on the 15th of May. The question now arose which—the north or the south, democratic or slave institutions, should first occupy, possess and control the thinly peopled territories, and organize them into States. It was a race for conquest between the people who lived south and the people who lived north of " Mason and Dixon's line." The territory lay close to the southern boundary, making the access from Missouri easy. The sons of freedom lived at a distance, in the Middle and Eastern States. Now was the time for men of wealth, eloquence, influence and public spirit to bestir themselves. They did so, and effectually. Happy was Gerrit Smith now, to be at home, on his own ground, with his neighbors and friends about him, and his hands on the machinery he so well knew how to use. There was call for money; and that was a weapon he could wield to some purpose. There was call for plain speech, not addressed to lazy legislators, but sent straight to the heart of colonists; and such was the speech that he was master of. There was call for close intercourse among the leaders of the new crusade ; and this intercourse he had been forming for years. The centre of the activity in sending emigrants to Kansas and Nebraska was New England, for there the zeal was hottest ; there the population was most dense, and organizations were compact. In the middle of New York, such concentrated action was not possible. A man like Gerrit Smith stood alone, and worked by his own methods. We have seen enough of him to know that he could not use other men's ideas or arrangements. With the record of his life before us, we cannot agree with Mr. Thurlow Weed, that he was "wildly possessed by one idea," that "he lived for nearly thirty years of his life in a state of political hallucination," that "his mind had hovered on the brink of insanity for more than a quarter of a century." He was as far as it is possible for a man to be from fanaticism ; and so many ideas occupied his mind that no one could get possession of him. This is one reason why he could not work with a party ; he saw too many aspects of every question. He was almost, if not quite alone, among abolitionists, in reasonableness of sentiment towards the south. At the close of the war, when the south was beaten and prostrate, he was but one of many to recal the fact that the guilt of the rebellion and the responsibility for the causes which resulted in the rebellion, were not exclusively hers. Before the war, and while the virulent causes were at work, exasperating the friends of freedom, he was able to make allowance for the slaveholder, to comprehend his embarrassments, to understand his position. In the heat of the Kansas trouble, at a meeting held at Syracuse, Oct. 1856, to commemorate the rescue of Jerry, he said : "I pity the poor

slaveholder! I pity him more than I do the slave!"
"More than you do the slave?" cried an excited lis-
tener. "Yes," was the reply, "much more; for the
slaveholder is the victim of a fatal delusion which is endorsed by most of the churches and clergy of this country—a delusion which is ruining the slaveholder, soul
and body, for time and eternity! God will take care of
the slave; but the poor slaveholder will never know till
he stands before his God, the evil he has done." The
effects of education in making men unconscious of wrong
doing and morally protecting them against personal
contamination from its guilt, should be familiar enough
to every man never to be forgotten; but they are forgotten continually; few remember them when most they
need to be borne in mind. He was never oblivious of
them; nor did he ever lose sight of the fact—this was
one of the most remarkable features of his unsectarian
church—that character may be independent, not of creeds
merely, but even of conduct; that good men and women,
—as good as any, perhaps, — may be found among
people who are implicated in evil institutions, not as
victims, but as supporters of them.

Nor was he blind to the weaknesses of the negro
character. For many years, the vicious moral condition
of the blacks, whether in slavery or out of it, was a
heavy burden on his heart. In 1842, he issued an address to the slaves, exhorting them to cultivate the dis-
positions becoming to poor, afflicted men, patience,
trust, hopefulness. Dr. Channing found fault with it as
being disturbing, exciting, even revolutionary in its tendency; but really it evinced a deep concern for their rational being, and an apprehension lest they might, in

their desire for freedom, neglect the qualities that would render them fit for it. To the liberated blacks of the northern States, he was unsparing of counsel and admonition. The " Address of the Liberty Party to the Colored People of the northern States," presented at the Buffalo Convention, in 1848, shows no lack of information respecting their infirmities and infidelities, and no lack of frankness in imparting it; their natural inclination to idleness and shiftlessness, their carelessness of rights and duties, addictedness to animal pleasures, dishonesty, untruthfulness, unchastity; their stupid docility in following the guidance of political and religious leaders, their general want of self-respect, their insensibility to personal and social duties, are set forth with a plainness which would have been exceedingly unpalatable, had the censor been less unquestionably a friend. The resolutions offered at the National Convention of the colored people, at Troy, thanking him for his gift of one hundred and forty thousand acres of land, drew from him a letter which contains language like this :

" The free colored people of this country have lost their self-respect. Hence my gravest doubt of their redemption. Hence too, my gravest doubt that they will ever exert an effectual influence for the redemption of their enslaved brethren. . . . Could I but get the ear of my northern colored brethren,—could I but get it away from their flatterers and deceivers—I would say to them : ' Cultivate self-respect ; cultivate self-respect,'—for by that means, and not without that means, can you peaceably regain your own rights, or the rights of your race at the south."

In January 1851, there was a meeting at Syracuse, to consider the duties imposed by the Fugitive Slave Bill,—Frederick Douglass presiding.—Gerrit Smith presented the same address and resolutions he had reported at the

State Convention, in the same city, the day before. Again his voice rings out:

"Would to God, brethren, that you were inspired with self-respect! Then would others be inspired with respect for you;—and then would the days of American slavery be numbered. We entreat you to rise up and, quit yourselves like men, in all your political and ecclesiastical and social relations. You admit your degradation;— but you seek to excuse it on the ground that it is forced—that it is involuntary. An involuntary degradation! We are half disposed to deny its possibility, and to treat the language as a solecism. At any rate, we feel comparatively no concern for what of your degradation comes from the hands of others. It is your *self-degradation* which fills us with sorrow—sorrow for yourselves, and still more for the millions whose fate turns so largely on your bearing. We know, and it grieves us to know, that white men are your murderers. But, our far deeper grief is that you are suicides."

There is no fanaticism in that.

Equally manful is the comment on the liberators. Thus the Abolitionist writes to Wendell Phillips, the prince of Abolitionists, in 1855:

"Considerable as have been the pecuniary sacrifices of abolitionists in their cause, they fall far short of the merits of that precious cause. It is but a small proportion of them who refuse to purchase the cotton and sugar and rice that are wet with the tears and sweat and blood of the slave. And when we count up those who have sealed with their blood their consecration to the anti-slavery cause, we find their whole number to be scarcely half a dozen.

"In none of the qualities of the best style of men—and that is the style of men needed to effectuate the bloodless termination of American slavery—have the abolitionists shown themselves more deficient than in magnanimity, confidence, charity. They have judged neither the slaveholders nor each other, generously. . . . The quarrels of abolitionists with each other, and their jealousy and abuse of each other would be far less had they more magnanimity, confidence, charity. Many of them delight in casting each other down, rather than in building each other up. Complain of each other they must; and when there is no occasion for complaint, their ill-natured ingenuity can manufacture an occasion out of the very smallest materials.

Were even you, whose trueness to the slave is never to be doubted, to be sent to Congress, many of your abolition brethren would be on the alert to find some occasion for calling your integrity in question. . . . It is no wonder that slaveholders despise both us and our cause. Our cowardice and vacillation, and innumerable follies have, a.most necessarily, made both us and it contemptible. The way for us to bring slaveholders right on slavery is to be right on it ourselves. The way for us to command the respect, ay, and to win the love of slaveholders, is to act honestly, in regard to slavery and to all things else. Do I mean to say that slaveholders can be brought to love abolitionists? Oh yes! and I add, that abolitionists should love slaveholders. We are all brothers; and we are all sinners too; and the difference between ourselves, as sinners, is not so great, as in our prejudice on the one hand and our self-complacency on the other, we are wont to imagine it to be."

Another evidence of the temperate character ot his mind is his opinion—entertained until the outbreak of the war—that, in the event of emancipation, the North should share with the South the expense incident to the sacrifice of so much property. This he maintained in a speech at a " National Compensation Convention " held in Cleveland, Ohio, August 25, 26 and 27, 1857:

"We are met," he said, "to initiate—I might perhaps, rather say, to inaugurate—a great movement, one that is full of promise to the slave and the slaveholder, and our whole country. It is not so much to awaken interest in their behalf that we have come together, as it is to give expression to such interest—a practical and effective expression.

"We are here for the purpose of making a public and formal, and, as we hope, an impressive confession that the North ought to share with the South in the temporary losses that will result from the abolition of slavery. Indeed, such are our relations to the South in the matter of slavery, that, on the score of simple honesty, we ought to share in these losses."

No man took stronger ground in regard to Kansas than Gerrit Smith; no man spoke braver words, or backed them by more consistent deeds. The scrapbooks, about this period—1855, 1856—contain a record of thoughts and actions that might satisfy the most ar-dent warrior. A few extracts from the long printed let-ters and speeches are all that can be given here. This is from a speech delivered at a Kansas meeting held at the Capitol in Albany, March 13, 1856:

"I hear one thing of the people of Kansas which I am sorry to hear. I hope it is not true. It is that they shall be willing to sub-mit to this ruffian government, provided the Federal government shall require them to do so. But in no event, must they submit to it. They must resist it, even if in doing so, they have to resist both Congress and President. And we must stand by them in their re-sistance. Let us bring the case home to ourselves. Suppose the legislators who meet in this building, were to enact a statute depriv-ing us of the freedom of speech, and making it a penitentiary offence to express an opinion against the rightfulness of slaveholding—would we submit to the statute? No, we would much rather march into this building, and hurl from their seats the men guilty of such a perversion of their official powers. And we would be no less prompt to do this, even though all the congresses and presidents on earth were backing them."

The following is from a letter printed in the Syracuse *Daily Journal* dated May 31, 1856, addressed to the callers of a Kansas Convention there:

"I wish the convention would go with me in voting slavery to death. But I tell you, gentlemen, with all my heart, that if the con-vention is not ready to go with me in voting slavery to death, I am ready to go with it in putting slavery to a violent death. . . Con-cluding that your convention will decide to fight rather than to vote against slavery, I hope it will originate a movement as broad as our whole State, and taxing the courage, energy and liberality of every part of the State. I hope to hear that it has adopted measures to raise one million of dollars and one thousand men. I will not doubt that both can be readily obtained. If they cannot be, then are the people of New York so degenerate and abject as to invite the yoke of slavery on their own necks.

"A word in regard to the thousand men. They should not be

whiskey drinkers, nor profane swearers. They should have the purity and zeal of Cromwell's armies, and, therefore, would they have the invincibility of those armies.

"For myself, I am too old, and too ignorant of arms, to fight. I scarcely know how to load a gun, and I am not certain that I ever saw a Sharpe's rifle, or a revolver, or a bowie knife. I could not have encouraged others to fight, had not slavery invaded the free State of Kansas. Which of the Free States it will next seek to conquer, I cannot conjecture. Hitherto I have opposed the bloody abolition of slavery. But now, when it begins to march its conquering bands into the Free States, I and ten thousand other peace men are not only ready to have it repulsed with violence, but pursued even unto death, with violence. Remember, however, that anti-slavery voting—real, not sham anti-slavery voting—would have prevented all need of this.

"I said that I am unfit to fight. Nevertheless I can do something for the good cause. Some can give to it brave hearts and strong arms, and military skill; others can give to it the power of prayer with Him 'who shall break in pieces the oppressor;' and others can give money to it,—the cheapest indeed, and least meritorious of all the gifts—nevertheless indispensable. I am among those who can help the cause with this poorest of gifts. It is true that my very frequent contributions during the past year in aid of our suffering people in Kansas, have exhausted my current means. Nevertheless, I authorize you to put me down for ten thousand dollars of the million."

On August 16, 1858, when the Kansas war was substantially ended, he wrote and spoke thus :

"I have often thought that the industrious efforts to persuade the people that I have been untrue to freedom in Kansas, present the most remarkable instances of the success of a lie against the truth. Having done what I could for her in Congress, I came home to do much more for her. My use of men and money to keep slavery out of that territory has been limited only by my ability.

"The true history of Kansas is yet to be written. The impression that she has been preserved from the grasp of slavery by the skill of party leaders and by speeches in Congress, is as false as it is common. She has been preserved from it by her own brave spirits and strong arms. To no man living is so much praise due for beating back the tide of border ruffianism and slavery as to my old and dear friend John Brown of Osowatomie. Though he has had at no time under his command more than one hundred and fifty fighting men, yet by his unsurpassed skill and courage he has accomplished wonders for the cause of freedom. Small as have been the armed forces, which have saved Kansas, their maintenance has nevertheless taxed some persons heavily. My eye at this moment is on one merchant in Boston, who has contributed several thousand dollars to this object. What, compared with him, has gaseous oratory, in or out of Congress, done for Kansas ?"

Again:

" No man out of Kansas has done so much as Eli Thayer to save her ; and no man in Kansas as John Brown—Old John Brown. the fighter. Kansas owes her salvation to no party—to no speeches and no votes either in Congress or elsewhere. She owes it to her ample preparations to repel by physical force the aggressions of slavery. She believed slavery to be a pirate—the superlative pirate ; and she prepared herself to deal with it in just that common sense way that every persistent pirate is to be dealt with."

The tribute to John Brown was sincere. He was essentially a man after Gerrit Smith's own heart. They were alike, and yet unlike. Both were men of purpose, direct, simple, earnest, upright. Both lived for humanity. Both held dear the cause of the poor, the lowly, the afflicted, the oppressed. Both believed in justice and righteousness. Both revered one law; the law of rectitude. Both believed in the divine institution of government. Both detested slavery, regarded it as an outlaw, and incessantly prayed and worked for its extinction. But they were of different temperaments and constitutions. The one was large and stately, of expansive and superb presence, sunny, beaming, melodious, open of hand and heart, trusting and sanguine ; the other was also above middle height, but close, concentrated and intense, taciturn, serious, gentle, but alert and circumspect. Both were sincerely religious ; both were bible men ; but one had watched and waited at the base of Sinai, the other had sate among the complacent listeners to the Sermon on the Mount. Both were peace men, though neither was non-resistant ; yet practically their feelings were differently turned, as was strikingly apparent in the circumstance that the one was innocent of all knowledge of firearms and warlike weapons of any sort, while the other was a resolute fighter and a leader of armed men. The sword that Smith relied on was the sword of the Spirit, the essential might of truth, the power of principles, the superior force of the moral sentiments ; the sword that Brown appealed to was " the sword of the Lord and of Gideon," principles edged and pointed with steel. Brown was the more visionary of the two, his enthusiasm being streaked with a vein of fanaticism which was absent from his friend's composition ; his humor was grim ; his hope was not sunny like the morning, but pensive and grave.

These resemblances and differences explain the mutual attraction between the two men, and also their failure to understand one another entirely. For it seems that the Kansas hero was at first restrained by an instinct from disclosing his whole mind to his fellow-abolitionist, and one has an impression that the latter was constitutionally unable to take in the full scope and significance of the Covenanter's idea.

They made acquaintance on the 8th of April, 1848, when Brown came from Springfield, Mass., where he resided, to make a home for himself among the colored people to whom the great land-holder had distributed one hundred and twenty thousand acres. His kindness to the poor colonists as shown in gifts of produce, in coun-

sel and direction, and in general friendliness gained the
respect and love of the warm-hearted benefactor. Brown
bought his own farm and two others besides, and took
his family to North Elba, in Essex County. On the
opening of Kansas to the colonizing freemen, Brown
went there, as is well known, to do his part in rescuing
the state from slavery. Peterboro lay in his way, and
he stopped to talk over his affairs with his friend there.
Smith gave him money, without asking what uses in
particular he designed to make of it, being interested in
his operations at both ends of the line,—small sums at
first ranging from twenty to fifty dollars, whatever might
be required, sometimes one or two hundred, but never
at this time enough for any considerable scheme or enterprise,—in all, it is believed, about one thousand dollars. In 1855, Brown attended an anti-slavery meeting
in Syracuse, presented the cause of the Kansas emigrants, described their hardships and dangers, and asked
for aid to relieve their sufferings and supply them with
means of resistance to the ruffians who assailed them.
Lewis Tappan and S. J. May approved of sending relief
to the sufferers, but opposed gifts of money to be spent
for arms. Smith in the meeting concurred with them,
and it was stipulated that a portion of the money raised
should be used for charitable purposes alone. It was
his frequent boast that the rescue of " Jerry " had been
accomplished without the shedding of blood, and there
are many to bear witness that he had ever deprecated
the resort to violent measures in liberating slaves. The
outrages in Kansas more than reconciled him, as we have
seen, to armed resistance to invasion, and excited him
to the degree that he avowed his readiness to pursue

slavery even unto death. But this was not his habitual frame of mind; and when the stress of Kansas peril was over, his feeling settled into its usual channels. With John Brown's work in Kansas he expressed no discontent. The military operations justified themselves. The following records are in the diary:

July 24, 1857. "Col. Hugh Forbes arrives at 11 A. M., on his way to Kansas to assist my friend Capt. John Brown in military operations. I put some money into his hands. I have put some this season into the hands of Capt. Brown.

Feb. 18, 1858. "Our old and noble friend, Captain John Brown of Kansas arrives this evening."

22. "F. B. Sanborn of Concord, Massachusetts, arrives."

24. "Mr. Sanborn leaves us this morning."

25. "Our friend, Captain Brown, leaves us to-day."

April 2, 1858. "My esteemed friend, Captain John Brown and his son John came at 10 A. M. Leave next morning at 6."

April 11, 1859. "Captain John Brown of Kansas, and his friend Mr. Anderson came at 11 A. M."

14. "Captain Brown and Mr. Anderson leave us at 6 this morning."

These entries are made without comment, along with others of similar character. Guests were continually coming and going without prearrangement. On the occasion of his last recorded visit, April 11–14, 1859, Brown held a public meeting, at which he told the story of his exploit in carrying a number of slaves from Missouri to Canada and asked help to prosecute the work on a larger scale. Mr. Smith was moved to tears by the veteran's eloquence—headed the subscription paper with four hundred dollars, and made an impressive speech, in which he said—"If I were asked to point out—I will say it in his presence—to point out the man in all this world I think most truly a Christian, I would point out John

Brown. I was once doubtful in my own mind as to Captain Brown's course. I now approve of it heartily, having given my mind to it more of late."

But all this work in Kansas was incidental and provisional, in view of a grander scheme which for years Brown's mind had been revolving and maturing, and which had been already communicated to two or three trusted friends. This was no less than an assault on slavery itself in its own dominions by opening a breach in its wall and planting freedom in the heart of its territory. His purpose was to unsettle the foundations of the institution, and so compel its abandonment; and his plan was to effect a lodgment in the mountains of a border state fortify his position by proper defences, circulate appeals to the people, near and far, black and white, including the military of the United States, summon the blacks to his retreat, give them arms to defend themselves against state and government troops, keeping open a way of escape to the North but working steadily to the South. Thus in time the slave country would be, he thought, reclaimed and redeemed. It was an immense plan, involving a multitude of contingencies and embracing years, perhaps decades of time, with possibilities, nay certainties, of insurrection and bloodshed. But it was conceived in such a spirit of faith in the divine providence, in the supremacy of justice, and the coöperation of moral agencies, that those who heard it were fascinated in spite of themselves. The encouragements came into light. The discouragements fell into shadow. The moral aspect was illuminated, the immoral aspects of disorder, violence, anarchy and murder were thrown into the background; and the splendor of the anticipated deliverance cast a soft glow over the path through which it was to be reached. The enthusiast had meditated his scheme until every detail of its execution was completed and set in its place. Every objection had been anticipated, every question had been raised and answered to his satisfaction. He had even gone so far as to frame a provisional government for the administration of his free dominion, the draft whereof was first submitted at a " very quiet convention " of the " true friends of freedom," in Chatham, Canada. It was written out in January of 1858, at the house of Frederick Douglass in Rochester. This plan he was anxious to submit to friends, and with this view he asked Theodore Parker, George L. Stearns, T. W. Higginson and F. B. Sanborn to meet him at Gerrit Smith's house in Peterboro. Sanborn alone came ; he had been there before to visit a classmate, Edwin Morton, who, as tutor to young Greene Smith, was one of the household. This is the visit of February 22, mentioned above. In Morton's room, aloof from the other guests in the house, Brown detailed his plan ; Smith going in and out, but being present during the reading of the paper, with which he was probably already familiar, as Brown had been four days his guest, and taking part in the discussion that followed. The colloquy lasted till late that night, and was resumed the following day. To the amazed auditors the plan looked not so much audacious as chimerical. The obvious objections were disposed of ; the old man was prepared and met them at once, until at last, silenced, awed, fascinated, but not convinced, they succumbed to the hero's faith. As the winter sun went down behind the lonely snow-covered hills, Smith and Sanborn walked for an

hour talking over the strange scheme. Smith said to
Sanborn : "You see how it is ; our old friend has made
up his mind to this course of action, and cannot be
turned from it. We cannot give him up to die alone ;
we must stand by him. I will raise so many hundred
dollars for him ; you must lay the case before your friends
in Massachusetts, and see if they will do the same."

Sanborn returned to Boston and laid the matter before his friends, with what result is told in the Atlantic
Monthly for July, 1872. On the 24th of the next May,
Smith being in Boston on other business, the "secret
committee" held a meeting at his room in the Revere
House, at which Brown was not present, when the situation was discussed, and the conclusion reached that the
enterprise should be deferred, in consequence of threatened disclosures, till the spring of the next year. Smith
no doubt pledged his share of the sum the committee
agreed to raise for Brown. The matter of the rifles
which Brown had asked for did not concern him, as they
belonged to George L. Stearns. On June 4, 1859, he
wrote a note to Brown, which is printed in the Atlantic
Monthly for May, 1875. And that the thought of Brown's
invasion was then on his mind is all but certain from the
letter to the chairman of the Jerry Rescue Committee,
August 27, 1859, which has already been quoted. In
that letter he uses the following language which discloses
an expectation of some impending blow :

"For many years I have feared, and published my fears that slavery must go out in blood. My speech in Congress on the Nebraska
Bill was strongly marked by such fears. These fears have grown
into belief. So debauched are the white people by slavery, that there
is not virtue enough left in them to put it down. . . . The feeling among the blacks that they must deliver themselves, gains

strength with fearful rapidity. . . . No wonder is it that in this state of facts which I have sketched (the failure of the Liberty Party, the Free Soil Party, the Republican Party to do anything for the slaves) intelligent black men in the States and Canada should see no hope for their race in the practice and policy of white men. No wonder they are brought to the conclusion that no resource is left to them but in God and insurrections. For insurrection then we may look any year, any month, any day. A terrible remedy for a terrible wrong! But come it must unless anticipated by repentance, and the putting away of the terrible wrong.

"It will be said that these insurrections will be failures—that they will be put down. Yes, but nevertheless, will not slavery be put down by them? For what portions are there of the South that will cling to slavery after two or three considerable insurrections shall have filled the whole South with horror? And is it entirely certain that these insurrections will be put down promptly, and before they can have spread far? Will telegraphs and railroads be too swift for even the swiftest insurrections? Remember that telegraphs and railroads can be rendered useless in an hour. Remember too, that many who would be glad to face the insurgents, would be busy in transporting their wives and daughters to places where they would be safe from that worst fate which husbands and fathers can imagine for their wives and daughters."

It is hard to believe that the writer of these passages had not John Brown's general project in mind. There was no visible sign of peril. The blacks, North and South, were to all appearances quiet. The Secretary of War at Washington, Mr. Floyd, a southern man, hating and fearing the Abolitionists, did not deign to take notice of a menacing letter, putting him on his guard against this very redoubtable John Brown. The surface of society was not stirred by an uneasy ripple. No one suspected an uprising. But Sanborn, Stearns, Higginson, Howe, Gerrit Smith, and others who had been long in the secret, knew that a scheme was on foot that would convulse the country. The Cassandra spoke from certainty.

11

Moreover that Smith was in communication with Brown till close upon the actual attack on Harper's Ferry, seems probable from the circumstance of his sending money to him directly and indirectly, and receiving advices through others, particularly through Mr. Sanborn. But for the whole-handed destruction of documents immediately on the failure of the project, Mr. Smith's participation in John Brown's general plans could be made to appear still closer. It would probably be revealed that he knew as much as anybody did, sympathized as much and aided as much. A check for one hundred dollars, on the State Bank at Albany, found in Brown's possession at his capture and sent by Smith to Chambersburg at the suggestion of Mr. Sanborn, who transmitted to Peterboro the note in which Brown stated his condition, establishes the fact that his presence there was known to Smith, and authorizes the inference that the object of his presence there was also known. The intention to enter the Slave States at Harper's Ferry was known to but two or three men. Theodore Parker was perhaps aware of it. F. B. Sanborn was. That Gerrit Smith was may be conjectured from his knowledge of Brown's presence at Chambersburg, and from the remarkable language above quoted. On the 7th of June, 1859, Edwin Morton wrote to his friend Sanborn from Mr. Smith's house at Peterboro, "I suppose you know the place where this matter is to be adjudicated; H. T. suggested the Fourth of July as a good time to raise the Mill." Is it probable that Morton, living in Smith's house, and intimate with his thoughts on these subjects, knew what Smith did not? This is possible; for in a confidential talk at Peterboro, with Mr. Sanborn, as late

as July 1874, he disclaimed all recollection of the special
scope and drift of Brown's plans; he recalled only their
general outlines, had the impression that the invasion
was to take place further west than Virginia, and that
it contemplated simply the establishment of a grand
southern depot, where slaves should be collected for
transportation northward. The testimony of Frederick
Douglass is to the same effect.

The hue and cry made after the miscarriage at Harper's Ferry caused the destruction of valuable private
documents relating to John Brown and his confederates.
His friends and coadjutors were compelled to protect
themselves by covering over the traces of their operations. To escape arrest they took various precautions.
Dr. Howe went to Canada; so, for a short time did G.
L. Stearns. F. B. Sanborn was arrested at his house in
Concord, but released by a writ of *habeas corpus*, backed
by his fellow-townsmen, who assembled in formidable
numbers at the sound of the alarm bell and refused to
let him be taken away; he too had previously found
refuge in Canada; so had Frederick Douglass; Edwin
Morton went to England. Theodore Parker was seeking health in Europe. Gerrit Smith staid at home and
was a conspicuous object of attack.

His friends were more fearful on his account than he
was on his own. His house was guarded. The male
occupants of it carried arms by day, and slept with weapons within reach. The parcels that were left for him,
at the house, were carefully opened lest they might contain infernal machines. "The New York Democratic
Vigilance Association," issued a ferocious manifesto
designed to bring condign punishment on him in connec-

tion with others supposed to be implicated in a plot to rouse the slaves. This paper he did not see at the time of its publication, and the meditated blow did not fall. The intended victim was already beyond the reach of his enemies.

The shock occasioned by the tidings of the assault at Harper's Ferry and its failure, grief for the disaster of his friend, agony in contemplation of his inevitable doom, horror at the uproar and carnage, distress at the prospect of new difficulties in the way of the cause he had so deeply at heart, were too much for a nervous system already overstrained. Dr. John P. Gray, the distinguished superintendent of the asylum of Utica, declares that in the first half of 1859, he had reached the stage in the progress of insanity known as " exaltation of mind." He never read, studied or wrote with more pleasure. He never had, so he said himself, such confidence in his powers. He boasted that he could do more than at forty. An unnatural brilliancy marked all his productions. He seemed capable of living without food or sleep. He was exhausted, and did not know it. With feet so swollen that he had to wear moccasins, he persisted in walking, when always before he had been driven in a carriage. In 1857 a severe attack of typhoid fever had taken at disadvantage a frame worn by heavy labors and incessant cares. This was accompanied by acute neuralgic pains in the head. The fever was succeeded by dropsy ; the dropsy by dyspepsia. In the year 1858, he underwent the immense fatigues of a Gubernatorial campaign in which he spoke fifty-three times, each averaging two hours and a half. This ended, he threw himself into his religious speculations, studying, writing, thinking, taking brutal blows from people he loved, lampooned, caricatured, cursed, jeered at; in the worst of all excitements, a theological ferment. Overworked, sleepless, strung to the point of breaking, the last trouble of his noble friend's discomfiture overthrew him, and after vainly struggling for several days with the malady he went down under a troop of hallucinations. He was an outcast; reduced to poverty; he was hunted for his life; those were in pursuit of him who meant to carry him about the country in a cage and submit him to horrible tortures. He was gentle as usual, but melancholy. Several times he was suspected of having designs on his own life. Silent and brooding he sat for hours together. At length on the 7th of November, he was taken to the asylum for the insane, at Utica, his consent being obtained by humoring the notion that he was going to Virginia to vindicate or share the fate of John Brown. When the officials came to remove him he opened the door to them, said gravely, " walk in, gentlemen," and quietly surrendered himself.

The case was a serious one. On reaching the asylum, Dr. Gray remarked that he had not come a moment too soon ; that a delay of even forty-eight hours might have been fatal. The physical prostration of the patient was so extreme that the beating of the pulse was hardly perceptible. The whole physical economy was deranged. The fever, the dyspepsia, the sleeplessness had done their work slowly but thoroughly. The stress of toil and care and sorrow had been laid on the most sensitive part of the organization, and it could bear the strain no longer. But the constitution being strong, and the disorder physical, a judicious use of anodynes and stimulants, with quiet, and nourishing food, in a few weeks restored sanity though not strength. Four weeks at the asylum, and a few days in the family of Dr. Gray, so far recruited the system that, on the 29th of December, he was driven back to his home. There, still excessively weak, too weak to read the daily papers, or to converse on public affairs, he was watched and tended till vital power returned. The first production of his pen after his restoration, was a long letter written May 1, 1860, to his dear abolition friend, and his dire theological foe, William Goodell, giving an account of his condition, detailing the causes of the insanity, moralizing on it, and protesting against the cruel insinuations which had been thrown out against him on the occurrence of it. As the letter rehearses what in substance has been told already, the republication may be dispensed with.

The excitement incident to this calamity was so terrible that for years even a casual reference to it or any thing connected with it, menaced a return of the insanity. In 1872, F. B. Sanborn addressed to him a quiet note asking if he did not think it timely to collect and publish whatever was known of John Brown's plans, as those who knew them were, one after another, passing away. To this note Mrs. Smith replied, deprecating any unnecessary use of names, for the reason that excessive nervous sensibility made dangerous any revival of her husband's mental excitement. The experiences of his insanity were so closely intertwined one with another, that reference to one portion of them, precipitated upon him the whole.

Mr. Smith himself, wrote to Mr. Sanborn, October 19, 1872, to the same effect:

" I am not competent to advise in the case. When the Harper's Ferry affair occurred, I was sick, and my brain somewhat diseased. That affair excited and shocked me, and a few weeks after I was taken to a lunatic asylum. From that day to this, I have had but a hazy view of dear John Brown's great work. . . . My brain has continued to the present time to be sensitive on this John Brown matter, and every now and then I get little or no sleep in consequence of it. It was so when I read the articles in the Atlantic you refer to, and now, your bare proposition to write of this matter has given me another sleepless turn. In every fresh turn I fear a recurrence of my insanity."

The note closes with the significant request that the full history of the transaction might be withheld from the public until after his death ; or in the event of its being published earlier, that the use of his name might be as sparing as possible.

Thus, deepest and uppermost in Gerrit Smith's mind was the sentiment of horror, and a dread of returning insanity. This impelled him to detach himself as much as he could from personal associations with the tragedy at Harper's Ferry and its author. But this was probably not all. In point of fact, the John Brown tragedy occupied a subordinate place in his distempered mind. In forty-eight hours after his arrival at the asylum, it had ceased to haunt him, and had given place to tormentors of another character, from other spheres. On his recovery a new set of considerations came in to turn the instinctive repugnance into a purpose, and the purpose into a policy. He was an enthusiast and at the same time a man of business ; as an enthusiast passionate to a degree that made him oblivious of practical conditions ; as a man of business practical to a degree that made him oblivious of his enthusiasm. Men of his temperament are subject to reactions that may properly be termed revulsions; he was subject to these. But he was subject, besides, to oscillations from the practical to the sentimental side, or the reverse way, by reason of the powerful bent of his mind in opposite directions. He was a singular combination of emotion and common sense, of feeling and shrewdness. When feeling was in the ascendant there were no lengths he would not go. When common sense and shrewdness prevailed, the course he pursued was characterized by a sagacity that bordered on craft. In one case he was all wings, in the other he was all eyes. In the days of John Brown's activity, when he saw him, heard him talk, was under the spell of his moral influence, and felt his anti-slavery enthusiam thrill in every fibre, he surrendered unconditionally, or with but slight and spasmodic protest, to the spirit that inflamed the man. At moments, his judgment hesitated, even recalcitrated, but interposed no serious obstacle. Heart and soul he was with the old hero. There is nothing to show that he at the last discouraged or tried to restrain him; he was even prepared for some such enterprise as the one actually made at Harper's Ferry, and was unwilling that it should be thwarted by Hugh Forbes or Henry Wilson or any other marplot. The secret was kept in his own breast, as it should have been; but there it was cherished with hope, till hope could be entertained no longer. Had John Brown succeeded in gaining a foothold in Virginia, in making a stand, and inaugurating his project, it is probable that his ally at Peterboro would have remained constant, for he was no coward, and the practical demonstration of the hero's shrewdness would have laid to rest the cavillings of his judgment. But the enterprise disastrously failed. The first step was not planted. There was not so much as a beginning made. On emerging from the mental obscuration at Utica, the whole scheme or tissue of schemes had vanished and become visionary. Brown was in his grave; his band dispersed; his colleagues were thrown into confusion and scattered. At Washington the authorities were busy, or were ceasing to be busy at treading out the sparks. It was a dream, a mass of recollections tumultuous and indistinct.

Then cool reflection came in. The practical objections to the enterprise which had flitted across his mind before, settled down heavily upon it. The ill-judged nature of the plan in its details and in its general scope forced itself upon his consideration, and made him wish he had never been privy to it. The wish was father to a thought, the thought to a purpose. His old horror of blood, his old disbelief in violence as a means of redressing wrong, resumed its sway over his feelings. The man of business repelled the association with the visionary and tried to persuade himself that he had taken no part in operations that were so easily disconcerted. He set himself to the task of making the shadowy recollections more shadowy still, and reducing his terms of alliance with the audacious conspirator to sentiments of personal sympathy and admiration. It was already becoming the fashion among conservatives to praise Brown's nobility of character; and among radicals it was becoming the fashion to condemn his " folly," thus allowing scope for enthusiasm on the one hand, and for criticism on the other. Smith instinctively fell into this mood, gave his heart to Brown, but kept his judgment to himself.

Had he been content to hold this attitude privately,

11*

he could have done so without difficulty. The evidence of his complicity was all but totally destroyed. The accomplices were safe against bearing witness. The members of his family knew nothing. But he could not be still. He could not consider himself a private man. A wish to be in the confidence of the public, a passion to rush into print, to interchange thoughts with the leaders of opinion, to unbosom himself to all the world, was one of his infirmities.

Why then did he not make a clean breast of it and frankly confess the whole state of his mind? Why did he not own the infatuation he had lain under, describing it as an infatuation he had outgrown, acknowledging at the same time the desire of his heart and the repentance of his understanding? Because at this point the magnanimity failed him. Here came in the love of public approbation, which was a strong feature in his character. Along with his self-respect went a corresponding self-esteem. Self-approval was indispensable to his happiness ; so was the approval of his friends and neighbors. In a clear issue between right and wrong his conscience was a fortress within which he feared no foes. But in a mixed issue between wisdom and folly, there was no such judicial umpire, and he could feel keenly the separation from the controlling opinion of the "world." Hence a desire to persuade others as well as himself of his innocence of all complicity with the particular schemes of John Brown,—a desire that became an importunate demand as it was cherished. The note, already quoted, to Mr. Sanborn, of Oct. 1872, in which he begs that his name may be used sparingly in any account that may be given of Brown's plans, admits the existence of facts that he was anxious to have concealed, and his determination to conceal them, if he could. As is so often the case, the eagerness of his denial was a confession of his secret.

The first demonstration was made against the managers of the "Democratic Vigilance Committee," whose proclamation has already been alluded to. It was a wild, intemperate, foolish manifesto, an incoherent jumble of truth and falsehood, put forth in the main for party purposes, and of no significance aside from them. It was dangerous at first, no doubt, because the public mind was greatly excited, and extreme measures might be carried into effect against individuals who were obnoxious to the administration. The Democratic party leaders would have been glad to conciliate favor by apprehending prominent men, like Wendell Phillips, Dr. S. G. Howe or Gerrit Smith, and shutting them up in jail, or worse. But this danger, whatever it may have been at first, was over in less than three months. In six months the storm had so far passed by that ordinary quiet would have ensured safety. But Mr. Smith could not remain quiet, weak as he was. The blunders of the democratic manifesto were glaring and could be securely denied. The truths could not be substantiated by documents or witnesses. The committee were open to assault, and the assault was made boldly and with force, by Charles D. Miller, Mr. Smith's son-in-law, who knew nothing of the extent of Mr. Smith's complicity.

Peterboro, February 13, 1860.

WATTS SHERMAN, Esq.:

Sir : — My father-in-law, Mr. Gerrit Smith, has at length so far waked up from the eclipse of his intellect as to be able to read and to hear reading. He has just now seen, for the first time, the

"Manifesto of the New York Democratic Vigilance Association," published last October, in which you connect his name with a certain "Central Association," of bloody and horrible purposes.

As Mr. Smith belongs to no society, has always opposed secret societies, had never before heard of this "Central Association," and condemns all shedding of human blood, save by government, he necessarily feels himself to be deeply wronged by you and your associates. He holds you and them responsible, for calling in effect upon the people both of the north and south to detest and abhor him.

Mr. Smith wishes to know without any delay, whether you and your associates will persist in your libel, or make the unqualified and ample retraction which the case calls for.

Yours respectfully,

CHAS. D. MILLER.

Similar letters were addressed to Royal Phelps and S. L. M. Barlow, calling forth diplomatic replies, which were so far from satisfactory that Messrs. Sedgwick, Andrews and Kennedy were instructed to bring suits against those three gentlemen, laying the damages at fifty thousand dollars in each case. It is needless to say that the suits were never brought to trial. The correspondence was published in a little pamphlet, which put the Vigilance Committee entirely in the wrong, and placed Mr. Smith before the public in the attitude he desired.

With this, he might, it would seem, have been satisfied. His objections had been well taken, his antagonists fairly discomfited. From that quarter no further danger was to be apprehended. From no other quarter was there a menace. But the newspapers still kept alive the memory of John Brown and his exploits; the public curiosity was hungry for more information. Mr. Smith was unable to preserve a discreet silence, and after eight years had elapsed,—in 1867—he put forth a manifesto purporting to be a full, frank, final account of his connection with John Brown. At this date there was no danger or even inconvenience from the fullest acknowledgment of such connection. The war had resulted triumphantly for the north. It had become the fashion for people to call themselves abolitionists. Old pro-slavery Democrats were singing " Glory, Hallelujah ! " and copiously volunteering the information that the soul of John Brown was " marching on." The hero would have received an ovation in Wall Street. Gerrit Smith takes this time to disclaim knowledge of his plans. Here is the Manifesto :

JOHN BROWN.

As the newspapers are speaking of my relations to John Brown and of his purposes, it may not be amiss for me also to speak of them.

April 8, 1848, Brown came to my house. His residence, at that time, was in Springfield, Massachusetts. I had recently distributed one hundred and twenty thousand acres of land among three thousand colored men. This land was in a number of counties of the State of New York. Some of the grantees had already removed to their parcels in Essex and Franklin counties, where lay the great body of it. It was among these that Brown purposed to find a home for himself and family ; and that purpose was soon realized. In this wise began my acquaintance with that remarkable man—an acquaintance, which soon ripened into a warm and enduring friendship. His kindnesses to the little colored colony in gifts of barrels of flour and other necessaries, and, above all, in advice and guidance, were numberless. His care for it was incessant. He was, in a word, its friend and father. There was his home until his death ; and there, on one of the farms he obtained from me, sleeps his body.

April 11, 1859, on his way from Kansas to his home, he visited Peterboro. Here, as in some other places through which he passed, he held a public meeting, in which he related his recent success in running off slaves to Canada, and asked contributions toward continuing his good work on a much larger scale.

John Brown talked to me—but he never counselled with me—

respecting his plans for freeing slaves. Then too, for reasons which
he mentioned to some of his friends, he did not feel as free to tell
me, as he did to tell others, the details of these plans. But I learned
enough of them to believe that, in addition to his former ways of
helping off slaves, he meant to go into a mountain or mountains of
a Slave State, and invite slaves to flee to him, and give them arms
to resist attempts at their recapture. I confess that, with all my
leanings to " non-resistance," I did not object to this use of arms.
For if a fugitive slave may not fight for his liberty, and stand for his
life, who may ? If blood is shed in pursuit of him, the whole sin of
it is on the pursuer. But that Brown intended a general insurrection, or the taking of any life except his, who was foolish and wicked
enough to attempt to drag back into the pit of slavery those who
had escaped from it, there is not the slightest reason to believe. Not
the least evidence of it is there either in his words or deeds. Brown
had a great horror of bloodshed. He said in my hearing, and said
it, too, from the depths of his humane and religious heart, that he
would never, in any instance, take life, save in the strictest self-defence. It was his consolation that, in delivering slaves, he had
never hurt the person of any one. A great crime against the sacred
memory of John Brown is the charge, that he embarked in any other
insurrection (if that may be called one) than helping off slaves and
protecting them.

Brown left Peterboro, April 14, 1859 ; and never returned to it.
I never saw him again ; and never again had I any communication
with him, direct or indirect, touching his plans or movements. His
only letter to me after that time was a few lines respecting his inability to obtain the payment of a note I had given him. This note
for two hundred and fifty dollars was against one of his old friends
and fellow-laborers in Kansas. For months after I received that
letter, I was at a loss to know where he was. When he left Peterboro, he had not yet decided whether to go into an Eastern or a
Western Slave State.

I think it was in August, that I learned, in some indirect way—
perhaps from mere rumor—that Brown was in Chambersburg. In
a similar way, I learned, only a very few weeks, perhaps only a very
few days, before his descent upon Harper's Ferry, that Brown had
gone into a Slave State. I well remember looking into an atlas to
see what mountain or mountains he had probably gone to. I hoped
that the next news would be the welcome one of a stampede of slaves.
But, instead of that, it was the painful news of the Harper's Ferry
affair. I had not myself the slightest knowledge nor intimation of

Brown's intended invasion of Harper's Ferry :—and when I saw that George L. Stearns of Boston (that noble man who was so intimate with Brown) testified before the Senate Committee, that he too knew nothing of that intended invasion, I questioned whether a single person in all the North knew anything of it. Thus, also, testified that other excellent friend of Brown—Dr. Howe of Boston. Indeed, not one person testified before the Committee that he knew aught of the intended invasion. Nor was this universal ignorance in the matter, in the least degree strange. For it turns out that it was only a very few weeks before his descent upon Harper's Ferry that Brown had decided upon it. By the way, Brown himself, as he was reported, expressed deep regret at this change in his plans.

Having heard that some persons understand that Brown's words, in his two-days' interview with Mr. Frederick Douglass at Chambersburg, serve to connect me with his invasion of Harper's Ferry ; to convict him of a plot of general insurrection ; and myself of the knowledge of it, I asked Mr. Douglass to write me respecting that interview. As his letter goes to confirm the most important parts of what I have thus far written, I herewith give it to the public :

Rochester, August 9, 1867.

Hon. GERRIT SMITH :

My Dear Sir — I wish to say distinctly, that John Brown never declared nor intimated to me that he was about to embark in a grand or unqualified insurrection ; and that the only insurrection he proposed was the escaping of slaves, and their standing for their lives against any who should pursue them. For years before, Captain Brown's long-entertained plan was to go to the mountains in the Slave States, and invite the slaves to flee there and stand for their freedom. His object was to make slave property unprofitable by making it insecure. He told me he had given to you a general idea of this plan—but that he had not given you the full particulars, lest you might turn from him as a visionary and dangerous man Three or four weeks previous to his invasion of Harper's Ferry, Captain Brown requested me to have an interview with him at Chambersburg, Pennsylvania. I had it ; and in that interview he informed me that he had determined upon that invasion, instead of carrying out his old plan of going into the mountains. He did not tell me that you knew anything of this new plan. I do not suppose that any of his friends at the North, outside of his own family, knew of it.

Captain Brown never told me that you knew anything of his guns or other weapons.

You are at full liberty to make use of this statement in any way you may deem proper.

As ever, yours very truly,

FREDERICK DOUGLASS.

Much has been said of Brown's guns, and how he got them. I do not recollect that he ever spoke to me of them. I remember how surprised I was to find, after the Harper's Ferry affair, that he had obtained possession of the Kansas rifles. As to the pikes—I had the strong impression that he had told me, several years before, that he purposed getting them to put into the hands of the honest settlers in Kansas. I was surprised but, I confess, not at all displeased, when I found, among the revelations of Harper's Ferry, that he meant to put pikes into the hands of fugitive slaves, with which to defend themselves against pursuing dogs, and pursuing men. Of course, I would not have it implied from what I have here said, that I supposed John Brown would enter upon his work unarmed. I add that I distinctly remember having heard (but I cannot recall in what way) that, at or about the time Brown entered the land of slaves, boxes of disguised arms entered with him.

But it is said that I gave money to Brown in the year 1859; and it is inferred that I gave it to help his invasion of Harper's Ferry and to help him produce an insurrection. Unwarrantable inference! It is also inferred from my giving him money in 1859, that I gave him *much* money in that year. Another unwarrantable inference! I met Brown in Syracuse in 1855, on his way to Kansas. I handed him twenty dollars to buy bread for some starving ones in Kansas he might fall in with. Every year from that to his last, he was one of the distributors of my surplus means. He often asked me for small sums, I never refused him. And yet, the whole amount of what I gave him, from first to last, including one gift of two hundred dollars, was hardly a thousand dollars—an amount not greater than what I might well have given him in return for his gifts and goodness to my colored colonists. Ever after he began his brave and effective labors in Kansas, I told him to use, at his discretion, what he received from me. I must, however, admit that I trusted he would use it chiefly for the deliverance of the oppressed.

The reader is, perhaps, surprised that I gave by the many thousands to the Kansas and other Anti-Slavery Associations, and yet, made my gifts so small to even the worthiest individuals, who labored with me in the cause of these associations. The explanation is found in my far greater reliance on the collective wisdom in these associations than in the wisdom of the wisest individual.

To return, was it wrong in me to give Brown money to help the oppressed with? If so, how then can it be right in me to give money to Daniel O'Connell, to Polish Committees, to Italian Republicans, to the Greeks now, and also more than forty years ago? Was it wrong because my oppressed countrymen were black men? But with me "a man's a man." Was it wrong because there was law for slavery? I knew no law for any piracy—least of all for slavery, which is the superlative piracy. Not for the less injurious crime of murder would I recognize a law. I say less injurious—for what right-minded person would not rather his child were murdered than enslaved? Law is a sacred thing—and I, therefore, deny that the abomination of slavery can be embodied in it. Such, by the way, would be the denial of every man, who should be so unhappy as to fall under the yoke of slavery—and, therefore, should it be his denial now.

But my gifts to Brown show only a small part of my relations with him. For many years, and down to the last year of his life, he had business transactions with me. He borrowed money from me. He deposited money with me. He bought farms from me. The title to eighty acres of land, which he bought from me in 1858 and then paid for, he left in my name, when he bade me " Farewell! " on the 14th of April 1859 ; and in my name it remained at the time of his death. I did not hold the land subject to the repayment of the sums he drew from me in 1858 and 1859. These sums were not advances or loans, but gifts—and gifts too, I admit, to help him deliver his and my enslaved brethren.

I must not omit to say that my money dealings and land dealings with Brown did not all pass through my own hands. More of them passed through the hands of Mr. Calkins, who has been my clerk for the last thirty years and my chief clerk for the last twenty-five years. He knew more of my business with Brown than I did. I might add that he knew more of Brown himself than I did, as he saw much of him not only in my land office, but also at Brown's residence, where I never saw him.

Now that I have done speaking of my relations to John Brown and of his purposes, let me say that I cast no blame on any one for supposing that I had a full knowledge of Brown's plans and of his changes in them. That I had is, I admit, a not very unreasonable inference from the intimate relations both of business and friendship existing between us. Nevertheless, so it is, that I had but a partial

knowledge of these plans and not the least knowledge of his ex-
changing them for others. Right here, too, let me say that I do not
feel myself at all dishonored by the coupling of my name with any
of Brown's endeavors for the liberation of the slave. Even where
truth forbids the coupling, regard for my reputation does not forbid
it. The more the public identifies me with John Brown, the more
it honors me. As I knew Brown so well and loved him so well, it
was not unreasonable to suppose that I, too, would give his character to the public. Thank God ! Brown did that himself. His life,
crowned by his well-nigh matchless death, shows unmistakably and
fully, what was his character. His words, all the way from his capture to his death, sweeter or sublimer than which there have been
none since Jesus walked the earth, leave no room for mistake or ignorance of his character. And here let me say, that Jesus was in
Brown's heart, the Blessed and Loved One. Were I asked to say,
in the fewest and plainest words, what Brown was, my answer
would be that he was *a religious man.* He had ever a deep sense
of the claims of God and man upon him and his whole life was a
prompt, practical recognition of them. Brown was entirely and I
might perhaps add, stiffly orthodox. I do not believe that he doubted
the truth of one line of the Bible. Twice he attended the religious
conversational meeting, which we hold in Peterboro, and each time,
he criticised remarks of mine, which he regarded as theologically
unsound. His ever favorite hymn was that beginning : "Blow ye
the trumpet, blow ! "

All the members of my family held Brown in high regard. Beneath that stern look beat one of the kindest hearts. He loved children ; and they loved him. My little granddaughter was often in
his lap.

A more scrupulously just man in matters of property I never
knew. In 1858 he and a Mr. Thompson, who was his neighbor in
Essex County, came to my office. He had purchased Mr. Thompson's interest in a farm. While I was making out the papers which
they needed, Brown certainly twice and, I believe, three times, asked
Thompson if the price were great enough :—telling him to make it
greater if he thought proper. It occurred to me, at the moment,
that Brown went beyond the Christian precept, and cared even more
for his neighbor's rights than for his own. Let me add that Thompson beautifully declined to increase the price.

It is quite probable that John Brown will be the most admired
person in American history. Washington worked well—but it was
for his own race—only for his equals. William Lloyd Garrison had

lived for a despised and outraged race. John Brown both lived and died for it : and few names, even in the *world's* history, will stand as high as his.

Men begin to ask why a monument to the memory of John Brown has not yet been built. The day for building John Brown's monument has not yet come. It will be built where stood his gallows ; and it would not yet be welcome there. Its base will be broad and its shaft will pierce the skies. But the appreciation of his sublime character is not yet sufficiently just and widespread, to call for the rearing of such a structure. In executing this work of love and admiration, Southern hands will join with Northern hands. In rendering this tribute to the grandest man of the age, Southern zeal will not fall behind Northern zeal. Indeed, it may well be expected that the generous and ardent South will, ere the cool and calculating North is ready to do so, confess the enormous crime of the nation —of the whole nation—against the black man. Nay, it is just because the North is not yet ready to confess it, that there is not yet peace between her and the South. That confession would surely bring the peace. For it would involve the further confession of the common responsibility of North and South for the cause of the war : and it is the sense of that common responsibility which would impel the North to afford such relief to the war-impoverished South as would win her heart, and result in a true and enduring peace.

But the North and South will both come right. They will both repent of having, for generations, trodden out the life of the black man. And then they will love each other. And then God will make them the happiest nation in all the earth. And then to have enjoyed the confidence of John Brown, as did Howe and Parker and Stearns and Douglass and Sanborn and Morton and many others, will no longer be counted dishonest, but, on the contrary, high honor. Blessed indeed will be the day which shall witness these things ! Then John Brown's day will have come :—and then will John Brown's monument be built !

GERRIT SMITH.

Peterboro, August 15, 1867.

Did Gerrit Smith really think that this was a complete account of his relations with John Brown ? A statement wherein nothing true was suppressed, and nothing untrue suggested ? A statement that would be satisfactory to Edwin Morton and F. B. Sanborn, and

Dr. Howe and other friends of the martyr? Possibly he did think so, though his letter to Mr. Sanborn in 1872, above quoted, is inconsistent with the belief that he did. Possibly he did think so; but if he did, his case is as curious as any recorded in medical books. We must believe that his insanity obliterated a certain class of impressions, while another class of impressions, on the same subject, remained perfectly distinct, dates being remembered, and small particulars of incident recalled. We must believe that a department of the brain was paralyzed, without affecting the department that lay adjacent to it, and in closest sympathy with it. Nothing precisely like this is known to the intelligent general reader. Dr. Gray, his physician, has met with no such case, and in the absence of well established proof, such an account of the matter will not be accepted.

Is it not more likely that Mr. Smith made the statement by which he was ready finally to stand? The statement which his whole mind, on full reflection, accepted and ratified? Is it not possible that he chose to set aside the literal details of history, which did violence to his sober judgment, in order that he might present a case, satisfactory to judgment and feeling alike? To the candid, clear, direct mind this looks like subterfuge. It is not surprising that some of his friends were shocked and grieved, that some were indignant, that some were of opinion that the insanity was not wholly cured. He probably remained satisfied with an account of the matter that was consonant with all his moods of feeling, and left him at peace with himself. He could not rest contented with a divided mind, and the only way of securing an undivided mind was to suppress the tormenting side which his judgment presented.

Two years before the Manifesto was issued,—in 1865,—the Chicago "Tribune" gave editorial currency to a popular suspicion that Gerrit Smith's insanity was feigned, in order, as was vulgarly surmised, to escape arrest. The insinuation was shocking in the extreme to Mr. Smith, who remembered only too keenly the agony of that experience. It implied cowardice, hypocrisy, meanness, falsehood of the basest sort. His remonstrance was instantaneous and vehement. The editor declined to make an apology that was satisfactory to Mr. Smith, and a suit was brought for libel. Horace White, the responsible editor, accepted the challenge, and prepared himself by gleaning facts in relation to Mr. Smith's connection with John Brown, which Smith himself had been anxious to conceal.

In March 1867, at Utica, where evidence was taken in regard to his insanity, he heard from witnesses details which were wholly new to him, and which so shocked and excited him that a recurrence of the dementia was threatened. Dr. Gray was again called in. The gloom returned; the family were once more apprehensive; he too, feared that the thought of self-murder might occur to him, and told his grandson to remove his razors. Later in the spring, having received hints of what the other side expected to prove, he made a western tour, called at the office of the "Tribune," had an interview with the editor in charge, Mr. White being absent, persuaded him of the groundlessness and iniquity of the charge of feigning insanity, and obtained a satisfactory recantation. The editor in chief on his return to Chicago, found himself outgeneraled, and expressed his vexation in the following " card," followed the next day,

July 28th, by an editorial article to the effect that the
charge of feigning insanity, even if made, as it was not,
implied no moral turpitude, but was merely a statement of historical fact, from which no inference in regard
to character could be drawn.   Here is the " card," from
the " Tribune " of July 27th.

During my absence from home I learned with surprise that the
libel suit of Gerrit Smith versus the "Tribune Company" and others,
had been settled and the case dismissed, upon the publication of a
quasi retraction of the article upon which it was founded.   I immediately telegraphed my earnest protest against such proceeding,
but the settlement being an accomplished fact there was nothing
further to be done.   It is proper to remark that Mr. Dexter and Mr.
Van Arman, the two attorneys who had been actively employed in
the case, were both absent from the city at the time, and as the
plaintiff, Mr. Smith, refused to postpone the negotiation until any of
the absentees could be heard from, it was consummated upon imperfect information and in a summary manner.   While I perceive
that my associates in the "Tribune Company" were governed by
motives both honorable and praiseworthy in the course which they
pursued, it is nevertheless true that if they had been in possession
of the same facts as myself the terms of settlement would have been
somewhat different from those which were agreed upon.

For the many estimable qualities of Mr. Gerrit Smith I have a
high regard.   I recall his benevolence to the free State settlers of
Kansas, and his long but somewhat erratic service in the anti-slavery
cause with admiration.   But I am bound to say that the ferocity
with which Mr. Smith, during nearly two years, pursued his action
against the "Tribune," founded as it was upon a technicality too
narrow to stand alone, but requiring to be bolstered up with collat-
eral matter, had caused me to take the resolution to have a trial of
the case upon the merits, for the double purpose of vindicating the
truth of history and the rights of publishers.

Whether Mr. Gerrit Smith feigned insanity ; whether the "Tribune" charged that he feigned insanity ; whether such a charge, if
made, would be actionable, are questions of no public importance.
I find, however, in the article which embodies the so-called retraction, the following statement which was inserted at Mr. Smith's
instance:

"While he (Mr. Smith) affirms that he had no previous knowledge or intimation of John Brown's invasion of Harper's Ferry, he nevertheless states that he loved John Brown, his spirit and his principles, and that he now warmly cherishes his memory."

Now I am in possession of information which enables me to affirm that Mr. Gerrit Smith was fully advised of John Brown's purpose to make an armed invasion or raid upon Virginia for a long time prior to such invasion or raid ; that the said Gerrit Smith assented to and coöperated in such invasion or raid, with advice, money and counsel ; that interviews took place between John Brown and Gerrit Smith at the residence of the latter, in Peterboro, New York, in the summer of 1859, at which John Brown unfolded to Gerrit Smith his plan so far as it was then matured, informing him particularly that Chambersburg, Pennsylvania, had been fixed upon as the place to which arms should be first sent ; that the plan contemplated not merely a method of running off slaves, but a military occupation of the country and a general insurrection of slaves, accompanied by violence and bloodshed, and that Gerrit Smith knew it, assented to it and furnished money to carry it forward. I leave the public to judge how far this state of facts coincides with the statement that Gerrit Smith had no previous knowledge or intimation of John Brown's invasion of Harper's Ferry. I leave the public to judge also how much honor he does to the memory of John Brown under the circumstances.

The opportunity of vindicating the rights of publishers in the premises is no longer open ; but that of establishing an important fact in history remains. I have no other purpose in recurring to the case than this, and shall not again allude to it unless called upon to do so. HORACE WHITE.

Chicago, July 26, 1867.

This statement, brought to Mr. Smith's notice by a relative, again revived the mental agitation. He wrote immediately, August 15, to Mr. White, enclosing a copy of the manifesto printed above, in relation to his connection with John Brown, remonstrated against the new accusation of unveracity, and earnestly begged him to unsay what he had said, or to disavow the dreadful insinuations suggested by his language. To this touching note the editor returned the following curt reply :

Hon. GERRIT SMITH :   Chicago, August 20, 1867.

Sir — Your letter of the 15th instant, with enclosure is received.

As I have not charged you with falsehood, I do not see why I should retract such a charge. I stated certain facts which I am able to prove. The force and bearing of those facts I did not undertake to define. Your printed statement does not take issue with anything in my card. In its general tenor it corroborates rather than controverts it. It would be extremely foolish for me to say that you did not tell a falsehood, when I never alleged that you did. I would not thank anybody to render me that service.

I have neither charged you with feigning insanity, nor made light of your mental condition. I made light of the libel suit, but nothing more.

If it will afford you any relief to be assured that I shall not controvert, nor combat nor notice your printed statement, I cheerfully give you that assurance. I was a friend of John Brown during his life-time, and I honor his memory as much as any man.

> Very respectfully,
> Your obedient servant,
> HORACE WHITE.

The biographer leaves the matter here, sensible that his version of it is open to dispute, not professing to be entirely satisfied with it himself, but certain that he has spared no pains to get at the facts and to give a rational interpretation of them. The charge of moral cowardice could never be made against Gerrit Smith. He could never be accused of deliberate, persistent, aimless unveracity. But he may have been capable of making things wear a plausible aspect, and of thrusting into the background, with some violence, the things he did not choose should stand in front. How far the cerebral disturbance he suffered from affected his memory or confused the regular operations of his mind, cannot be told. Such a man is entitled to the benefit of every reasonable doubt. From every thing like moral turpitude he must be absolved. His conduct in this singular affair affected no-

body else ; he compromised none ; he cast reflections on
none ; the memory of John Brown received no detriment
at his hands. No kinsman, ally, or friend of John Brown
can complain of injustice, or of inconsiderateness for his
character or reputation. No interest suffered, no cause
was hindered by what he said, or did not say. The
principles he had always cherished, he cherished still ;
the models he had always kept before him, were still
revered. His weakness, whatever it was, did not touch
the essential qualities of his character. It was a constitutional inheritance that did not pervert the substantial
greatness of the man. Whatever the motive that
prompted him to conceal his complicity with the martyr
whose blood was the seed of the Union, it was not dis-
graceful to his character, and should not injure his fame.
It was a weakness, but it was not a baseness ; a fault,
but neither a crime, nor a guilt. That he was faultless,
it would be foolish to affirm. His faults were conspicuous, and even showy. He was not always candid ; he
was not always generous ; he was not always fair. He
lived too consciously in the world's eye. He was too
large a figure in his own regard. He lacked somewhat
the reserve of modesty. His fidelity to himself occasionally betrayed him into apparent insincerity to others.
But he was not false to others ; he never betrayed a
principle, or deserted a friend. His anti-slavery record
is manly and honorable, by all confession. It is much
to say that in so long and public a career, there is found
but one spot he desired to conceal, and that this one
he covered, not in order to escape personal danger or
public contempt, but in order that he might stand well
with himself ; in order that he might satisfy the claims

10

of his judgment, as well as the demands of his heart.
To the appeal of history, made through Mr. Sanborn, he,
as we have seen, turned a deaf ear. Biography was to
him more important than history ; and more important
than the biography that might never be written, was
the private record that lay daily beneath his own eye.
This was an infirmity.   Personal feeling should never be
permitted to obscure historical truth.   It is the biographer's privilege to draw aside the veil, and to do justice
to both.

CHAPTER VII.

THE WAR.

GERRIT SMITH was a man of peace and a "peace man;" but he was not a non-resistant. That is, he believed in the divine institution of government, consequently in the divine ministration of force. But believing that the ministration of force was divine, he would take the exercise of it out of profane hands and commit it to the best hands. The public executioner should be the most honored citizen. The community's "armed police" should be composed of the most orderly, sober, grave, just and humane men. The army should represent the disciplined virtue of the country, not its undisciplined vice. On all occasions he improved his opportunity to divulge this idea. When an infatuated Christendom was glorifying General Havelock, one of the heroes of the Sepoy rebellion, Gerrit Smith wrote :

" I am free to admit that a few men connected with the army and navy have amiable and beautiful traits of character ; that a few of them are the subjects of strong religious emotion. Such were Colonel Gardiner, Captain Vicars, and General Havelock. But that even Havelock, 'whose praise is in all the churches,' was a Christian, I am compelled to doubt. I will not doubt that he deeply loved and devoutly worshipped his own ideal of Jesus Christ, that his orthodoxy was valiant for the 'doctrine,' that he was full of zeal for his Baptist church, and that he abounded in prayers for all men. But in that enlightened and better day when the true religion shall be seen to be, not a sentiment to weep and joy over, nor a doctrine to quarrel

for, but a principle to be governed by in all our relations, and a life
to be lived out everywhere and always, not the fervors which are
kindled by fancies of God, but that acknowledgment of him which
is made practical, and is proved by justice to man; then the Havelock type of piety, which is so bewitching in an age of war religion,
will be reckoned of little worth. Havelock was an unjust man, as
is every one who identifies himself with war, and holds himself to do
the devilism it bids. This unreserved submission to human authority
is of itself sufficient to prove that the warrior cannot be a just man,
and that war and Christianity are incompatible with each other.
Havelock was among the foremost murderers of the Affghans, the
poor Affghans, against whom the British waged a war as surpassingly cruel as it was utterly causeless. His own pen describes its
revolting horrors.

"Havelock was self-deceived. His religion was a superstition;
for it was the current misrepresentation of Christianity. When he
says that in a certain battle he 'felt that the Lord Jesus Christ was
at his (my) side,' he was misled by a fancy scarcely less wild and
wicked than slave-holding piety; and instead of sharing his delusion,
we are deeply to pity and as deeply to loathe it. That Havelock
was more an ambitious soldier than a follower of Christ, is told out
of his own heart when he says in a letter: 'One of the prayers, oft
repeated throughout my life since my school days, has been answered, and I have lived to command in a successful action.'"

A similar infatuation in regard to "Stonewall" Jackson, provoked a similar protest:

"I am amazed," he writes to Henry Ward Beecher, in 1863,
"that you make so much of Jackson's theological bundle, and of
his being 'an active member of the Presbyterian church of which he
was a ruling elder,' These, in your esteem, suffice to carry him
straight to heaven. I had supposed that your strong common sense
and large intelligence had long ago lifted you up out of the superstitious faith that any such things can carry any man to heaven. I
had taken it for granted that you believed that it is his character
however induced—whether by himself, or by Christ or otherwise—
that alone qualifies a man for heaven :—so obvious is it in the light of
reason that every man must go to his own place, and that what shall
be his place must be determined not by his theology but by his character. But I was mistaken. For in the same breath in which you
send Jackson to heaven, you argue out for him a thoroughly base

and abominable character, even, to use your own strong and eloquent words, ' a comprehensive and fundamental degradation of heart and mind and soul.' "

The civil war did not take Gerrit Smith by surprise. He had long anticipated and predicted that slavery would come to an end in blood. Being in itself a perpetual war against human rights, an outlaw from humanity, a foe to civilization, the offspring of malignity, hard-hearted, violent, savage, no other doom was meet or possible for it. The war therefore had been allowed for, adopted into his scheme of social development in the United States, as the inevitable issue of the barbarism that had been cherished. This was his theory of the war, his whole theory. It was a coming out of devils, which tore and convulsed the nation, casting it into the fire and water to destroy it. That it was a struggle between the principle of States' Rights, and the principle of National Union, did not apparently occur to him. It was a rebellion of anarchy against order, of iniquity against justice, of evil against good. But one event was to be looked for, the extermination of slavery. But one course was open to the north, the prosecution of the war till the south was completely subdued, and slavery utterly abolished. This was the only alternative ; but this must be pursued in a spirit, resolute and unfaltering indeed, but neither vindictive nor pitiless. He writes to Dr. Beckwith, Secretary of the American Peace Society :

"Let us thank God that anything, even though it had to be the insanity of the whole south, has brought slavery to its dying hour. Never more will the American Peace Society witness the need of raising armies to put down a treasonable onslaught upon our government. For the one cause of so formidable an onslaught will be gone when slavery is gone. Besides, when slavery is gone from the whole world, the whole world will then be freed, not only from a source of war, but from the most cruel and horrid form of war. For slavery is war as well as the source of war. Thus has the Peace Society as well as the Abolition Society, much to hope for from this grand uprising of the north. For while the whole north rejoices in the direct and immediate object of the uprising—the maintenance of government ; and while the abolitionists do, in addition to this object, cherish the further one of the abolition of slavery, the Peace men are happy to know that the abolition of slavery will be the abolition of one form of war, the drying up 'of one source of war, and of one source of occasions for raising armies."

At a war meeting in Peterboro, April 27, 1861, he said :

" The end of American slavery is at hand. That it is to end in blood does not surprise me. For fifteen years I have been constantly predicting that it would be. . . . *The first gun fired at Fort Sumter announced the fact that the last fugitive slave had been returned.* . . . And what if, when Congress shall come together in this extra session, the slave States shall all have ceased from their treason, and shall all ask that they may be suffered to go from us. Shall Congress let them go ? Certainly. But only on the condition that those States shall first abolish slavery. Congress has clearly no constitutional right to let them go on any conditions. But I believe that the people would approve of the proceedings, and would be ready to confirm it in the most formal and sufficient manner. A few weeks ago I would have consented to let the slave States go without requiring the abolition of slavery, . . . But now, since the southern tiger has smeared himself with our blood, we will not, if we get him in our power, let him go until we have drawn his teeth and his claws. . . .

" A word in respect to the armed men who go south. They should go more in sorrow than in anger. The sad necessity should be their only excuse for going. They must still love the south. We must all still love her. Conquer her, and most completely too, we must, both for her sake and our own. But does it not ill become us to talk of punishing her ? Slavery, which has infatuated her, is the crime of the north as well as of the south. As her chiefs shall one after another, fall into our hands, let us be restrained from dealing revengefully, and moved to deal tenderly with them, by our remembrance of the large share which the north has had in blinding them. The conspiracy of northern merchants and manufacturers, northern publishers, priests and politicians, against the slave-holders, carried on under the guise of friendship, has been mighty to benumb their conscience, and darken their understanding in regard to slavery."

He saw no cause for the Rebellion, on the part of the south; none in the tariff, which had never been so low; none in the election of Lincoln, who was constitutionally chosen; none in the northern agitation on the question of slavery, for that was simply an exercise of the right of free speech which the south indulged in as freely as the north; none in northern legislation against slavery, of which there was little enough; none in the intemperance of the abolitionists or the invasion of John Brown, for the abolitionists were a despised minority of radicals, and John Brown was repudiated as a madman by the all but entire north. The Rebellion was causeless, save for the one essential cause, the irrepressible violence of slavery which would have everything or nothing.

At the outset, therefore, Gerrit Smith's part was appointed. He accepted it without hesitation or misgiving. He put himself unreservedly on the side of the government, spent money, made speeches, published letters and appeals, all to one end, *the putting down of the Rebellion.* Before any one proposed it, before the government was prepared for it, while yet the idea was new and startling, Gerrit Smith offered to equip a colored regiment. Instead of objecting to the enlistment of his only son, Greene, he applauded it, and insisted that he should serve without the soldier's pay. The Rebellion must, at all costs, be put down. Till the Rebellion was put down, nothing else was worth thinking of. All expenditure of power, material, intellectual, political, moral, that did not promote this object, was, in his opinion, wasted. He discountenanced all abstract speculations, all general discussions, all internal dissensions, that every nerve might be strung to the utmost tension to the work of crushing the South.

When the draft was decreed, in 1863, his only objection to it was that the conditions were too merciful. With the attempts to evade it he had no patience :

" Oh, how base must they have become who, when rebels are at the throat of their nation, can hie themselves to the constitution to see how little it will let them off with doing against those rebels— how little with doing for the life of that nation ! Our noble constitution should be used to nourish our patriotism ; but alas it is perverted to kill it ! . . . I admit the duty of the wealthy to avail themselves of this commutation clause to save, here and there, from going to the war the man to whom it would be a peculiar hardship to go. I also admit that every city disposed to do so, can very properly vote the three hundred dollars to every drafted man who serves, or to his substitute. I care not how much the cities help the soldiers. The more the better. I am glad that Oswego voted ten thousand dollars two years ago and five thousand last spring to the families of her soldiers. Let her vote hereafter, as much as she pleases to the soldiers and their families. I will pay cheerfully what share of the tax shall fall on my property in the city ; and more cheerfully would I take part in voluntary contributions. . . . I am not sorry that so many rich men have gone to the war. Nevertheless, let as many rich men as will, remain at home to continue to give employment to the poor in manufactories and elsewhere, and to maintain a business and a prosperity which can be heavily taxed to meet the expenses of the war. Men of property should be heavily taxed to this end ; and my only objection to the income tax is that it is not more than half large enough. It should be six and ten, instead of three and five per cent. . . . The love of country, the love of country, this is what we lack."

As the presidential election of 1864 drew nigh he dreaded and deprecated the approaching excitement and distraction :

"I still say, as through the past winter I have frequently said, written and printed—that the presidential question should not have been talked of, no, nor so much as thought of, until midsummer. The first of September is quite early enough to make the nomination; and in the meantime, undistracted by this so distracting subject, we should be working as one man for the one object of ending the Rebellion—and of ending it before reaching the perils of the presidential election."

The sanguine prediction that the war would be short was not fulfilled. The summer ended, the autumn came and we were not saved. The presidential election must be met. The two candidates were Lincoln and McClellan, the former the advocate of war, the latter the advocate of peace; the former the choice of those who held the North to be in the right, the latter the choice of those who held the North to be in the wrong. This, at all events, was Gerrit Smith's view of the situation; and such being his view, he threw his whole weight into the scale with Lincoln, as the surest support of the anti-slavery party; a fragile support it sometimes appeared, this man of exasperating moderation and provoking prudence, whom the radicals did not bless when alive as much as they did when he was dead; a man whom fanatics would have put out of the way as too cautious, whom the Gerrit Smiths complained of as slow—still, the only champion of liberty then on the field. His reëlection insured, at least a prosecution of the war till the South should yield.

"The President of the United States is both a great and a good man. But neither greatness nor goodness would be manifest in consenting to a peace, which, however admirable in other respects, failed nevertheless to secure the ballot to the black man, and left him therefore, at the mercy of his enemy and ours—of his and our demonized enemy. Happily, among the highest proofs that the

12*

President is both great and good, is his willingness to grow and change. Such willingness is not found in little and mean men."

On the 22d July, 1861, the House of Representatives adopted, with but two dissenting voices, Mr. Crittenden's resolution to the effect that " this war is waged but to defend and maintain the supremacy of the constitution, and to preserve the union with all the dignity, equality and rights of the several States unimpaired; and that, as soon as those objects are accomplished, the war ought to cease." This resolution was, in Gerrit Smith's judgment, the most pernicious of all the mistakes made in the conduct of the war, for it turned the thoughts of earnest patriots away from the real issue, and it justified the luke-warm in their reluctance to push the war which the radicals were using as an instrument for the abolition of slavery. Obstructions of this kind made the philanthropist despond. It was the temporizing at the North he feared, not the valor at the South; it was the prudent President's deference to the Constitution and the Supreme Court, not the rebels' determination to set up another constitution, that boded ill for the country. The President he had faith in, as an honest, earnest man; the people he had faith in as sincerely attached to their institutions; the providential destiny of the nation he had faith in, for he could not believe that the fine experiment of a republic would fail. But the President's concessions to established traditions and popular scruples played into the hands of the enemy who took advantage of his policy to discredit his principle; the people allowed themselves to be duped by demagogues who cried patriotism and were eager for spoils; and the ways of providence were so mysterious and so devious, that it

seemed more than once as if the salvation of the country was to come, if it came at all, through what, to human
vision, was defeat and overthrow.

The excitement consequent on the seizure of Commissioners Mason and Slidell on board of the English
steamer " Trent " was, in his breast, a tumult of indignation ; against England for her arrogant menace of war
on such a pretext ; against the government for its supine
submission to England's demand that the commissioners
be surrendered, and the act of their seizure be disavowed.

Why is it that the English press threatens us with war ? It is
for compelling the English ship to give up the rebel commissioners,
so it says. This is the ostensible reason. But would not England
—she who is so famous for clinging to an almost entirely unqualified
and unlimited right of search—have done the same thing in like
circumstances ? If she would not, then she would not have been
herself. Had a part of her home counties revolted and sent a couple
of their rebels to America for help, would she not have caught
them if she could ? And in whatever circumstances they might
have been found ? If she says she would not, there is not on all the
earth one " Jew Apella " so credulous as to believe her. If she con-
fesses she would, then is she self-convicted, not only of trampling in
her boundless dishonesty on the great and never-to-be-violated principle of doing as we would be done by, but of insulting us by claiming that we ought to be tame and base enough to forbear to do that
which her self-respect and high spirit would prompt her to do. Her
naval captains have taken thousands of seamen from our ships—
these captains constituting themselves the sole accusers, witnesses
and judges in the cases. It was chiefly for such outrages that we
declared war against her in 1812. The instance of the San Jacinto
and Trent is not like these. In this instance there was no question,
because no doubt, of personal identity.

It is not possible that England will make war on us for what we
did to the Trent. . . . She could not make such a causeless war
upon us without deeply and broadly blotting her own character and
the character of modern civilization.

What do I hold that England should do in this case ?

1. Reprimand or more severely punish the captain of the Trent

for his very gross and very guilty violation of our rights in furnishing exceedingly important facilities to our enemy. This our government should have promptly insisted on, and not have suffered England to get the start of us with her absurd counter claim. . . .

2. The next thing that England should do is to give instructions, or rather repeat those in the Queen's Proclamation, that no more rebel commissioners be received into her vessels.

3. And then she should inform us whether, in the case of a vessel that shall hereafter offend in this wise, she would have us take the vessel itself, or take but the commissioners. It is true that whatever her preference, we would probably insist on taking the vessel in every case :—for it is not probable that we shall again expose ourselves in such a case to the charge of taking too little. . . .

I have said that England will not go to war with us in the case of the Trent. Nevertheless I am not without fear that her government will be driven to declare war against us. If an irresistible pressure comes upon the government, it will come from those portions of the people who long for the cotton and free trade of the South, and who have allowed themselves to get angry with the North by foolishly misconstruing our high tariff (which is simply a war measure) into a *hostile commercial measure.* . . .

Let us but know that England, to whom we have done no wrong, has resolved to come to the help of the Pro-slavery Rebellion, and our deep indignation against her combining with our deeper indignation against ourselves, will arm us with the spirit and the power to snap the "cords" and "green withes" and "new ropes" with which slavery has bound us, and to dash to the dust the foul idol whose worship has so demented and debased us. Yes, let us hear this month that England has declared war against us, and this month will witness our Proclamation of Liberty to every slave in our land. . . . Should England so causelessly, cruelly and meanly force a war upon us, there will be no divisions among us in regard to that war ;—nor indeed will there then be in regard to the other. And so deep and abiding will be our sense of her boundless injustice, that there will never be any among us to welcome propositions of peace with England, until her war with us shall have reached the result of our subjugation or of her expulsion from every part of the continent of North America. Moreover we shall rejoice to hear of the crushing of her power everywhere—for we shall feel that the nation which can be guilty of such a war is fit to govern nowhere—in the Eastern no more than in the Western Hemisphere.

When Gerrit Smith was nominated for governor, in 1858, Horace Greeley remarked that if the State were New Jerusalem instead of New York, such a governor would be admirably qualified. His method of administration was, in all cases, prescribed by the Golden Rule: an excellent rule for the ideal society of the Millennium for which it was intended; but no political state ever conformed to it, or ever will.

The story of Andersonville did not surprise him. It was precisely what might have been expected. Its horrors, taken at their worst, were but the natural result of causes that had been active for half a century. The counter statement of the southerners, could he have heard it, would have been intrinsically incredible to him, as contradicting the natural law that makes every effect follow its cause. Before he could accept the palliative representations of the opposing side, he must recant all he had said about the character of slavery; he must repudiate the convictions of half a century.

As long as Andersonville shall live in the world's memory, (and can its sins and sorrows ever be forgotten?) so long shall it warn men not to trample upon nor forget the rights of their fellow-men. By the way, the guilt of Andersonville rests not alone on the South. The North has countenanced and justified the Southern contempt and denial of the rights of the black man. Nor was this by Democrats only. The Republican Party, though not so extensively, was also involved in the guilt. The doctrine that the black man has no rights, is still virtually subscribed to, not only by the mass of the Democrats, but by multitudes of Republicans also. Many a Northern church is still defiled by it. The religion and politics, the commerce and social usages of the North are all to be held as having a part in fashioning the policy which rules at Andersonville; the policy of ignoring the rights of prisoners of war, and of starving and murdering them. Moreover, many a prisoner there, if his sufferings have sufficiently clarified his vision for it, is able to see that he is himself

chargeable with a responsible part in the production of those sufferings ;—ay, that he is " hoist with his own petard." In his political
or ecclesiastical party, and elsewhere also, he has contributed to uphold the southern policy of excluding the black man from all rights ;
and consequently, as events have proved, of excluding himself too
from them.

The war closed with the assassination of Lincoln ; a
fitting symbol of the spirit that began it, and pursued it
till manly resistance was no longer possible. The power
which fired the first cannon at Sumter, discharged the
last pistol at the back of the President. During this
time and the remainder of the unexpired term wherein
Andrew Johnson did his best to complete Lincoln's unfinished purpose without Lincoln's temper, Smith grieved
and watched. The situation caused him grave concern,
but no special exigencies stirred his spirit till the motion
to impeach the President called him back once more to
first principles. That the termination of active hostili-
ties did not leave national affairs as he hoped and believed it would, need not be affirmed ; so much will be
understood. That the "taking off" of Lincoln seemed
untimely and deplorable, may be surmised ; that the administration of his successor failed to carry out the real
intentions of the war-president might be inferred from
the circumstance that it offended every class of the
negro's friends. The proposal to impeach Johnson met
his approval, but it was characteristic of him to come
out in defence of those who voted against it, with upright
intention. The one thing he could not excuse was
partisan injustice, the proscription of good men because
they withstood the pressure of public opinion. He could
concede the possession of virtue to those who differed
widely and fundamentally from himself, to slaveholders,

to rebels; it was easy for him to concede virtue to true
men whose hearts, he knew, beat in sympathy with his
own, though their views of policy differed. Thus he
wrote of the "calumnious and contemptible treatment"
of men like Chief Justice Chase and senators Trumbull
and Fessenden:

The flood gates of defamation were opened upon Mr. Fessenden
and Mr. Trumbull because they voted for the acquittal of the President. I wish they had voted for his conviction. For, although I
had not, previously, taken much interest in the proposition to impeach him, nevertheless, after reading those parts of his last Annual
Message, in which he traduces the colored citizens of our country,
I was quite willing to have him removed from office. Were Victoria
to take such an outrageous liberty with the Irish, or Scotch or Welsh,
she would quickly be relieved of her crown. I do not forget that insulting the negro is an American usage. But not with impunity
should the President of the whole American people insult in his
official capacity, any of the races which make up that people ;—least
of all that race which is, already, the most deeply wronged. This
gross violation of the perfect impartiality which should ever mark
the administration of the President's high office—this ineffable meanness of assailing the persecuted and weak, whom he might rather
have consoled and cheered, should not have been overlooked, but
should have been promptly and sternly rebuked. Nevertheless, in
the light of their life long uprightness, I have not the least reason to
doubt, that they voted honestly. Nay, in the light of their eminent
wisdom, I am bound to pause and inquire of my candid judgment,
whether they did not vote wisely as well as honestly.

The clamor against the Chief Justice was not, as is pretended,
occasioned by his conduct in the impeachment trial. That this conduct was wise and impartial, scarcely one intelligent man can doubt.
This clamor proceeded for the purpose of preventing his nomination
to the Presidency. It is said that he desires to be President. But a
desire for this high office is not, necessarily, culpable. Instead of
being prompted in all instances by selfishness, it may in some instances, be born of a high patriotism and a disinterested philanthropy. For one, I should rejoice to see the Chief Justice in the
Presidency ;—and I say this after a-many years intimate acquaintance
with him—after much personal observation of the working of his

head and heart. I, however, expect to vote for Grant and Colfax.
I like them both, and in the main I like the platform on which they
stand. Nevertheless, if, contrary to my expectations, the democrats
shall have the wisdom to nominate the Chief Justice and along with
him a gentleman of similar views and spirit—a gentleman honest
both towards the nation's creditors and towards the negro—I shall
prefer to vote for the democratic candidate. If the democrats, at
last, sick and ashamed, as I have no doubt tens of thousands of
them are, of ministering to the mean spirit of caste, prating for a
"white man's government," and defying the sentiment of the civilized world,—shall give up their nonsense and wickedness and nominate for office such men as republicans have been eager to honor—
how wanting in magnanimity and in devotion to truth, and how enslaved to party would republicans show themselves to be, were
they not to welcome this overture, and generously respond to these
concessions.

The clause "honest towards the nation's creditors,"
which occurs in the foregoing passage, in connection
with the qualities requisite in a candidate for the office
of Vice-President of the United States, clearly refers to
the doctrine of repudiation, openly avowed in certain
parts of the country, particularly in the western States,
and generally associated with the policy of the democratic party. It will be remembered that, at an earlier
period, when the war with Mexico was in question, Gerrit
Smith countenanced this very doctrine, laid it down, in
fact, as a fixed rule that each generation should pay its
own debts, and should contract no debts it could not
pay; that each generation had a right to enter, unincumbered, on the career appointed to it, and is perfectly justified in refusing to pay bills which were contracted
without its consent or knowledge. This doctrine however, was advanced in view of *avoidable* expenses, such
as might be incurred by an administration in pursuance
of party interests, or by a community planning a project

of improvement like an Erie Canal or a Pacific Railroad, which can be commenced or not, or can be left at any stage uncompleted. The argument that as future generations are to share the benefit of the improvement, future generations may reasonably be required to bear their fair proportion of its cost, is met by the consideration that one generation cannot foretell whether the improvement will be advantageous or not, and even if it could, is unjustified in conferring sumptuous favors which have not been asked, and may not be acceptable. The next generation may, from some unforeseen reason, be too poor to pay for the boon, or may wish its money for other things, or may be compelled to consult other interests which have come up since the project was inaugurated. In the case of a wanton war, for party aggrandizement, or national conquest, it is quite likely that no public benefit will accrue; the money may be thrown away or worse; the next generation may be burdened not merely with a monstrous debt, but with a monstrous evil, which it would be cheaply relieved of at an expense of millions. Where it is a matter of choice, the principle of free will should be allowed to play its part, and each generation be permitted to decide for itself what it will have, and when it will have it. Under this rule, people will take charge of their own interests instead of committing them to governments, corporations or companies; they will have nothing they do not want, and will consider well before beginning what they may be unable to finish. The Mexican war would never have been begun had the people understood in advance that if they undertook it, they must pay every dollar of its cost; for in that case, the few who wanted it would be outnumbered by the thousands who did not want it at all, or who wanted it to the amount of six-pence. This was the sum of Gerrit Smith's doctrine of repudiation. It was a doctrine held in the interest of justice, as a check to the powers of government, and an education of the people in carefulness and judgment. There was no taint, no suspicion of dishonesty in it. It looked to the diminution of indebtedness, not to the disclaimer of it. It bade people be cautious in contracting debts, not slack in paying them when once contracted. Its aim was not repudiation, but economy. The school to which Mr. Smith belonged, in this particular, is a school of thinkers who stand for honesty pure and simple, and at the same time for personal independence of the absolute sort. They believe in the duty of paying what is due, but only what is due, not what other people see fit to impose. Have what you want, when you can pay for it, —is their motto. On that rule, you will study what you really do want, and will test your desires by the sacrifice necessary to gratify them. They bid people to forego even the things that seem indispensable, rather than incur debt for them which future ages must pay. Schools, academies, libraries, museums, institutes, asylums, hospitals, however necessary to appearance, must wait, or be imperfect, till they are justified by present desire and wealth. Canals must remain in project on the engineer's table, railroads must be ideas in the schemer's brain until they are actually demanded for traffic. Then, as they are called for they will be constructed.

Such a doctrine has nothing in common with the doctrine of repudiation which was in vogue immediately after the Civil War. For the war was no luxury but an

unavoidable necessity. It was not the act of the administration, but the doom of the people. It accomplished
no sectional benefit, but saved the life of the nation. It
was precipitated upon a single generation, but was the
concern of all. The generation that had it forced upon
them, and that spent money and blood to carry it through
was not the generation that enjoyed its benefits. This
generation must pass away and perhaps yet another before the essential gains will be appreciable; and in such
a case the expense may fairly be levied on succeeding
ages. According to one theory, the people of the South
who inaugurated and conducted the war, should be compelled to pay for it by wholesale confiscation of estates;
but this solution occurred to few, and was never proposed
as a party measure; the thought of conquest was repudiated from the beginning; every act of the government
denounced it; the Democratic party was too friendly to
the South to oppress it; the Republican party was too
tenacious of the rights of revolution and the principles
of humanity to recommend arbitrary and stern reprisals.
According to another theory, the industry of the country, prostrated by the war, required exemption from the
burden of unusual taxation, in order to recover itself,
and to this end, the burden should be thrown off without hesitation or apology. The present generation had
spent enough in treasure and blood; the flower of its
youth and the vigor of its manhood had been destroyed;
the fields had been untilled; the mineral resources were
undeveloped; and the means for maintaining, or even
for starting enterprise were wanting. A few years of
untaxed labor would work wonders of reparation; a few
years of taxed labor would retard if not obstruct hope-

lessly the future progress of the country. Therefore, the policy of repudiation found favor, especially at the West, with people who were not concerned about the next generation, but were absorbed in the actual situation; they wished, themselves, to be free. The proposal that a number of immensely wealthy men, whom the war had not impoverished but enriched, should reduce the war debt, met with no response from the only gentlemen directly interested in such a plan.

The doctrine of repudiation on the principle of sparing those *that should come after*, was hardly suggested, if at all. Gerrit Smith was ready to do his part and more, to make the transmitted burden as little as need be, but there is no evidence that he deemed it incumbent on the generation that had saved the nation by subduing the slave power, to bequeath, along with the unspeakable blessings of that achievement, a plenary dispensation from the necessity of discharging their portion of the expense. Feeling as he did about the inestimable advantage of emancipation to all coming ages of men, on this continent and elsewhere in all the world, fidelity to his ideas rather required that these coming ages should pay their own debt, and not force or permit the discharge of it by those who had all the sorrow, and could expect little or none of the joy.

"As a general thing," he wrote when the continuance or discontinuance of the validity of the ' Legal Tender Act' was under discussion, "They who in the late war fought for the salvation of our country, were poor. Included in this salvation were the estates of our rich men. It would be an expression of justice and gratitude toward the poor, and at the same time not at all oppressive to the rich, were our large estates made to pay, for a few years to come, a greater proportion than they now pay of the annual payment on our war debt. Moreover both the benevolence and patriotism of our rich men should make it a pleasure to them to pay ten per cent on incomes exceeding ten thousand dollars, and twenty per cent on incomes exceeding twenty thousand dollars."

THE GOLDEN RULE AGAIN.—The validity of the Legal Tender Act, as a war measure, he admitted without debate. The question of its constitutionality he considered to be impertinent, because the war which made it necessary, was unimpeachable by the constitution. The continuance of the powers of the act beyond the period actually covered by the war was demanded, in his judgment, by the exigencies of business, which would suffer seriously by a sudden return to specie payments. He applauded the existing banking system as the best possible in the existing emergency. He advised that no limits be set to the creation of new banks, and none to the issues of banks, new or old, beyond the present restrictions. But he believed in a gradual and fast return to specie payments, to begin in 1870 and be completed in 1873, the redemption being accomplished in four successive instalments. So sanguine was he of the energy and recuperative power of the country, of the firmness of the national credit, and the rapidity of accumulations under an honest administration of government, that up to the date of "the infamous fraud of repudiation," he foresaw the clearance of the entire debt in twenty or thirty years.

In the darkest days of the war he confessed but one fear, and that was lest the people should not be permitted to think and act freely. His faith in the people was so strong, his faith in human nature, in the fundamental rectitude of the "masses," in the saving virtue

of liberal institutions which left men free to employ all
the faculty there was in them in the regulation of their
public and private concerns, in the laws of equity, and
the regenerating influences of justice, that he was sure
all would be well, if the politicians, the wire pullers,
managers, jobbers, demagogues, could be induced or
compelled to retire from the field, and let affairs regulate
themselves.   Defeat and disaster furnished no evidence
that the northern cause was bad or weak; they merely
confirmed the judgment that it was prevented from dis-
playing its strength and excellence.   There was enough
of valor, patriotism, generosity, devotion; there was
enough of this before the war to make the war needless;
but the mercenary ambition of politicians was interested
that it should not assert itself, and so, to the end, the
redeeming forces were restrained.   Again and again, he
was driven back upon the resources of hope, when the
resources of evidence gave out; but the hope was brave
and bright to the last.

The absorbing interest of the war did not make this
man unmindful of the other interests that lay near his
heart.   The cause of temperance was as dear as ever.
The cause of intellectual emancipation from the bondage
of superstition and sectarianism had its share of his attention.   The controversy with Albert Barnes on the
dogmas of the Christian theology began in 1867 and continued till August, 1868.   His letter to John Stuart Mill
on the subject of temperance was written in 1869, subsequent, indeed, to the close of the war, but during the
heat of the discussions which the war engendered.   The
letter to Mill, though scarcely more than a recapitulation
of positions sufficiently indicated already, is worth

printing, as exhibiting the points of agreement and the points of contrast between the man of feeling and the man of thought, the warm-blooded friend of human nature and the clear-headed student of human opinions.

State of New York, Peterboro, February 5, 1869.

JOHN STUART MILL, England:

Honored and Dear Sir, — A gentleman in England, who is rendering eminent service to the cause of temperance, requests me to criticise your attitude toward that cause. So profound is my sense of your preëminent wisdom—perhaps, well-nigh as profound as was Buckle's sense of it—that I could not, without heavily taxing my diffidence, presume to criticise you in any respect. Nevertheless, I venture to comply with the request.

The gentleman I refer to would have government shut up the dramshop. You would have government leave it open. How shall so wide a difference on a subject of so vast importance be explained? Is he more radical in his theories than you are? Probably not. Few of the world's great writers are less cramped than yourself by the spirit of conservatism. Are you less disposed than he to reduce radical theories to practice? Your admirable pleas for woman's voting prove that you do not shrink from the boldest practical innovations. This wide difference must be otherwise accounted for. Perhaps, while his philanthropy is particularly moved by intemperance, yours is by some other vice or suffering. Or, perhaps, it is to be accounted for, in part or entirely, by the supposition that you are especially jealous of the interference of society with the rights and practices of the individual, and he, of the interference of the individual with the interests and welfare of society. On this supposition it is quite natural that one of you should argue the right of the individual to buy or sell drams, and the other the right of society to punish him for such buying or selling.

You make the province of civil government much narrower than most do. I (though not forgetting that, in doing so, I go against the judgment of many a man far wiser and better than myself) make it still narrower. For instance, while you would have government compel the idler to work, I would let him remain an idler, should moral influences prove inadequate to change him: and while you would have the parent compelled to educate his child, I, with my dread of all possibly avoidable compulsion, would look to his enlightened and benevolent neighbors to supply, as far as they can, the unnatural parental lack. Again, I would have government shut out not only from the church but also from the school. It should have nothing to do with either. Then, too, I would have the right to buy and sell so free, as not to leave a custom-house upon the earth. Nor would I allow government to concern itself with the cause of temperance, nor with any other moral reform, nor with asylums for the blind or the deaf mutes, nor with any other benevolent institutions. Why, then, you will ask me, am I in favor of the enactment of sumptuary laws? I am not. Families should be left to dress as they please, and to eat and drink what they please. There should be no laws to regulate living. If, in saying so, I open the way for the question—how I can then consistently be in favor of government's shutting up the dramshops—my reply is that this question will be answered in what I shall say of the province of government. I have said what is not its province—in other words, what it should not do. I will now say what is its province—in other words, what it should do. It should protect persons and property; and it should attempt nothing more. Its one work is to hold a shield over its subjects beneath which they can, unjostled by each other, and secure from foreign aggressions, pursue each his own chosen calling, and each live out his own views of life. The protection of person and property being its sole office, government is to protect society not only from the criminal but from the insane, be it liquor or disease that has produced the insanity. Hence, while we are to look to enlightened and benevolent persons for asylums for the sick and poor, we are to regard lunatic asylums, including inebriate asylums, as a part of the machinery of government. By the way, the almshouse and kindred institutions would scarcely be needed were the dramshops abolished. Rare, in that case, would be the person who is so impoverished or debased, as to cast himself upon the public charity; and rare too, in that case, would be the person, whose friends are so impoverished or debased as to allow him to be cast upon it.

If I have rightly defined the office of civil government, then, manifestly, were every part of the earth to be blessed with a true civil government, there would not be so much as one dramshop left in any part of the earth. For what is the dramshop but the great manufactory of incendiaries, madmen and murderers? Its staggering army in Great Britain counts up nearly a million; in America scarcely less. Because of the dramshop hundreds of thousands of British and American families are deep-sunk in misery, stricken with terror, and not a very small proportion of them besmeared with blood. Because of the dramshop night is so often made hideous in Britain and America by screams of "murder," and sunrise made sorrowful by its revelations of the deeds of drunkenness. And, yet, even John Stuart Mill will not have government suppress the dramshop! Its evils, surpassing the sum total of all other evils, stare him in the face—and, yet, he allows himself to be swayed by the microscopic view, which detects in such suppression a particle of seeming sumptuary legislation! Pardon me for being reminded by your hypercritical and fastidious objection to the only way of salvation in this life and death case, of the old story of the extreme ceremoniousness of the gentleman, who made his never-having-been-introduced to the drowning man his excuse for not rescuing him. Even if there is in this proposed suppression of the dramshop something of the form or semblance of sumptuary legislation, there nevertheless is not the least of the spirit of it. Moreover, were it so that, incidental to this supposition, there must be violations of some minor rights and inconsiderable interests, no account should be made of the violations, but all of them should be forgotten in the joy of the accomplished object.

I admit that the shutting up of the dramshops might put some families to a little inconvenience, if not also to a slightly additional expense, in obtaining alcoholic liquor. I admit, too, that, while it is not only unnecessary but pernicious to persons in health, there is occasionally a bodily ailment, in which, provided there are not other remedial agents of similar effect at hand, such liquor is useful. But to make trifles like these excuses for keeping open the flood-gates of the deadly dramshop argues the impossibility of finding worthier excuses for continuing the murderous wrong.

I do not forget that, although you would leave the dramseller unpunished for keeping a soul-and-body slaughter-house, you would have his customer punished for the violence of which he may have been guilty in his drunkenness. But to make this the only security against such violence is too much like stipulating with the men, reckless or malignant enough to bring fire into the powder-house, that they shall not be punished until an actual explosion has come of their recklessness or malignity. Surely, surely, London is entitled to more security against dramshop-violence than this which you propose—yes, to immeasurably more, seeing that, probably, never a day passes without some of her dramshops being chargeable with one or more deaths. The deaths may be from suicide or murder—produced suddenly or gradually—nevertheless, they are all dramshop deaths.

13

I do not forget the frequent cavil, that, even were the dramshop shut up, drinking and drunkenness would not thereby be diminished. Nevertheless overwhelming are the proofs, that the drinking and drunkenness are in proportion to the temptation—in proportion to the frequency and attractiveness of the places for gratifying the unhappy appetite. Of course, no one is less chargeable with such cavil than yourself. For your argument against shutting up the dramshop is the solemn one that human rights would thereby be invaded—invaded by lessening the facilities for tippling and drunkenness! I scarcely need add that the cavillers I refer to entirely ignore your argument. With your fear of the increased difficulty of getting rum they have no sympathy. Their confidence that rum will still be within as easy reach as ever remains undiminished.

How sad it is that even the wisest and best of men do, by getting used to crimes—to the presence of criminal usages—become patient with them! Possibly, before the year is ended, thousands of shops may be opened in London for the sale of a newly discovered gas. It will craze no small part of their frequenters. Some of them it will turn into incendiaries and some into murderers. Nevertheless, so attractive will be the gas that scores of thousands will go to inhale it. No sooner, however, will the effect of it be well ascertained than petitions for shutting up these gas-shops will pour into parliament. Among the most influential names upon them will be your own. The gas-shops, unsustained by the plea of custom, would be tried solely by their character, and would, therefore, be as quickly and as thoroughly condemned as would be the dramshops, were they also unsheltered by this plea, and put on trial for their character only —their emphatically infernal character.

We are both in favor of having the people own government instead of being, as is the case in many nations, owned by it. Hence, we both deprecate government's travelling beyond its legitimate limits. Could it be kept within them, it would be a blessing above all price. Travelling beyond them, it becomes an evil, not only from its meddling with matters which do not belong to it, but from its consequent neglect of its own proper duty. Has it never occurred to you, that the most effective way to recall government from its meddlings is to hold it firmly and constantly to the discharge of its one duty to protect person and property? When it shall have been brought to see that, in leaving the dramshop to pour out destruction and death, it leaves person and property more unprotected than from any or all other causes; and when it shall, consequently, have been brought to see that it has no higher duty to perform than to shut up this fountain of woe, then will civil government be in a process of education and change that will leave it no taste nor time nor talent for continuing its usurpations. And then, with hands filled with its legitimate work, and with heart filled with zeal to perform it, and destitute alike of affinity and ability for every other work, civil government will realize the sublimest expectations of the most enlightened and philanthropic statesmen. In that day, it will be held, not only that civil government has the right to shut up the dramshops, but that, wherever it fails to exercise this right, it fails to prove itself worthy of the name of civil government.

With the highest regard, yours,

GERRIT' SMITH.

That the surrender at Appomattox, though nominally ending the war, did not put an end to the virulent causes that produced the war, or allay the patriot's apprehension of another trouble, is apparent in the following letter to Gen. Lee.

Peterboro, September 25th, 1868.

GENERAL R. E. LEE, Virginia :

I honored General Rosecrans for his patriotism and bravery in the war. Nevertheless, his letter to you is so exceedingly offensive on account of the servile, flattering, false spirit with which it overflows, that I found it quite easy to toss it aside and forget it. I would forget him also. For when a man has done good service to his country, it is painful to remember him, if to remember him is but to loathe his apostacy. But your reply to General Rosecrans is what I cannot forget, nor cease to grieve over. I have thought of it, perhaps, every day since I read it. Very sorry am I that you wrote it. Very sorry am I that you did not continue your dignified, beautiful and exemplary silence in regard to the political affairs of the country.

And is it so, that General Lee, with all his wisdom, has nothing better to offer us, as the result of this slavery-begotten and slavery-overthrowing war, than the re-instatement of slavery?—nothing better to offer us, in return for all this expenditure of treasure and blood, than the restoration of the horrid cause of this horrid war? Your letter shows that it is even so. Far am I from calling in question your sincerity, when you disclaim all expectation of the re-establishment of chattel-slavery. But to argue to you that slavery, virtual, if not literal, must ever attend the disfranchisement of a race, and especially when it is the only disfranchised race, would be a superfluity insulting to your excellent understanding. Slavery attended the disfranchisement of your blacks before the war. It also attended it, after the war. Under the governments, which President Johnson set up at the south—and which, by the way, he had no more right to set up than you or I had—under, in other words, his policy of confining all the political power to the whites—a policy immediately espoused by the whole democratic party—a type of slavery, more cruel and crushing than the former one, was at once entered upon. As a matter of course, if this party shall succeed at the coming election, and shall be able to execute its General Blair threat of bloody disfranchisement, and of bloody restoration of the white man's government, your blacks will, because, amongst other things, of the deep and undying enmity kindled against them by their having taken up arms against their oppressors, be more grievously oppressed than they were when in chattel-slavery.

But why should it be doubted that you and such as signed your letter, would, if circumstances invited it, be in favor of reviving chattel-slavery? Your letter virtually denies that to enslave your fellow-men is to "oppress them." Nay it goes so far as, in effect, to declare that to doom them and their endless posterity to stripes and chains and unrequited toil and rayless ignorance and the loss of every right, is "to look upon them with kindness." If you gentlemen do not see that to enslave men in the past was to "oppress them," and to lack "kindness" toward them, why should it be supposed that you would see oppression or unkindness in their future enslavement? If you justify, instead of condemning yourselves for having heretofore crushed the negro, what is there in your hearts to hold you back from crushing him hereafter? If slavery is pleasant to look back upon, why should it not, also, be pleasant for you to look forward to?

Deeply have I deplored the short-comings of the north toward the south. When the south, because less than the north, not in bravery, but in numbers and resources, had to surrender, the north should have recognized and confessed herself to be the fellow-sinner of the south—to be as guiltily responsible for its cause. The north should not have found it in her heart to charge any one with treason for his part in the war. She should have felt herself to be morally incompetent to put any of the southern leaders, even yourself or Jefferson Davis, on trial for treason ; and she should have been eager to expend, if need be, a hundred millions from the national treasury in relieving the most urgent wants of her war-impoverished sister. But, General Lee! the lack of the north, in these and other respects, does not justify the failure of the south to repent of slavery;—least of all, does it justify the union of her white men with the democratic party for the purpose of reëstablishing slavery. It is true that the republican party did not do its whole duty toward the south. It would, however, ere this time, have relieved your disfranchised classes, and produced peace between the north and south, and restored the credit of the nation, and reduced to four or less than four per cent the interest she pays, had it not been for the hinderance it encountered in a hostile President and the encouragement to embarrass and resist it, afforded by those hinderances. It was this encouragement which stirred up the whites of the south to their unreasonable demands. Did ever any other conquered people take so insulting an attitude toward their conqueror, as did this toward the mildest of conquerors? But I would not judge my southern brethren too harshly at this point. They were, at first, entirely willing to "accept the situation." But they were tempted by the northern democrats to cast off a becoming modesty and decency, and to be guilty of bad faith and a defiant spirit.

How sad that the white men of the south should look upon the republican party as the enemy of the south! In the success of this party—in the election of those just and wise men, Grant and Colfax —is the salvation of the south. Peace—a righteous and enduring Peace—would come of it. The white men of the south have but two enemies. The republican party is neither of them. Their own wicked hearts—wicked because still refusing to repent of slavery— is one of them; and the other, and far wickeder one, is the democratic party, which, its only hope of re-ascendancy being in the resurrection of slavery, is ever at work to inflame those wicked hearts, and to counsel and contrive that resurrection.

You white men of the south have made your choice. This choice is to go for the democratic party. You will, probably, be disappointed in the election. For the north, though extensively corrupted by the arts of the leaders of the democratic party, can hardly be brought to give a majority of her votes to a party which goes openly for cheating the nation's creditors and for taking up arms to bring back under the yoke of slavery a race to whose magnanimous forgetfulness of their immeasurable wrongs and to whose brave hearts and stalwart arms the salvation of our country is so largely due.

I said that you would, probably, be disappointed in the election. Happy, thrice happy, for you if you shall be. For the war that would come of the success of the democratic party, would be very different in its character and results from what you dream of. You who were slave-masters, are deceived in your calculations by the facility with which you formerly disposed of your blacks. You forget that, whilst they were then but your disposable chattels, they are now, your self-disposing fellow-freemen. You ignore history. You overlook the fact that the African, though easily kept under foot, is not easily after his rights have been restored to him, brought under foot again. You forget the torrents of blood in which France learned the lesson, when near the beginning of this century, she sought to bring back a few hundred thousand freedmen in the western part of St. Domingo, under the yoke of slavery, and in which Spain also learned it when, only a few years ago, she attempted a substantially like oppression in the case of a far smaller number of the same race in the eastern end of the same island. You will not succeed in wresting the ballot and freedom from four millions of blacks, whose women are as brave and hardy as their men, and all of whom can live in mountains and marshes.

I see, in a menacing and mean address of the democrats of Charleston to the blacks of that city, that the democrats of New York have again promised you help to fight your pro-slavery battles. They failed to fulfil their promise before. They will fail to fulfil their promise now. As before, they will talk for you, but shrink from fighting for you. If they have no conscience "to make cowards." of them, nevertheless they have a wholesome dread of encountering the millions, who will be as enraged by such a nefarious attempt to rob them of rights which it is for their life to retain, as would be the she bear or lioness by the attempt to rob her of her young.

Pro-slavery gentlemen of the south ! you cannot too soon give up your purpose to plunder the blacks of the ballot. Your attempt to put it in execution will bring on a scene of horrors, such as living man has never witnessed. There will be "blood even unto the horse bridles." Besides that it will be an attempt against an infuriate foe, it will encounter the sympathies of nearly all of Earth as well as quite all of Heaven. Give up the attempt ! Cease from your hatred and scorn of your colored brother. Take him by the hand. Instruct and guide him—and so will he bless you by his freedom and his ballot. The sooner you bring yourself to admit that the right to vote is entirely irrespective of complexion, the better. You sir, and the other gentlemen, who signed your letter, would have us believe that the blacks of the south are too ignorant to vote. Allow me to reply, that it does not lie in the mouth of those who used their superior knowledge to destroy their country, to speak disparagingly of the inferior knowledge which others used in saving that country.

But I need write no more. Indeed, I had no encouragement to write at all. For, when was it ever known that the oppressing race did not underrate and despise the strength and resources of the oppressed race? And when, too, was it ever known that the oppressor accustomed as he ever is, to flatter himself and be flattered by others, would consent to open his ear to the words of warning? Ere closing however, I must say three things to you, which if not as polite as they are personal, are nevertheless, things which I trust, can be said without going counter to the rule of good-breeding.

First, when you accepted the easy terms on which Gen. Grant, as generous as he is brave and just, allowed you to surrender, neither the prophet who foretold the crimes of Hazael, nor any other prophet, could have persuaded you that, in little more than three years, you would in return for the generosity shown to you and your army, be found in league with the worst enemy of this nation. For the democratic party is incomparably its worst enemy. By the way, I rejoiced in those easy terms of surrender; and one of my strongest desires for the election of Grant springs from my confidence, that President Grant will be as generous and conceding to the south as was Gen. Grant. He will be as ready in his civil, as he was in his military capacity to make every concession to her that is not forbidden by justice and reason.

Second, bred as you were, in a school of honor, and all your life disdaining to do aught, which your judgment pronounced dishonorable, you could not have foreseen that you woud be guilty of calling on this nation to do a meaner, as well as wickeder thing, than has ever been done by any nation. The crimes of this nation against the colored race are beyond description, and yet this race, surpassing every other in affectionateness and patience and forgiveness, dropped those crimes from its memory, and took up arms to save the nation that had so wronged it. Now, for this nation to undertake to throw this race under the feet of its old oppressors is to undertake to reach the very climax of perfidy and meanness and wickedness. Nevertheless, this is just what you advise it to do. I know that the leaders of the democratic party are but in keeping with their character, when they go forward in this undertaking—for there is no wrong, however flagrant, which they hesitate to perpetrate, if only the interests of their party call for the perpetration. But I also know that whoever else can consistently have part in this cruelty and baseness, a man of honor should refuse to stain himself with it. Let me, in this connection, say that since I have not, for between thirty and forty years, belonged to any one of the great political parties of the country, my speaking against the democratic party cannot be attributed to a party spirit.

Third, and when you surrendered, how little *did* you apprehend that you would claim, as you do in your letter, " their rights under the constitution," for those who had defied it and trampled it under foot. Preposterous claim! They have no rights at all under the constitution. As well might a devil in hell plead his rights under the Bible he has scouted. They have no rights under any law, save the law of war—no rights but those which the conqueror is bound, in justice and humanity, to concede to the conquered. Scarcely anything in the republican party has disgusted me more than its occasional loose talk about the *constitutional* mode of settling matters between the north and the south. The word " constitution," should never have been spoken between the north and the south until the war between them had ceased, and the return of peace had been mutually recognized. The war is not yet ended ; and there can never be peace in our land, until this alliance between northern democracy and southern pro-slavery shall be effectually and forever broken up. Never was their alliance closer than now ; and never was their purpose to crush the negro deeper or more malignant than now.

If the Southern uprising amounted to no more than a rebellion, then all involved in it were rebels and traitors. Then all of them had, still, rights under the constitution—especially and emphatically, the right to be punished under it. But if it is, as you assert, and as, in numberless arguments I have asserted, that this uprising attained to the dimensions and dignity of a civil war, then did it pass from under the constitution, and take its place under the " Law of War." Of course, it did not surprise me to find the northern democratic leaders telling the south, that she was still under the constitution. No falsehood, no baseness, on their part can surprise me. But, I confess, that it did surprise me to find high-minded southern gentlemen accepting this version of the matter; and thus degrading their valorous and mighty movement into a mere rebellion ; and, thus, with their own hands, putting halters around their own necks, by which to be hung as traitors, whenever the government might choose to hang them.   Respectfully yours,

GERRIT SMITH.

P. S.--In looking over what I have written, I see that I have not so much as mentioned the name of your presidential candidate. But the omission is not important. For, in the first place, there is scarcely a possibility that the Seymour and Blair ticket will be elected ; and, in the next place, if it should be, Mr. Seymour would not be President. In that event, the shedding of blood would, as was as frankly as brutally foretold by Mr. Blair, be the policy of the democratic party. But the gentle nature, bland manners and persuasive lips of Mr. Seymour would be entirely out of harmony with this barbarous policy. Whatever the difficulties to be disposed of, and however hard the knots to be untied, his reliance will ever be upon Blarney instead of Blood. Hence, Mr. Seymour, even if elected President, would not be the President. He would have either to stand aside, or be put aside. If this murder-party, which has, within the last three years, murdered for their political opinions, more than a thousand men at the south, shall come to be in the ascendant all over the land, murder may be well-nigh as common in the north as in the south. Human life in this country would be made cheap by the success of the party which, not in spite, but in consequence of his murderous programme, nominated General Blair for Vice President—ay, and emphatically, for President also.

The triumphant election of General Grant to the Presidency, in 1868, with Schuyler Colfax as his second, seemed the natural conclusion of the war. In his hands, one might expect the northern interests to be safe. It might be presumed that the man who had brought the conflict to a successful close, would guard, better than any civilian could do, the results which the war obtained. The crushing defeat of the democratic party justified the belief, at all events the hope, that the principles with which it had so strangely allied itself, were expelled from the political arena, and would no more dare to lift their serpent heads. Four years of peace, with an administration pledged to justice towards the freedmen, to equity towards the south, to honesty towards the national creditors, to the law of righteousness and the industries of peace, would, it might be confidently pre-

13*

dicted, suffice to place the country in a condition to make good its noblest pledges to the civilized world. In his usual outspoken way, Gerrit Smith congratulated the new President:

Peterboro, November 4, 1868.

PRESIDENT GRANT:

Honored and Dear Sir — Pardon this letter. Pardon my irrepressible impatience to write it. I learn to-day, that you are made President of the United States: and I cannot wait, even until tomorrow, to say to you what my whole soul urges me to say to you.

Before the election, your exhortation to your countrymen was: " Let us have Peace ! " To this exhortation, as sublime as it is concise, their reply, in the voice of the election, is also, " Let us have Peace ! " What you then asked of them, they now ask of you. What you then called on them to do, they have now put it in your power to do, and now call on you to do.

What, however, is the peace which you asked for, and which in turn, you are asked for ? Is it of a superficial and evanescent character ? or is it that deep and enduring peace, whose foundations are in nothing short of nature and reason, justice and religion ? The pride of race, of rank, of wealth has ever stood in the way of realizing this true peace. The pride of race is by far the greatest of these obstacles, and it is of this one that I would speak to you. Our New England fathers brought much religion with them to America. Unhappily, it was more of the Jewish than the Christian type ; for never was there a people in whom so much as in the Jews, the pride of race was controlling, contemptuous and cruel. These fathers saw in the American tribes only another set of heathen : and the laws of the Jews in dealing with *their* heathen became (more, it is true, in spirit than in letter), the laws for dealing with ours. By these laws the most learned and influential of the New England divines insisted that the family of even King Philip should be adjudged—of that King Philip, who wept when he heard that an Indian had shed the blood of a white man. The wife of Philip was sold into slavery, and into a foreign land. These Judaized teachers and judges, instead of entering upon the case with human hearts, pored upon the bloodiest pages of the Old Testament ; and instead of imbuing themselves with the spirit of that Blessed One to whom the Samaritan was as dear as the Jew, and in whose religion " there is neither Greek nor Jew, circumcision nor uncircumcision, Barbarian,

Scythian, bond nor free," set their revenge all ablaze by gazing at the worst examples of revenge.

There has never been a thorough peace between our white man and our red man. The lack of it is, doubtless, to be traced more or less, to this mistake of the white man in regarding himself as of the heaven-loved and heaven-favored race, and the red man as of the heaven-hated and heaven-cursed race. Perhaps we are never to have peace with our Indians. Perhaps no however just treatment of them on our part could avail to regain their confidence. There is but too much reason to fear that this confidence is lost forever; and that, in their utter distrust and undying hatred of us, they will continue to dash themselves against our superior power, until little or nothing shall remain of them. How different from all this would it have been had we and our ancestors, instead of indulging this pride of race, cordially recognized the equality of all men in the sight of their common Father !

Even more proudly and cruelly have we borne ourselves toward the black man than toward the red man. Very extensively has the belief obtained among us, that the Jewish part of our religion authorized us to make not only " a servant of servants " but property of him, and to strip him as bare of rights as is any kind of property. In that monstrous side of our religion we found, or fancied we found, that God had laid peculiarly heavy curses upon the black man.

Alas, what sorrow has come to our country from the indulgence of this murderous caste spirit toward the black man ! For many generations he has wet with his tears and blood the soil he has tilled. At length came the war, which was the natural, if not indeed necessary, culmination of our guilty nation's sufferings—a war costing many thousands of millions of dollars and filling several hundred thousands of graves. This war is not yet ended—and, mainly, for the reason that the indulgence of this hatred of race is not yet ended. So rife and so ruling is this hatred, that murder is committed in our nation every day, if not indeed every hour.

Because of this hatred between races, how full of bloody contentions, for centuries, was Spain !—and how disastrous to her in all her subsequent history was the final victory of the Spaniard over the Moor ! How Greeks and Turks have hated and wasted each other ! And how severe and protracted has been the oppression of the Irish because they were Irish instead of English ! Until the Irish and English shall know each other as men rather than as Irishmen and Englishmen, there cannot be a sound and permanent peace between them. The treatment of the Chinese immigrants upon our western coast comes, also, of this pride of race. How cruel and infamous that treatment!

We often hear even men of culture declare that, in a war between their own and another race, they would take the side of their own, be it or be it not the side of justice. How base is such a declaration! On the other hand, how beautiful is the following of justice whithersoever it leads, and the honoring of it in whatever variety or section of our grand common humanity it may be found.

The chief thing for which I took up my pen was to remind you of the deep desire of many hundred thousands who voted for you, to have your administration signalized by its cordial recognition of the equal rights of all races of men: by its downright and effective assertion that no man loses rights by being born in a skin of one color instead of another; and by its faithful, warm-hearted and successful endeavors to rid our country of this low and brutal antagonism of races. What your administration shall be in other respects is of comparatively little consequence. Confident, however, may all be that, if right in this most comprehensive and vital respect, it will be right in every other essential one. No wonder that the democratic party was in favor of robbing the nation's creditors. The party that can rob a race of all the rights of manhood, and build and maintain itself on such robbery, is of course capable of every other robbery, because every other is infinitely less than this sweeping one. I said that this party *was* in favor of robbery—for it is, now, a party of the past only. It was not killed by the vote of yesterday. It was killed when slavery was killed. In losing slavery it lost its tap root, its indispensable nourishment. Its partial resurrection was solely because of the prospect of the reanimation of slavery. The prospect of this reanimation was blighted yesterday; and this pro-slavery democratic party has therefore fallen back into its grave, never again to rise, nor even to attempt to rise, from it. Many a " Democratic Party " there may, hereafter, be in our country—but no one of them will be a pro-slavery party, and, therefore, no one of them will be like this party, which was killed several years ago, and which lost yesterday all hope of a resurrection. Yesterday's vote has left no room for a pro-slavery party, either now or hereafter. Most emphatically true is this, if the measures and influence of your administration shall be withering and fatal to the caste-spirit—to that spirit which, more than all things else, begets and fosters slavery.

Entirely reasonable is the confidence that your administration, if it maintain the equal rights of all our races of men, will not fail of responding to all the essential claims of justice. Of no wrong to the nation's creditors will it be guilty. For universal suffrage it will be unyielding—not merely because, as the right to life, liberty, and property is natural, so participation in the choice of those at whose official disposal these possessions so largely lie, must also be a natural right; but, because all have seen that nothing short of the ballot in the hands of those who have recently emerged from slavery can save them from being thrust back into it. The governments which President Johnson set up in the south recognized no political rights in black men : and straightway these governments set to work to reënslave them. It matters not, as regards my argument, that this new slavery was not literal chattel-slavery. It has none of the alleviations incident to chattel-slavery, and was, on the whole, more oppressive and cruel.

In this connection let me add that, far above all the other good which will come from the purging of the nation of this malignant and cruel caste-spirit, will be the removal thereby of the greatest ob-stacle in the way of the Christ-religion. For the spirit of this religion cannot dwell in the bosom that cherishes the hatred of race. And, then, what so much as the spirit of this religion of nature and rea-son, justice and goodness, prepares the bosom to welcome sound political principles and cultivate sound political sentiments?

I saw, in your letter of August 1863, that you had not, in your early life, made human rights one of your studies. Nevertheless, that, in the high office to which you were chosen yesterday, you will prove yourself to be their enlightened, impartial and successful de-fender, I cannot doubt. For like the martyred and immortal Lin-coln, you are above the stupidity of not being able to change, and above the weakness of being ashamed to change. Indeed, while in your letter to which I have referred, you say that formerly you had not been " an abolitionist—not even what could be called anti-slavery "—you do, in the same letter, acknowledge yourself to have advanced so far as to insist on the abolition of slavery, and on there being no peace which permits the existence of slavery. Moreover, in another of your letters written in the same month, you reach the altitude of declaring that " Human Liberty is the only foundation of Human Government." Better still is your recent declaration to Mr. Colfax that, in your Presidency, " we shall have the strong arm of the executive, representing the will and majesty of a mighty people, declaring and insuring to every citizen, black or white, rich or poor, be he humble or exalted, the safeguard of the nation, and protecting him from every wrong with the shield of our national strength."

But, best of all to prove your discernment and appreciation of human rights, and your fidelity to them, was your acceptance of your nomination and of the righteous principles of the republican party. The grandest of all these principles is not no-slavery—but universal suffrage : for the ballot is the mightiest protection of its possessor not only from slavery but from every other wrong. That universal suffrage is one of the principles of the republican party is manifest from its being set up in the District of Columbia. Had this party as clear a constitutional right to set it up in the loyal states, all those states would, also, have been blessed with it. The acting of Congress on the question of suffrage in the disloyal states was under the Law of War—was the exercise of the right of the conqueror.

Nor in your early life did you take the lead in saving a nation. But, when the time came for you to do so, you did so ; and did so successfully, triumphantly. Nor in early life, had you heard the call to help drive out of your country this mean and murderous antagonism of races. Since then however, you have heard it, and have been obeying it. And now, safely can your country rely on your wisdom and justice for what more she needs at your hands. The qualities so eminent in you, have faithfully and fully met all the claims which your country has in quick succession laid upon you. Not less faithfully and fully will they meet all her remaining claims upon you. And well too, may she trust that He who has brought you into the Chief Magistracy " for such a time as this," will both show you your true work, and give you head, heart and hand to it.

I cannot forbear saying that no small ground of my rejoicing in your election is your charitable judgment and generous treatment of the south. Warmly did I approve the easy terms on which you allowed General Lee to surrender. Your subsequent report of the temper of the south, after a too hasty tour through it, showed that you were capable of forming a charitable judgment of even a recent foe. Far too favorable as this report was thought to be, it nevertheless would have been borne out in a high degree, had not these bad men amongst the leaders of the northern democracy held back the south from accepting the situation, and pushed her forward to the indecent and preposterous inversion of claiming for the conquered the right to dictate ᵗerms to the conqueror. And how monstrous these claims ! Nothing less than that the nation should again put under the ᵗeet of the wicked white men, the black men who had taken up arms to save her ! No fear need be entertained that, in your measures for peaceable and affectionate relations between the north and the south, you will lay all the blame of our civil war on the south. Inasmuch as the north is scarcely less responsible than the south for slavery, you will judge and rightly too, that she is scarcely less responsible for the war, which grew out of it. Wherever there is a man who, because he became the enemy of his country, was subjected to political disabilities, there is a man whom you would have relieved of them as soon as there is proof that he has again become its friend. But, on the other hand, you will regard no man as the friend of the country, who wars upon his neighbor because that neighbor is from a race different from his own, or because that neighbor stands up for the equal rights of all the races of men.

I close my letter with saying that I like to believe that the motto of your administration will be : " A man's a man." The spirit of such a motto pervading our land will make it a land of peace. The white man and the black man will be at peace with each other ; the north and the south ;—and this peace, because founded in unchangeable nature instead of shifting human expediency,—in the Divine constitution of things instead of human and conventional arrangements, will be a thorough and a permanent peace. I scarcely need add that the identifying of your administration with the sublime and Christian doctrine of the oneness of the children of men— with the sublime and Christian doctrine that every man is every other man's brother and God the common and equal Father of them all—will not only make ours the happiest nation on earth, but will make it to all other nations a surpassingly grand and influential example of casting down the barriers of race and setting up in their stead the law of impartial justice and the reign of fraternal love.

With the highest respect for your virtues, and the deepest gratitude for your services to our beloved country.

GERRIT SMITH.

CHAPTER VIII.

THE PEACE.

ALL problems are simple to the Idealist. From the mount of beatitudes one looks out on a world unclouded by sorrow or sin. " Blessed are the pure in spirit, for theirs is the kingdom of heaven." " Blessed are the meek, for they shall inherit the earth." " Blessed are the persecuted for righteousness' sake." " Blessed are the pure in heart." Gerrit Smith's panacea for the ills of the time was Love,—love for the southern enemy. If we only could love to order! If simply, we were something else than men and women! If we were past being human! Or if the prophet had the power to make men fulfil his prophecy!

Dates are of small consequence here. Principles are not regulated by epochs, do not consult time tables. Some of the words we shall quote were written at the close of the war, others several years later, but the tone of them all is the same. The declarations of principle lack variety.

" How unseemly not to say how intensely hypocritical, for the north to punish the south for holding the doctrine of secession, when those eminent advocates of it, Jefferson and Madison, have ever been as high political authorities for it at the north as at the south; and when too, the doctrine had become so popular at the north that some of her national conventions endorsed it, and how unseemly, not to say how intensely hypocritical, for the north to punish the south for putting the doctrine in practice! For what impelled the south to do so but the spirit of slavery ? that spirit for the generating and fostering of which the north is scarcely less responsible than the south ? Nay, in the light of her smaller and less direct temptation, she is far more wickedly responsible for that spirit. . .

" Were the north penitent, she would instantly recoil from the proposition to punish the south. For she would see, in the light of such facts as I have glanced at, her partnership with the south in the political fallacies and moral wrongs which have brought this great sorrow on the land. . . .

" There is nothing in this connection in which the north appears worse than in her endeavors by the pulpit and the press, by popular meetings and by visiting committees, to fire the President with vengeance. How she repeats and gloats over his admission that treason is a crime to be punished ! No one denies that treason is a crime—a great crime—and that, as a general proposition, it should be punished—severely punished. But in this case there is no treason to punish. I do not say that there is no moral treason in this case. Of this there is an abundance. What I say is that there is no treason in the eye of law. When the Rebellion broke out, all the rebels were traitors ; and we had the legal right to punish them as such. But, however slowly and reluctantly, we nevertheless became at last, convinced that we could not carry on the contest and save our country unless we allowed these rebels to come up from traitors in a Rebellion into enemies in a civil war,—and a civil war, too, differing in respect to none of its rights from a war with a foreign nation."

From a letter to Chief Justice Chase, dated May 28, 1866 :

" I have said that we must deal with the south in the spirit of impartial justice. We must also deal with her in the spirit of great generosity and great love. We must claim no indemnity for the past. We must exact no unnecessary security for the future. We must subject her to no changes and no disabilities which are not indispensable. If the breaking up of her large landed estates to parcel them out to her white and black poor is not demanded by her people, we must not insist on it. If, by putting the ballot into the hands of her blacks, it will not be necessary, in order to save her, to withhold it for a season, from her whites who were involved in the guilt of the war, then are there strong reasons why we should not insist upon the probation. One thing more, the south is poor, and the north is still rich. Would it be too large an expression of paternal love, to save the south for some five or ten years from the imposition of direct national taxes ? "

That such views were interesting to prominent men of various schools of opinion, and were thought of sufficient importance to be presented formally to the public, is proved by the correspondence printed herewith :

June, 1865.

GERRIT SMITH, Esq., New York :

Dear Sir, — The events which, with increasing emphasis are inscribing our national history, attract and impress the public mind. We think that information is needed and counsel required. We know that the interest which you have felt in the conflict which is passed, continues to the stages of its pacification and close.

Understanding your willingness to communicate with your fellow citizens on national topics, we would be pleased could you address a public meeting in this city, at the Cooper Institute, on the evening of next Thursday, the 8th instant, on the present attitude of the country.

HORACE GREELEY,	C. GODFREY GUNTHER,
E. H. CHAPIN,	HENRY WARD BEECHER,
RICH'D O'GORMAN,	DAVID DUDLEY FIELD,
SAM'L L. M. BARLOW,	HENRY W. BELLOWS,
HIRAM KETCHUM.	

Bearing in mind the sharp controversy between Gerrit Smith and Horace Greeley on the subject of the course of the former, when in Congress, in relation to the Nebraska Bill;—remembering that S. L. M. Barlow was a member of the " Democratic Vigilance Association," which arraigned and would have tried Gerrit Smith for treasonable complicity with John Brown;—considering the keen criticism that Gerrit Smith had visited on Henry Ward Beecher for his eulogium on "Stonewall" Jackson, and for his impulsive expressions of sentimental compassion with the south; taking into account the political attitude of other signers of the invitation, this tribute is remarkable. Mr. Smith accepted it without hesitation.

Gentlemen — An invitation from such names to make a speech on "National Affairs" I regard as a great honor. Gladly do I accept it. GERRIT SMITH.

The speech was given, and it contained a repetition of the views with which we are familiar on the causes of the war, the past and present relations of the north and the south, the duty of conciliation, reconstruction by the frank recognition of the rights of the freedmen. A speech of like purport was delivered in the autumn of the same year at Chicago. A long letter to William Lloyd Garrison and Wendell Phillips on the attitude of the abolitionists toward the impending issues, dated September 12, 1865, puts the question from their point of view, and contends, 1st. That the nation is perishing because she persists in not letting the negro into the human family, 2d. That the horrors of the worst of wars —a war of races—await the south in return for the nation's crime of withholding the ballot from the black man. Letters to Thaddeus Stevens, Charles Sumner, Herschel V. Johnson and numerous communications to newspapers are evidence that this matter was uppermost in his mind.

In the spring of 1867, Mr. Smith made a remarkable speech in the city of Richmond, in which he reiterated his cardinal belief that "love will everywhere, and even in the province of statesmanship, prove itself to be 'the fulfilling of the law.'" The north and the south must be bound together in mutual love. The south must not try to get away from the moderate terms imposed by the conpueror, but must in good faith accept the situa-

tion, and make not the worst, but the best of it. The
north must deal with the south justly and generously ;
must honestly admit her complicity in guilt, and confess
her share of responsibility ; must feel deep pity for the
south in view of her impoverishment and desolation, and
do what she can to heal her wounds, by handsome appropriations of money and by exempting the prostrate
states from taxation. The whites, remembering the un-
paid toil of the blacks, their suffering and tears, should
in every just and reasonable way, assist them to secure
homes of their own, sell them land at moderate prices,
make them welcome to the ballot, provide them with
schools, and promote impartial legislation. The blacks,
remembering that their former masters inherited the institution that had so lately been broken up, and bearing
in mind the lasting influence of prejudice and the stub-
bornness of habit, must be patient, considerate, gentle,
ready to believe that the wrongs of the past will not be
perpetuated in the future.

"Do not cultivate, nor let others cultivate in you, a spirit of jealousy. Far better will it be both for your own temper and the temper
of your best friends, that you generously confide in them. Let me
here say, to the end of guarding you against an undiscriminating and
unwise confidence : Trust no man, white or black, vote for no man,
be he of the republican or democratic party, who does not acquiesce
in your possession of the ballot, and rejoice in your deliverance from
the yoke of slavery. Respect yourselves and you are safe. Failing
of this, you are lost. Give no countenance to confiscation. . . .
A numerously signed petition to Congress from the blacks of the
south to relieve the old leaders of the south of their political disabilities, would be one of the handsomest and happiest things in the
world. . . . Black men of the south, give no occasion for even
your enemies to call you rioters. Never, never again, let a black
man disgrace himself and mortify his northern and southern friends,
by either an open or a sly part in a mob. . . . Keep clear of

rum. Keep clear of it if you would keep clear of riots. Keep clear
of it, if you would have homes of your own. I would that all negroes
kept themselves so clear of rum as to make *a man who doesn't drink
rum* a suitable definition of a negro."

The first condition of peace, in Gerrit Smith's judgment, should .be that "no people in the rebel states
shall ever either lose or gain civil or political rights by
reason of their race or origin." The next condition
should be

"that our black allies in the south—those saviours of our nation—
shall share with their poor white neighbors in the subdivisions of the
large landed estates of the south. And this, not merely to compensate them for what we owe them; and not merely because they are
destitute of property; and not merely because they have ever been
robbed of their earnings, and denied the acquisition of property;—
but, more than all these, because the title to the whole soil of the
south is equitably in them who have ever tilled it, and profusely shed
upon it their sweat and tears and blood. There are who would have
our soldiers also, share in these subdivisions. But, besides that such
a quartering of soldiers and strangers upon the south would be offensive to her; we are abundantly able to reward them otherwise."

The third and last condition should be, "that the rebel masses
shall not, for, say a dozen years, be allowed access to the ballot box,
or be eligible to office; and that the like restrictions be for life on
their political and military leaders. . . . I do not say that I
would have all black men vote, I certainly would, were the rebels
allowed to vote. But with the proposed restrictions on rebel suffrage, I would be quite content that none, black or white, who cannot read their vote, should be permitted to cast it. As a general
principle, and in ordinary circumstances, I would not have the ability
to read a qualification for voting."

The adoption of Gerrit Smith's doctrine of the ballot
would have prevented the disgrace and demoralization
of the past ten years. He contended that, in a normally
constituted society, the right to the ballot was universal
and natural, not a creation of the social state, not a conventional privilege, but a prerogative incident to human-

ity, corresponding with the right to life and property, like that unlimited, though, like that, alienable for cause. But the condition of the southern States after the war was in every respect abnormal ;—the whites were in a mood of anger and rebellion ; the blacks were too recently, as a rule, emancipated from a disabling and demoralizing servitude. In such a predicament, only the calm and intelligent, of either race, were capable of voting judiciously. The only test of calmness and intelligence being some measure of education, an ability to read became indispensable as a prerequisite to the ballot ;—an inadequate test, to be sure, but the best at command. The application of it would disfranchise many whites and exclude many blacks, but the disfranchisement would neutralize the exclusion, and the admission of both races on equal terms would place both upon the same plane of advantage, and ensure, so far as any thing could, their mutual consideration. The point to be gained was the elevation of the blacks to the same political level with the whites ; the recognition of the common manhood, the abolition of the principle of caste. The thought of placing the blacks *above* the whites, of reducing the whites to an inferiority,— the notion that astute politicians hit on, and acted on, and committed the ruling party to—was not entertained by this " visionary," who was satisfied with the admission that one man was *as good* as another, without addition of the clause " and better too."

Gerrit Smith had no fear lest the blacks, still being under the influence of the whites whom they had so long served as a superior race, should vote as their former masters advised.

" Why should they not ? When the blacks shall be possessed of the ballot, they will be respected by the whites, and will be advised by them to do but what is respectable. The ballot in the hand of the black man will gain for him the respect of the white man ; and in return for this respect will be the confidence of the black man in the white man. And so full will be this confidence that he will follow the superior intelligence of the white man at the polls as well as elsewhere. Say not that he will follow it to wrong. For the putting of the ballot in the hand of the black man will extensively have the effect to bring the white man to consecrate that superior intelligence to the right. It is by this way, far more than any other, that the southern white can be brought up into a just man."

THE GOLDEN RULE AGAIN.—The recognition of the African's manhood was the beginning, middle and end of the true plan of reconstruction. That involved every thing else ; and the symbol of the recognition of the African's manhood was, in Gerrit Smith's eyes, the bestowal on him of the ballot, on a perfect equality with the whites, the conditions of loyalty and intelligence being the same with both. The ballot meant responsibility, self-reliance and self-respect. It was a summons to independent action, a call to the school, the reading room, the newspaper. It was a lien on civilization. Every gift was subordinate in value to this. Even the Civil Rights Bill was of secondary importance, for all the Civil Rights Bill promised to secure would be won by the ballot, and rights won were better than privileges conferred. In a letter to Henry Wilson, dated March 26, 1866, Mr. Smith says with his usual emphasis :

" The Civil Rights Bill, like much other legislation in our country, and in the world, proceeds on the false principle that government is to be the main reliance for the protection of its subjects. But the true principle is that in the main, they are to be left to be their own protectors. Now, in a Republic, the great means of self-protection is the ballot. Hence, when our government robs one of our races of the ballot or suffers the robbery, all in vain will it attempt to make up for the robbery by promising protection to the victims. The Civil Rights Bill cannot serve the black man in place of the ballot. But the ballot in his hands would make the bill superfluous.

"Can you believe that the 'Civil Rights Bill' will suffice to protect the negro and the white loyalist of the south? Strange if you can. You well know that no laws sufficed to protect from being sold into slavery your Massachusetts black seamen, who, in their lawful pursuits were so unfortunate as to touch southern soil. You well know, too, that Massachusetts sent her eminent citizens, Mr. Hoar and Mr. Hubbard to the south to look after the rights of these outraged seamen ; and that notwithstanding the abundant and even organic law on the side of those commissioners, they had to fly back to the north to save themselves from being murdered. Do you say that the Rebellion has improved the temper of the south? It has made that temper much worse. Never before was her hatred of the negro and the white loyalist so intense. . . . Rely on that bill or upon anything short of impartial suffrage for peace and justice at the south, and there will be no peace or justice there."

This was written in a mood of despondency. The hope of the philanthropist is weakening. He is anticipating nothing better than persistence in the foolishness of inhumanity, and the defeat of the efforts made by the friends of the negro. He does not believe that "a God of Justice" will permit the nation to prosper in such wickedness or to long survive in defiance of the law of equity. "Her survival would supply the atheist with a new argument."

Had suffrage been honestly granted to the blacks by the States as well as by the National government, and practically secured to him, this view of the Civil Rights Bill would not probably have been modified. But the right of suffrage was embarrassed by conditions which rendered it virtually inoperative. Political casuistry found a distinction with a difference between national and state citizenship. By virtue of this discrimination, the rights conferred by national citizenship could be defeated by the laws of any state not republican in its Constitution. No black man or woman, having occasion to go to Washington on business, could pass through one of the old slave states without encountering obstacles of a formidable if not absolutely disconcerting and forbidding character. The owner of horses would let no vehicle or beast; the inns refused hospitality; the taverns refused refreshment; the story told was not credited; the proofs of national citizenship were not accepted. The blacks were liable to annoyances that none but the most resolute could face, and to insults such as none but the most hardened or the most saintly could submit to. At home, where they were known, the obstacles though less formidable were serious, and to people so recently emancipated and still timid, were discouraging. Evidently, the boon of the ballot was one of doubtful value in such cases, indeed, in all cases, and the friends of the negro, however hostile to the paternal theory of government, were driven to the resort of additional and special regulation in behalf of the freedmen. Hence the zeal for the " Civil Rights Bill " that grew so hot and strong in the breasts of anti-slavery people. Gerrit Smith at last felt it as much as anybody, though he did not speak of it in terms as unqualified as some of its partisans employed. He disclaimed for it all bearing on matters purely *social*—matters that concerned personal preference, private partialities, likes and dislikes, the sympathies and antipathies natural to temperament, culture, condition, blood and breeding. The power he claimed for the bill was the guarantee of full protection for the blacks in the exercise of the rights bestowed on

14

them as citizens of the United States, the enforcement of this security, where such enforcement was necessary, by the authority of the national government. The repeated outrages against the freedmen in the south excited his indignation. Not so much however, as the outrages against the blacks, at the north, in places where the spirit of caste still prevailed as it had prevailed before the war. The Military Academy at West Point was the chief of these places. The spirit of the south was, and always had been, military. The southern whites were trained in the use of arms, and in the habit of carrying deadly weapons. The practice of duelling was popular in their best circles; their institutions rested on force. Like all "barbarians," as Mathew Arnold calls the nobility of England, and as one is fairly entitled to call the *quasi* nobility of Virginia and the Carolinas, they employed their leisure in war and the chase. The Academy at West Point was, as a rule, filled with the sons of the southern gentry. The south furnished the large proportion of cadets; it inspired the institution with its sentiments; it kept alive the distinctions of caste, and the notions of "honor," which distinguish the army and navy all over the earth.

In his speech of January 18, 1854, in Congress, on the bill making appropriations for the Academy, Mr. Smith spoke earnestly against the war-spirit, implored the house not to pass any war-bills, and deprecated the existence of such institutions as that at West Point on the ground that they perpetuated the enormities of war by making war a profession. Not that he would, if he could, abolish military and naval schools where fit men should receive the scientific, literary and moral education that would qualify them for effective service against the enemies of the human race; he believed such schools to be necessary, but he would have them detached from the war-system; schools for the humanities not for the inhumanities; schools for the maintenance of the principles of peace; schools where the arts of peace should be cultivated, and the sacredness of peace should be respected; where the civility which is the soul of peace should be studied, and the brotherhood which is the bond of peace, should be practiced; schools of gentlemanliness and character. Such the Academy at West Point never had been, and never promised to be. If this was his feeling before the war, it was more intense afterward, when the south, beaten in the field, insisted on maintaining its social supremacy in places where it had never been disputed. The mean persecutions of the black cadets by the whites, simply on the ground of race, aroused in him a hot indignation. He called now for the complete suppression of the Academy as a nursery of the caste spirit. Its habit of scorn was incorrigible. Cruelty, cowardice and contempt were inseparable from it. Its existence implied the perpetual violation of principles which lie at the foundation of republican institutions. Neither religion nor society can be what they should be in America so long as such an institution is maintained by government, for its maintenance by government is its countenance by the nation. New principles must take on new forms, and new forms cannot be fashioned while old forms are accepted. Philanthropy is radical or it is nothing.

Gerrit Smith's offer to put his name to the bail bond for Jefferson Davis brought on him as well as on Mr.

Greeley a storm of abuse from the patriots, so called, of the north. But no intelligent person, who had the least understanding of the men, was surprised ; and no sound-hearted person, capable of distinguishing between partisanship and principle, had reason to be offended. As this is a point of historical importance, the following papers will be of interest :

Private.   Office of the Tribune, New York, August 22, 1866.

To the Hon. GERRIT SMITH :

Dear Sir, — I enclose a memorial of which Mr. Greeley is the author, and which I send to you at his request, hoping that it will receive your signature also. It explains itself. It is proposed with no mere political purpose, but in the cause of humanity and justice ; and therefore it is designed that it shall be subscribed by those only who have been persistent friends of the black man and who urged his emancipation. I trust, and in this hope Mr. Greeley shares, that it will be promptly signed by you.

Let me say for myself that I know it would add greatly to the efficiency of the memorial if it were presented by yourself personally to the President. And if you could go at once to Washington on this mission you would, whether the prayer is successful or not, do an act which would have a happy and healing effect upon the prostrate people of the south, and be another step in that magnanimous cause which has already won for you their abiding gratitude.

Please send the memorial to Mr. Greeley, Tribune office, by *return mail* and believe me,

Yours with great esteem,

GEO. SHEA.

Of counsel for Jefferson Davis.

                                        Peterboro, Aug. 24, 1866.

GEORGE SHEA, Esq. :

Dear Sir, — This morning's mail brings me your esteemed and welcome letter, accompanied by a memorial to the President. Without hesitancy and with great satisfaction I have put my name to the memorial.

Were I convinced (which I cannot be) that one of so little influence as my own with public men, could by visiting the President, promote the object of the memorial, I would not delay to visit him.

Some one of a name and faith less offensive than mine, must be the bearer of the memorial. I venture however, to address a note to the President which, as you and Mr. Greeley may prefer, can be sent or withheld. I am, dear sir,

Very respectfully yours, etc.,

GERRIT SMITH.

MEMORIAL.

TO THE PRESIDENT OF THE UNITED STATES:

The undersigned earnestly solicit your attention to the condition of Jefferson Davis, a citizen of Mississippi, now held a prisoner of state in Fortress Monroe.

We understand these to be facts : that Jefferson Davis was captured on the 11th day of May 1865, and has for over fifteen months been a close prisoner in the fortress aforesaid.

That he stands publicly charged on the highest authority with the atrocious crime of conspiracy to murder our late President Lincoln, and is popularly accounted guilty of other high crimes and misdemeanors.

That he persistently and vehemently declares himself not guilty of any of the offenses laid to his charge, and most earnestly demands an early and impartial trial on any indictment that has been or may be found against him.

That learned and able counsel believe him to be innocent at least of the more heinous offense wherewith he is charged, and unite in the demand that he be speedily accorded a fair trial by a court of civil judicature.

That though he was fifteen months in prison awaiting and calling for a trial, he has not even been indicted except for treason, nor can we learn that even an attempt has been made to indict him on any other charge.

That his counsel have duly endeavored by all the means known to the law to bring his case before some competent legal tribunal for adjudication whether by writ of habeas corpus or otherwise, and have been baffled and defeated therein.

That they have been unable to obtain from the legal representatives of the government even a promise that he should be put on trial at some specified future day.

That his health is suffering from his protracted confinement, so that his physicians deem his life endangered thereby. Believing these to be facts, the undersigned, having neither personal nor political affinities with the prisoner, but on the contrary utterly and intensely adverse to the political views which have led him to his present position, do yet most respectfully represent, in the interest alike of humanity, public justice and the rights of person secured to every citizen by law, that Jefferson Davis the prisoner aforesaid should either be speedily arraigned and tried, or else admitted to bail.

We are your fellow-citizens.

Dated Aug. 14, 1866.

Peterboro, N. Y., August 24, 1866.

PRESIDENT JOHNSON:

Honored Sir — I have this day subscribed a memorial to yourself in behalf of Jefferson Davis. I have done so with great satisfaction; for I deem his very long confinement in prison, without a trial, an insult to the south, a very deep injustice to himself, and a no less deep dishonor to the government and the country.

I trust that Mr. Davis may either have a speedy trial or be admitted to bail. There are many men who have no sympathy with his political views, and who opposed slavery as strenuously as he upheld it, that would eagerly become his bail. I am one of them.

Your obedient servant,

GERRIT SMITH.

This was strictly in accordance with the belief that none of the leaders of the Rebellion could be legally punished or tried for treason. The acknowledgment of the state of war took them out of the category of conspirators against the government, and ranked them with strangers or foreigners. This point Mr. Smith had argued in a letter to Chief Justice Chase, dated May 28, 1866, wherein he fortified his position by the authority of Hallam, Vattel, Welcker, Macaulay, Lieber. The position was natural to him. His religious, moral and personal sentiments enforced it upon him. The law of love constrained him, so that he could not have done otherwise. Horace Greeley was notoriously a politician, and therefore exposed to the suspicion of political intentions. But both men were notoriously philanthropists, and were on this ground unassailable.

It was not out of character for these men to plead for kindness towards " Ku Klux " prisoners, as the letters which follow, written at the suggestion of Mr. Greeley, did.

Long Branch, N. J., July 28, 1872.

Dear Sir, — Your letter of the 9th inst. in relation to your visit to the Ku Klux convicts in the Albany penitentiary was duly received. I should have acknowledged the receipt of it and of the copy or copies of your admirable speech to your neighbors of the 22d of June, earlier. I shall send your letter to the Attorney General, with directions to send some one to Albany to visit those prisoners, and from the report made, together with the testimony against them, in his possession, submit such recommendation in regard to them as he may think proper. Any pardon now before the North Carolina election, would be misinterpreted. I therefore should not like to act now. But if any innocent persons are being punished, or any whose punishment is not calculated to spare innocent persons for the future from the acts of the K. Ks, I have no desire to keep them longer in confinement.

My oft expressed desire is that all citizens, white or black, native or foreign born, may be left free in all parts of our common country to vote, speak or act, in obedience to law, without intimidation or ostracism on account of views, color or nativity. With these privileges secured, there is no particular offence that I would not advocate forgiveness and forgetfulness of, so far as the latter is possible.

I thank you very kindly for giving me the result of your observations during your visit to these prisoners, and also for the many kind words I have read of your utterance towards my official acts.

With great respect, your obedient servant,

U. S. GRANT.

Long Branch, N. J., Aug. 26, 1872.

Hon. GERRIT SMITH :

My Dear Sir, — I received your letter enclosing applications for the pardon of the Ku Klux prisoners, and have handed the petition to the Attorney General, who is daily in receipt of many similar ones, but who thinks, with you, that such pardons should be few and far between.

Please accept my thanks for your kindness and thoughtfulness in sending copies of your letter. The President has read, with great interest, all you have uttered in regard to the present campaign, and has been deeply touched by the kind mention you have made of him. It really seems now that honest men are arranging themselves on one side and knaves on the other ; and during Gen. Grant's next four years, he will not only not be likely to appoint any rascals to office, but none of them will have sufficient political affiliation with him to be in a condition to ask him for office.

Very respectfully and truly yours,
HORACE PORTER.

The note that follows seems to be in reply to a letter of abuse or of misconception on this subject.

Peterboro, N. Y., August 19, 1872.

Dear Sir, — This evening's mail brings me your letter of the 14th inst. So far from my believing that "a majority of the Ku Klux prisoners now confined at Albany are innocent of any crime," I do not believe that even one of them is innocent. I take it for granted that they all had fair trials and were justly convicted.

There is amongst these prisoners a youth who, because he is hopelessly sick, I should like to have pardoned ; and also a man past middle age who, because of his weak intellect, I would commend to the President's clemency. There is also, an aged man who, perhaps, but only perhaps, should be left in prison not more than a year or two longer.

I can have no part in white-washing Ku Kluxism. I deem it the greatest crime on earth, and the party that upholds it or is identified with it, as the cruelest and worst party on earth.

Respectfully yours,
GERRIT SMITH.

In 1854 Gerrit Smith had favored the acquisition of Cuba as a part of the United States, in the belief that the humanity of republican institutions would redeem the island from its wretched condition under the Spanish laws, and secure the emancipation at once of the whites and the blacks. In 1870, when the question of the acquisition of San Domingo was agitated, his views had changed. The experience of fifteen years, especially the exhibition of the whites, northern and southern, towards the blacks, had satisfied him that the rapacity of the whites was more than a match for the humanity of republican institutions, and that no good to the dwellers in the tropics would come from the annexation of any portion of them to the United States. While he had no prejudice against the intermingling of blacks and whites and saw no objections to it in the nature of things, he had come to think that the joint partnership of blacks and whites in the same soil, and their joint possession of the same territory, could not be fortunate. The blacks, if not enslaved, would be robbed, plundered, crowded out, and at length annihilated. Their only chance for such existence as was to them desirable, lay in their having to themselves the climate and land of the tropics where they lived happily, and where the white races could not live at all, except with the institution of slavery to supply their labor. The President's scheme of annexation therefore had no favor in his sight. On the President's patriotism he cast no reflection; none on his integrity or humanity. That he was making political capital or seeking party diversion, or playing recklessly the game of empire does not seem to have occurred to him. He may have thought that the President's imagination was dazzled by visions of national splendor or national wealth, but that he would willingly sacrifice any great human interest was far from his suspicion. His own conviction was that before annexing new territories we had better learn to establish equal laws over what we had. Expansion northward might be well enough if expansion were necessary, be-

14*

cause in that direction there was legitimate field for conquest over Nature and brute mankind. But expansion southward implied the annihilation of docile races and the robbing of islands which Providence has destined to be homes for the otherwise harmless. The pity for the negro is still uppermost in this man's heart. No national aggrandizement, no national wealth are in his estimation sufficient to compensate for any additional wrong done to these unfortunates.

The condition of the blacks in the United States was far from satisfactory, and excited the philanthropist's utmost solicitude. As the first term of General Grant's administration drew to a close the prospect became appalling. All that the war had accomplished seemed to be at stake. The aspiration to power of the democratic party threatened to overturn the achievements and defeat the hopes of the abolitionists. General Grant, it was felt, could be relied on, at least so far as to maintain the ground already won, and to prevent the undoing of the work the completion whereof was his title to renown. His name was still a powerful one to conjure by. No other roused enthusiasm at all, and it must be under his leadership that the army of the republic must still move on, if victory is finally to perch upon its banners. Gerrit Smith threw himself with his usual ardor into the campaign for Grant's reëlection, deploring and resisting all the efforts that were made to thwart his career, more especially the efforts of the independents to create a diversion in favor of Mr. Greeley, which, he was confident could not succeed as a separate movement, and must strengthen the democrats in proportion as it weakened the republicans.

In judging the conduct of Gerrit Smith during the
years 1871 and 1872, it is but fair to bear in mind the
natural working of his disposition, as illustrated in the
" eccentricities " as they were called, of his earlier career.
He was a man of feeling, and consequently not amena-
ble to the rules of ordinary consistency. His guide was
moral conviction which men of his school dignified by
the title of " natural instincts." He said and did things
in perfect honesty and good will, unconscious of their
effect on others, and careless of their inconsistency with
the act of his previous career. He was not stupid; he
was not deceitful; he was not vacillating. He was simply self-assured. And his self-assurance proceeded from
that reliance on the " moral sense " which gives its
possessor the much overrated, much abused prerogative
of prophecy. He was never a party-man; never remained long in any party; never would be bound by
party nominations; always felt at liberty to adopt and
support any candidate who represented his idea, whether
set up by one party or another. Thus, in 1868, he announced his intention of voting for S. P. Chase, should
the democratic party give him the nomination, conclud-
ing that the candidate in that instance committed the
party which set him up. In 1872 he refused to follow
Sumner, Schurz and Greeley, because they would help
indirectly the success of the democratic party, which
they abhorred as much as he did. The press charged
him with inconsistency, and tauntingly magnified the
grandeur of the intellect that could rise so superior to
the vice of small minds. But he saw no inconsistency,
and for him there was none. In 1868 he was persuaded
that moral causes were disintegrating party combinations

to such a degree that the entire conversion of the democrats was not too strange an occurrence to be looked
for. He would have hailed the nomination of Chase as
conclusive evidence of a change of heart. In 1872 this
illusion had been dispelled, and the democrats, though
placing a saint's name on their banner, would have been
distrusted.

" May not the democratic party be allowed to put up and vote for
republicans? Yes. But republicans should, as a ·general thing,
pause long before voting for them. But suppose that party puts up
for president so pronounced and eminent a republican as Horace
Greeley—cannot republicans consistently vote for him? Certainly
not. For his election would as surely be the success of the democratic party as the election of President Grant will be the success of
the republican party. The election of Mr. Greeley will not turn the
democratic party into a republican party, but it will turn him into a
democrat—not, I trust, into one of the worst type—but still into a
democrat. Mr. Greeley's election would not assimilate the democratic party to him, but him to it. So it has ever been in such cases
—and how, with his kindly and obliging spirit, can he prove an exception? . . . But what if Mr. Greeley should notwithstanding
his candidacy and election, remain miraculously unchanged? It
does not follow that his election would not be the success of the
democratic party. The President is not all the government. Congress is far more nearly all of it : and Mr. Greeley's election would
be quite likely to result in a democratic Congress. . . . As the
candidate for however high an office at the hands of the republican
party, I would readily have voted for Mr. Greeley. I only lament
that he should have sought his honors by lending his name and influence to the democratic party, and by damaging and endangering
that other party which he had loved so long and so well."

Mr. Sumner's quarrel with the President implicated
Gerrit Smith at the very beginning. Constitutionally
unable to suspect evil of any, constitutionally inclined to
think the best of all, having before him the one invaluable service which General Grant had rendered to the
country in compelling the surrender of General Lee, full

of the conviction that he and he only could maintain
the supremacy of the republic over the oligarchy in
which lay the moral triumph of the north over the south,
and persuaded, that whatever Grant's personal deficien-
cies might be, he was sincerely loyal to the cause he had
led to final victory; in a word, having his heart fixed on
a single issue, and being certain that this issue was possible in but one way, what Mr. Sumner said, though he
could not answer it, made no impression on his mind
that remained when the weight of his friend's hand was
withdrawn.

He honored Mr. Sumner, respected him, loved him;
never imputed unworthy sentiments or motives to him,
never believed him to be actuated by private animosities
or moved by personal ambition, had no sympathy with
the partisans who ascribed his invectives to jealousy or
pique or base detraction, and explained the mutual re-
pulsion between him and the President by the natural
antipathy between two men so differently endowed, nur-
tured, trained and dealt with; so unlike in temperament,
capacity, taste and purpose; so dissimilar as to be precisely the opposites of each other, and standing more
sharply over against one another as years and experience, conflict and struggle, disappointment and success
brought their characteristic traits into relief, and threw
out the craggy masses above the stormy waters of circumstance. During the war General Grant had shown
the qualities of the soldier, which military life fostered,
and none could foresee what qualities latent so far in him,
civil life might develop. For twenty years Charles Sumner had been piling up the massive structure of moral
will, until at length he had become the embodiment of

intellectual purpose, straight, uncompromising, unsympathetic, ponderous, stately and impressive, but forbidding. Even his admirers looked on him with awe. His dislikers, who were many, accused him of arrogance, intolerant and intolerable. His egotism was of the kind most offensive to cold natures and most easily offended by coarse ones.

Sumner and Smith were warm friends of many years. Though in nearly every respect unlike, in every respect, excepting their devotion to the slave, they met cordially at this central point of sympathy, the hopeful enthusiasm of the one happily contrasting with the unbending integrity of the other. Sumner had borne honorable testimony to the value of Smith's service in Congress, and Smith had written from Washington to Frederick Douglass, in 1854, " Sumner is as guileless and ingenuous as a child, and hence my astonishment at the base and ferocious feeling manifested toward him at one period of the session. Chase and Sumner are gentlemen—Christian gentlemen. Great is my love of them ; and were I to add ' passing the love of women ' I should not be guilty of great extravagance." The hospitality of Peterboro had been repeatedly pressed on the Massachusetts senator, and, once had been accepted, in what spirit the following note of acknowledgment gives evidence.

Private. Senate Chamber, 7th December, '70.

My Dear Friend — I think often of the pleasant Sunday I passed under your roof.

What you told me of your son interested me much. I wish that he could be encouraged to persevere and apply his rare gifts to that branch of science for which he has shown such attachment. In this way he can do much to acquire a good renown.

Can you not help the colored people in Hayti ? The Minister of the Black Republic is much disturbed by the attempts of our government to establish itself on their island. The persistence of the President must be encountered. Will you not write one of your letters or make an appeal for the colored race? Let us hear from you.

Ever sincerely yours,

CHARLES SUMNER.

In August 1871, Gerrit Smith printed a "broadside" entitled "The anti-Dramshop Party," calling on its members for fidelity to its name and principles, urging the claims of the temperance cause and the necessity of enlisting political forces on its side. In his argument, he criticised the attitude of the republican party as a party of progress in reform. He says:

"It is but too probable that the republican party will sink down into a low chase with the democratic party after votes. So far from going forward, and making itself more and more a reform party, its murmurings against President Grant and frequent signs of disaffection toward him *reveal its declining appreciation of even those great moral ideas it had already espoused.* For to which of the grand undertakings and precious interests of the republican party, at the time of his election, *has he been found unfaithful?* To not one of them. Identified, therefore, as he is, *with them all, and the most prominent upholder of them all* every one of them is *necessarily disparaged when he is traduced or undervalued.* For the republican party to turn its back upon President Grant is to turn its back upon its honorable past—upon the past of its *better and more patriotic days.* He remains *the same man he was in those days.* He has proved himself to be free from the *accursed spirit of caste, and true to the equal rights of all men*—of the red man and black man as well as the white man. *He has deferred to the popular will, instead of moulding and fostering* a policy of his own. He has proved, with what *entire sincerity* it was that, in entering upon its office, *he expressed his desire* for peace. The late treaty between England and America *in the credit of which he shares so largely,* is the grandest and most auspicious peace measure the world has ever seen. The rapidity with which we are paying our national debt is a high proof *of his wisdom and honesty.* And yet, such a

President, no very small share of the republican party—certainly no very small share of its leaders—seem willing to drop! We hear them say that General Grant cannot be re-elected. But if he, who confessedly, did more than any other man to save our country in the perils of war, and *whose great influence in peace has all gone to make that peace more perfect and more blessed,* cannot be made our next President, *what republican can be? Manifestly, either he or the democratic candidate will be our next President;* and if the democratic candidate shall be, and shall represent and be a specimen of the bad, very bad democratic party, what then can save our country from ruin?"

The italics in the above passage are Mr. Sumner's; he underlined the words, marked on the margin of the paper expressions of surprise or protest, and enclosed the sheet to the author. The ensuing letters came immediately.

Private.　　　　　　　　　　　　Nahant, Mass., 20th Aug. '71.

My Dear Friend, — Your note and its enclosure reached me at this retreat where I am with my friend Longfellow. I regret much that I cannot see the Presidential question as you see it.

I know few politicians who think that Grant can be re-elected. Greeley told me last week that he looked upon his defeat as inevitable, and Forney, who is friendly to him and has just accepted the collectorship of Philadelphia, told me that he did not see how he could be re-elected, although he thought he would obtain the nomination;—to which I replied that he would not be renominated if it appeared that he could not be re-elected.

Therefore when you ask me to withdraw opposition to Grant, you ask me to aid in the defeat of the republican party. I have too much interest in this party to do any such thing.

But waiving the question of his success—he does not deserve the nomination. "One term" is enough for any body—especially for one who, being tried, is found so incapable—so personal—so selfish —so vindictive,—and so entirely pre-occupied by himself. All who have known him best testify to his incapacity. Don't forget Stanton's judgment.

It is hard to see the Ku Klux raging, and a good people dying through his luke-warmness and indifference. It is my solemn judgment, which at the proper time I shall declare, that the much criticised legislation of the last Congress would have been *entirely un-necessary*, if this republican President had shown a decent energy in enforcing existing laws and in manifesting sympathy with the oppressed there. *On him is that innocent blood*, which flowed while he circulated at entertainments, excursions, horse-races. Instead of being at Long Branch, a good President would have been at Savannah, and Mobile, or at least he would have made himself felt in those places.

Consider then, the insincerity of his message about St. Domingo. One million of blacks are now kept in anxiety and terror by the republican President, whom you hail as representing " moral ideas ! " Instead of abandoning his ill-omened scheme, he is now pressing it —working at home, like Hamlet's ghost, under ground and at the island with a most expensive fleet. His war-dance about the island has cost several millions. Instead of making peace between the two contending parties, and setting each on its legs, in the spirit of disinterested benevolence, he sends money to Baez under pretence of a sham treaty, to keep alive civil war. Nothing has aroused me more since the Fugitive Slave Bill and the outrages in Kansas. The same old spirit is revived in the treatment of the Haytien Republic.

And I am asked to help the re-nomination of such a man. Impossible ! I love the republican party—love my country too well to have a hand in such a thing.

In these conclusions I am governed by no personal feelings—more than I had to Franklin Pierce or James Buchanan ! How can I, an old public servant, devoted to a cause, turn aside on any personal feeling ? No, my dear friend, I write in sadness and sincerity, hoping yet to do something by which the cause of our country shall be saved. Think of five years under his vindictive imperialism ! Surely *you* must hesitate.

Grant is full of personal enmities. He has quarrelled with two members of his cabinet—a minister to England—a chairman of a senate committee—one or two of the diplomatic corps—the governor of a territory—and numerous others, *all good and faithful republicans* or friendly to him. I was always his true friend—never breathing a word except in kindness and respect—anxious for the welfare of his administration—and yet when I felt it my duty to oppose his St. Domingo scheme, *always without one word of allusion to him*, he was moved to vindictiveness. Ask any member of the committee or any senator, if in the debate of the committee on extra service I made any allusion to him, except to express a regret that he had entered upon this mistaken policy. And yet the vengeance came.

Afterwards when he still persevered, I felt it my duty to arraign him openly. Had I been a representative I should have felt it my duty to move his impeachment. I shall be astonished if at the next session his impeachment is not moved. His chance of impeachment is better than that of reëlection. Why, then, press him for candidate? Unquestionably the hardest possible to elect—and unquestionably the poorest calling himself republican! There are forty good republicans in the Union, any one of whom can be nominated without hazard to the party, and, when elected will be a better president. So I believe on my conscience, and on this belief I must act. At proper time I shall communicate Mr. Stanton's and my judgment.

Ever sincerely yours,

CHARLES SUMNER.

Hon. CHARLES SUMNER: Peterboro, Aug. 23, 1871.

My Dear Friend — I thank you for your long, frank and friendly letter. I thank you also for the printed sheets you have recently sent to me.

We have both the same paramount object in view—viz., the preclusion of a democrat from the presidency. You are certain that this cannot be accomplished by the nomination of Grant: and I own that your letter makes me less confident that it can by this means. I must still think, however, that if his nomination would not have this effect, no nomination would. I must still think that more persons could be brought to acquiesce in his nomination than in Greeley's, or Trumbull's or your or any other person's nomination. The republican party unhappily seems to be breaking up. I fear that there is no one man for whom the whole party will go.

President Grant is certainly very far from faultless. And yet, in the light of his successful leadership of our armies, but little account should be made of most of his faults.

You and Schurz and Morrill showed the error of his scheme of annexation, and of, at least, a part of the means by which he sought to accomplish it. But I am not sure that, in all this, he was guilty of anything worse than a mistaken judgment. A mistaken judgment will probably account for his other missteps. I hope that you do not give credit to the story of his having three hundred thousand dollars in blooded stock. I hope, indeed, that you do not doubt his honesty in money matters.

I remember your telling me of Stanton's bad opinions of Grant. But Stanton was sick when he expressed them—and they were, at the most, but the opinions of one man.

With your very unfavorable, I trust too unfavorable, view of Grant, I cannot ask you to vote for him, nor even to forbear voting against him.

God bless you, my dear friend! May your wisdom, integrity and eloquence long continue to serve your still deeply imperilled country!

My kind regards to Mr. Longfellow, and my repeated thanks to him for the youthful and beautiful likeness of yourself which he so kindly sent me, several years ago.

With love as well as esteem,

Your friend,

GERRIT SMITH.

Private.   Nahant, 28th Aug. '71.

My Dear Friend, — I am happy that you do not take unkindly my very positive difference from yourself on an important question.

The more I reflect on the question, the more I am distressed for my country and the republican party at the idea of Grant's re-nomination. We could better have lost one of his bloody victories. His rule for the second term would be the imperialism of selfishness and vindictiveness,—without moral sense, without ideas, without knowledge.

I think you will admit that he is the lowest President, whether intellectually or morally, we have ever had. Undoubtedly he is the richest since Washington, although he was very poor at the beginning of the war.

Mr. Stanton's judgment of him was positive and given under circumstances of singular solemnity, and the same thing he said at great length and with much detail to Mr. Hooper some months before. He said that he knew Grant better than any other man or the country could know him—that it was his duty to study him, and he did study him night and day,—when he saw and when he did not see him he then declared his utter incapacity. And you are electioneering for this person's re-election!

Think of his vindictive quarrels, since he has been President. God does not quarrel. What right has the President of the United States to quarrel and pursue supporters with vindictive hate?

Do not charge me with personal feelings. My life is my witness, I am an old servant, who has always thought of the cause and of my country; never have I sought any thing for myself. I have simply worked and served. I was so doing when I felt it my duty to oppose what seemed to me a mistaken policy of the President;—

never in my life did I act more simply and sincerely. I could not have done otherwise without failing in my duty. Then came attacks, and all that a small nature surrounded and prompted by small men, could do! Such a man President for a second term, God forbid!

Is not the course for us plain?

(1) Do not nominate a man with a mill-stone about his neck.

(2) Find somebody whose capacity is above question.

(3) Somebody who will not insult and quarrel with his supporters.

(4) Somebody who can surely be elected.

(5) Somebody whose election will not be a real defeat.

(6) Somebody who will elevate politics, instead of degrading them.

(7) Somebody who will scorn to use patronage for the subjugation of Congress to his personal will.

Ever sincerely yours,
CHARLES SUMNER.

How any colored person can support the man who offers indignity to the Black Republic, I cannot understand. The ablest colored man in Massachusetts declares his indignant disgust at him. At the proper time, I shall appeal to the colored voters to reject him.

Peterboro, August 31, 1871.

Hon. CHAS. SUMNER:

My Dear Friend, — I have yours of 28th ult. You are happy to find that I take your words kindly. Why should I not, when I know that they all proceed from deep convictions and an honest heart?

The idea of Grant's renomination would be as painful to me as it is to you, if I held your exceedingly unfavorable opinions of him. Your long continued and intense brooding over his faults has transformed him into a weak-brained monster. You put him "intellectually" and "morally" below all our former Presidents—intellectually below the garrulous Harrison, and morally below the *infernally* pro-slavery Pierce!

Grant is not an educated statesman. But when, a few years ago, I read in the public letters of Sherman and Sheridan their high praises of his ability as a general, I could not doubt that he was a man of superior intellect. I felt that he was great, not alone by the accidents and good fortune of war, but also by his intrinsic merits. Then as to his morality, I do not suppose that he is a saint—but I certainly lack evidence that he is a corrupt man. He could be guilty of all his errors in the annexation matter, and yet not be corrupt. In receiving his rich presents, in his nepotism and bad appointments to office, he was not necessarily corrupt.

It was not necessary for you to vindicate yourself to me. You have lived for your country and for all mankind—and I thank God that he made you capable of doing this with such eminent (can I not truly say *preëminent*) efficiency.

I see that you continue to make great (too great) account of Mr. Stanton's condemnation of Grant.

The seven requirements with which you close your letter are, I admit, well put and very imposing. The fourth requirement is to nominate "somebody who can *surely* be elected." I apprehend that this cannot be done. All we can do is to nominate some *decent* somebody who will stand the best chance of being elected. I am aware that you do not let Grant come into the category of *decent* somebodies—but just here. you are at war with the judgment of the world. I wish that you or *p*ur old friend Chase could be our next president—but, as yet, the popular current does not run strong enough for such pronounced abolitionists to bring that about.

You say that I am "electioneering" for Grant—I answer that I am too old (seventy-four) to electioneer for any one. All I have said or done for him is to be found in the few words in my paper on the dramshop. I repeat it—my concern is not to elect Grant, but to keep out a democrat. You and I do not count Chase among democrats.

With the highest regard,

Your friend forever,

GERRIT SMITH.

Nahant, 3d Sept., '71.

My Dear Friend — I know not why my opinions expressed in answer to an appeal from you should be characterized as proceeding from "long continued and intense brooding over his (Grant's) faults." You asked me to abandon an opposition to which I have been driven by solemn conviction or knowledge with constant opportunities of information, and when I ventured to assign reasons for these opinions you attribute them to "long-continued and intense brooding." Here you do me injustice. My opinions are honestly formed—on my conscience—and communicated to you only in reply to your appeal. Had you not written to me on the subject be assured I should have said nothing about it.

I am here with friends seeking repose, and, in such time as I can command, reviewing the history of our Anti-slavery struggle, thinking little of count, except when my opinion is challenged, as by yourself. If I am "brooding" it is on our great battle where you did so much, and revising my own humble contributions to it.

You think Grant cannot be below the "*infernally* pro-slavery Pierce?" Why not? Was he not in the time of Pierce just as "infernally pro-slavery," and has he not done things worse than any attributed to Pierce?

I say nothing of him as a military character. I leave that to others. How rarely in history has a good general been a good statesman! See Buckle.

As for "morals," all his thoughts, ideas and sentiments are on a low plane—lower than any president before has reached.

You inquire if he is "corrupt." I have never said anything on this head. You know well that he does not hesitate to buy men by office, as no other president has done; nor does he hesitate to receive "gifts!"

You discard the testimony of Stanton, who had the best opportunity of knowing Grant, and you discard mine, although I have had some opportunity. Whose will you take? Will you name any person, not an actual present member of his cabinet, whose judgment or testimony is of any weight. Ask Chase, who knows him well. He will speak to you of his incompetency. Unhappily this incompetency runs into the moral region.

And yet you not only become his partisan, but rebuke me, in my seclusion, because I frankly confess that I cannot see the idol as you see it.

I tremble for my country at the thought of a second term by this vindictive selfish personality. I tremble for the African, whose Haytien relatives he keeps in distress, like another Kansas plagued by another Pierce! Never since those Kansas days has my soul been so tried as by his conduct to Hayti. To me it is heart-rending. The tears flow at the thought of it. And yet YOU sustain the author of this distress.

When the presidential contest came on, Mr. Smith took the field for Grant, and, in explanation of Mr. Sumner's opposition, laid stress on the contrast between the two men in point of birth, education and character. Mr.

Sumner, meeting with a version of his remarks in a western paper hostile to himself, addressed to him the following sharp letter.

Washington, 9th July, '72.

Dear Mr. Smith — You supposed that I should call your remarks unjust? Did you not feel that they were unjust?

I write for no controversy. You make a personal assault on me and charge me with personal motives—forgetting the elaborate conversations at your house and afterwards at my own, where I disclosed to you my deep sense of General Grant's unfitness and the extent to which my conscience had been shocked by his conduct. You forget how I unfolded to you my interest in Hayti and her struggling people, which I was taught in childhood to cherish, and how happy I was in carrying through the act acknowledging the independence of the Black Republic—how from that time I watched its fortunes and tried to serve it—how, when I became aware of the utterly heartless and insensate conduct of Grant to that people, I was indignant, as when Kansas was assailed, the case being as bad as that of Kansas—you forget how sympathetically you listened *then;* and when acting simply according to these convictions, hoping to do something for my country, you assail me by substituting personal motives for that honest judgment which on my conscience I was obliged to give. I never deserved your sympathy and support more than now, and never in the course of a life which has had your praise, was I more sincere and simple in the discharge of my duty.

In sustaining your allegation of personal "dislike," you are pleased to invent with regard to my early life. If you will kindly ask any body familiar with it, you will see how imaginative you have been. But I am at a loss to understand what my early life has to do with this.

I never disliked Grant. When you allege that you again invent. On the contrary I was his sincere friend and supporter until I became aware of his course in Hayti, and the more I think of that, the more utterly indefensible it appears. It is *revolting*—so I see it, and for this reason I began to judge him.

Is it just, when these things were known to you, that you should hunt for personal motives? I deny the whole imputation, in gross and detail.

Would it not have been more candid, more in accordance with the friendship which I had supposed safe against decay so long as life lasted, for you to have recognized the strength of my convictions, and not questioned their honesty or sought to weaken them by invention about my early life?

I believe Grant essentially unjust, and I am sorry to see that his defenders seem inspired by his character. This is natural.

I send you a speech marked, and ask if you are just to me with regard to the Douglass incident. It was because Douglass had received indignity on board the boat, that the neglect of the president became conspicuous. You say "certain it is that Mr. Douglass is *insensible of it.*" Believe me I did not refer to this incident until Mr. Douglass in my own house, a fortnight before the speech, had complained of it.

You are mistaken about Mr. Stanton. I have abundance of concurring testimony. His most intimate friend during the latter months of his life, Mr. Hooper, confirms it fully, and so do many others. And why should it not be known? I am in earnest. I wished to save the republican party from the infliction of a second term, and what I said was true.

In defending his gift-taking, you forget that it is "gift-taking compensated by office" which is the unprecedented offense.

I have before me your letters of last autumn, very different from the assault you now make, where you say in reply to my frank statements that you "*know* that they all proceed from deep convictions and an honest heart." You then add; "The idea of Grant's nomination would be as painful to me as it is to you, if I had your exceedingly unfavorable opinions of him." Then again you say; "It was not necessary for you to vindicate yourself to me. You have lived for your country and for all mankind." I will not quote the praise that follows. Besides all this you say, "I cannot ask you to vote for Grant, nor even to forbear voting against him."

Then you were not disposed to assail me and to find excuses in imagined contrasts of early life.

It is very painful for me to write this. But it seems to me that your own sense of justice will recognize its truth.

Once you stood by the slave; stand by Hayti now, which represents the slave.

Sincerely yours,
CHARLES SUMNER.

Washington, 7th Aug., '72.

My Dear Friend —I have yours of August 4. You denounce me as joining democrats, because I declare my preference for Horace Greeley. But you would have been open to the same charge, had you supported Chase if nominated by them. Have I not as much right to vote for Horace Greeley as you would have to vote for Chase without any denunciation? The cases are identical. *I have entire faith in Horace Greeley.* I am at a loss to understand how a lover of peace like Gerrit Smith can resist the opportunity of reconciliation and put back the outstretched hand. Think of democrats adopting the Cincinnati platform and an abolition candidate and you holding back instead of closing with them and keeping them to their promises! "Blessed are the peace-makers." My life has been of controversy. It is with infinite pain that I find it continued and with personality and vindictiveness unequalled. But I could not do otherwise. My conscience spoke and I obeyed.

Sincerely yours,
CHARLES SUMNER.

I have a good letter from Chase to-day approving especially my letter to the colored people and declaring that he shall vote for Horace Greeley in whom he has entire trust.

Washington, 6th Aug. '72.

My Dear Friend, — The kindness of your note is grateful.

Let me confess,—your speech seemed to me a strange assault. I saw no reason why you should seek to account for my opposition to Grant when I assigned specifically the reasons, which had been communicated to you one or two years ago,—and when you went further and to sustain your theory, assumed to make a statement about my early life, inconsistent with the fact,—I thought your course very strange and unfriendly.

The injury is done. Your speech enters into the bundle of misrepresentations which I must endure, at a moment when I am seeking to save the country from misrule and to restore concord.

Sincerely yours,
CHARLES SUMNER.

This mournful episode may be concluded by a letter from Andrew D. White, President of Cornell University, which gives his view of the controversy between U. S. Grant and Charles Sumner, and also his feeling toward Gerrit Smith as a peacemaker.

U. S. Steamer Tennessee, Jan'y 17, 1871.

My Dear Friend, — On leaving Mr. Sumner night before last, in Washington, I said to him, " I leave the country with a sad heart, indeed, for I have this day seen the two men in Washington, who have helped most directly to save the nation, and they misunderstand each other, and that misunderstanding is sure to cost the country dear. I shall write this to Gerrit Smith."

That is my feeling. I talked fully with President Grant ! I am not *very* old, but I have had to see many men, and judge their main qualities. President Grant is honest and patriotic, I *know*. He presents the St. Domingo question from his side, in a manner that shows him sincere. Think whatever we may of his theory, it is that of a sincere man, and earnestly held, and as such entitled to respect.

As to Mr. Sumner, I need not speak of his qualities and services. I love and honor him. But the sad thing is to see these two men separated and hostile—to hear the adherents of either filling the air with charges which *cannot* be true—to hear them stimulating the *amour propre* of each, and devising plans of vengeance.

I have stated my own conviction that President Grant is honest. I had gone to Washington with many misgivings. I had feared that, in the heat of this contest, it might be signified to me that the authorities at Washington *hoped* or trusted that the Report of the Commissioners would be favorable,—or that it might be hinted that duty to party or country might require some forbearance, etc., etc. : and had this been done, the rejoinder on my part must have been a painful one to make ; for I had quietly determined that I would make no sacrifice of my manhood in this matter.

But I am bound to say that there was not the shade of a hint or suggestion of the kind. The President said : " Probe everything to the bottom." " Make your investigations as full and fair as possible." " I am as ready to be converted to anti-annexationist doctrines as I hope others are ready to be converted to annexationist doctrines." " I want all the light I can get,"—and this with a manner that bespoke earnestness, if any man's manner ever did.

And now, my friend, I feel better to have told you this, even though it does no good. Neither can be approached now ; but if ever a moment comes for you to earn the blessing for the Peacemakers, I trust that you will not let the chance go by. I remain,

Most heartily yours,

To Gerrit Smith.   AND. D. WHITE.

We are just leaving port. Good bye, and God bless you and yours.   A. D. W.

Gerrit Smith's interest in the President and in his reëlection, assumed, as usually was the case with him, a personal form. Mr. Smith was never impersonal. It was not in his nature to be so. Whatever he felt towards individuals he spoke out. He felt the force of his own individuality, and recognized the worth of theirs. General Grant was not left in ignorance of this man's honest opinions.

Long Branch, N. J., Sept. 4, 1871.

My Dear Sir — Your favor of the 11th of August enclosing me a few copies of an article from your pen, favoring my re-nomination and election to the office of President, was duly received. I have no valid excuse for not acknowledging the receipt of it earlier and thanking you for your good opinion which I prize very much. The fact is I put your letter in my pocket, with many others, to prevent it being mislaid until an opportunity occurred to answer it. It has been there ever since. Please accept my thanks at this late day and overlook my negligence.

With great respect,

Your obedient servant,

Honorable Gerrit Smith.   U. S. GRANT.

———

Peterboro, Sept. 13, 1871.

PRESIDENT GRANT

My Dear Sir — On my return home after a short absence, I was happy to find myself honored with a letter from you. It is a much esteemed and very welcome letter.

The republican party saved our nation. But if this party shall now break up into factions and have a different presidential candidate for each faction, it will make itself guilty of giving up the nation to destruction. God grant that it may be kept back from such suicidal folly and sin ! There are a dozen men in the land, any one of whom would make a good President. But the republican party must unite on one of them, or fail. Manifestly, they can unite on no one but yourself—and on yourself I firmly believe they will unite.

Please make my very kind regards to Mrs. Grant.

Very respectfully, your friend,

GERRIT SMITH.

PRESIDENT GRANT:
Peterboro, November 13, 1872.

My Dear Sir — My congratulations on your reëlection are none the less warm and sincere because coming so late. I delayed sending them, for the reason that you must have been deluged with letters immediately after the election.

l rejoice in your reëlection for your own sake—for the sake of its ample vindication of your assailed wisdom and assailed integrity—but I rejoice in it more for our country's sake. What our country most needs is not prosperity in business, the speedy payment of her great debt and the increase of her wealth. Far more than this and than all things else she needs the cordial recognition and full protection of the equal rights of all her children—the black and red as well as the white. In the light of what you have already done to this end, I believe that ere the close of your next Presidential term, this recognition will be gained and this protection enjoyed. Then and not till then shall we be a favored nation. For then and not till then can God be at peace with it. May His wisdom continue to guide you! With the highest regard,

Your friend,

GERRIT SMITH.

PRESIDENT GRANT:
Peterboro, March 6th, 1873.

Dear Sir, — I felt myself to be too old (seventy-six this day) to attend the inauguration. But I am not too old to appreciate your inaugural address. For one thing especially in that address, which contains so many good things, I cannot forbear to thank you. This one thing is your calling attention to the nation's persistent wronging of the black man in continuing to withhold from him equal civil rights. To cease from this injustice and this ingratitude toward him and from this great sin against God is the nation's first duty. The nation cannot be safe,—most emphatically the republican party cannot be safe,—if the discharge of this duty shall be delayed much longer.

Congratulating you that you enter upon the second term of your great office under auspices so favorable,

I remain, your friend,

GERRIT SMITH.

CHAPTER IX.

PHILANTHROPY.

ALL this time the works of general philanthropy went on. The daily calls for charity were listened to. The hungry were fed, the naked clothed, the poor provided for, the sick visited. It was said of a prominent reformer, a friend of Gerrit Smith, that, being asked to contribute to the necessities of an individual sufferer, he replied that he was too much occupied with masses of wrong to heed particular instances of misfortune. On hearing which remark a witty woman exclaimed: "Well, that beats the divine Providence! God Almighty has not come to that!" Gerrit Smith never merited nor provoked such a criticism. No matter how severe the strain or how intricate the perplexities of public affairs, he had leisure for the unnoticed little ones, and in blessing them he found an unfailing solace. During the latter years of his life, his business required less of his personal attention, his chief clerk in Peterboro and his agent in Oswego being men of competency, in whom he had entire confidence, so that he was able to give his heart out freely at the invitations of human kindness. The providence that had so faithfully befriended the fugitive slaves was now extended to the freedmen, whose elevation he was greatly concerned for. The schools, academies, seminaries which sprang up in the former slave States, were watched by him with interest, and generally aided with contributions of money. Whatever had a moral and social significance for the community had an interest for him. His endeavors in behalf of the temperance reform were unceasing and assiduous as ever. He attended conventions of his anti-Dramshop party at Syracuse and elsewhere, speaking and writing, journeying from place to place, when his three score and fifteen years might have excused him.

There is an impression that he never took a practical interest in schemes of public improvement, save as they favored his private investments, and in the expectation of handsome pecuniary returns. But this is an entire mistake. There was not an enterprise that promised to aid the industries or to promote the commerce of central New York that he was not consulted about, and concerned in, whether it directly furthered his projects or not. He was willing to take his share and no more than his share of the general benefit. The Niagara Ship Canal, in which his old friend Alvan Bronson was so active an advocate, he regarded as an enterprise of the utmost importance to the State; not to the portion of the State in which the greater part of his own property lay, but to the city of New York in particular. To Auditor Benton, in 1866, he wrote:

"Taking you for authority, I should affirm with the utmost positiveness the wisdom of building the Niagara Ship Canal. If, as you say, the Erie Canal ' will not pay tolls enough to pay the expense of superintendence and repairing after the Niagara Ship Canal is in operation,' then why should not every one who believes you feel emboldened to declare that the Niagara Ship Canal ought, with all possible speed, to be hurried into operation? What a rich blessing in reserve for tens of millions of people in this canal, according to your view of the vast use it will be put to ! and how can you find it in your heart to postpone their enjoyment of it ! "

Then after arguing at some length, the advantages of the canal, he concluded :

" Is it not high time for us to rise up out of this unenlightened, selfish, narrow policy, which makes more account of tolls than of commerce, of local interests than of the general good, of a State than of a Nation ? If men will build us canals more useful than those we have, I do not say that we should help them,—but I do say that we should let them. Our present improvements are to be prized by us ; but we must not make them a finality. On the contrary, the door for greater improvements must be constantly left open."

In 1867 he wrote to Alvan Bronson, of Oswego :

" For one I never suspected that the Midland Road was to be turned aside for the benefit of any interests, even those of Oswego. We understood that the one great object in building it was to open to the products of the great west an avenue to the city of New York cheaper than any other which there was or could be in the State of New York. . . . Scarcely will the construction of the Niagara Ship Canal have been commenced, ere will also have commenced the construction of a railroad from New York across Chenango and Madison Counties to Oswego. It will be a road far more substantial and expensive than the contemplated one. It will not be a road zigzagging after bonds,—but the shortest there can be. The zigzagging road would not remove nor at all lessen the necessity of building the other. And when the other were built, what then would the zigzagging road be worth to its stockholders ? . . . There is complaint in some quarters that I do not increase to twenty-five thousand dollars my subscription to the Midland Road. I cannot see that, in any point of view, it is my duty to increase it. Had the proper route of the road been adopted, I should, from the fact of my ownership of property in Oswego, be morally bound to make a large subscription to the stock of the road. I should not then have objected to its being as large as twenty-five thousand dollars. But, a grossly improper route having been chosen, I am, on the other hand, morally bound not to add to my subscription. Nothing in my stewardship must I be guilty of wasting ; and I must not, by adding to the subscription, encourage others to waste their money upon this unwisely, nay, wildly located road."

The same year he wrote to John B. Edwards, of Oswego, who represented to him that most of the people of Oswego preferred the route adopted for the Midland Road, for city and county reasons:

" A far higher question than what is for the advantage of Oswego, is what does Honesty require of her. Is it honest in Oswego to desire to have the Midland Road turned ten miles out of its way, for the sake of these special favors to herself? . . . I suppose I have paid much more than any other stockholder. What I have paid I am willing to count as loss. But I am not willing to fling away any more money on this wild scheme of building a road from Oswego to New York by the way of the north shore of Oneida Lake. I took twenty-five thousand dollars in the stock of the present road from Oswego to the Rome and Watertown Road. If Oswego shall organize a company for building another road to the Rome and Watertown Road, I will yield to her wishes and be one of the company. But I am not willing to help her build any of her little side roads under cover or pretense of their being roads to the city of New York. . . . You refer to the proposed Lake Shore Road. I have subscribed three thousand dollars to it ; and I hope to increase my subscription to twenty thousand. But I shall feel myself to be neither morally nor legally bound to pay a penny of it, if your city shall, in order to gain more trade from her neighborhood or to prevent the division of her county, or for any other reason, succeed in getting the directors to turn the road through South Hannibal. I might be willing to help build a road from Oswego to South Hannibal. But I would not be, if it were built under the deceptive name of the Lake Shore Road."

Thus did Gerrit Smith reconcile business with regard for the benefit of his fellow-men. His business sagacity was seldom at fault, and it often turned out with him that the most public spirited, the most equitable, and the most humane thing was the most profitable. His prophecy in regard to the ill fortune of the Midland

Road came true and justified the moral grounds of his objection. Had the building of the Niagara Ship Canal been undertaken, his beloved city of Oswego might have risen, according to his prediction, to be the great and beautiful city of his dreams.

The faith in human brotherhood, in the harmony of human interests, in the mutual dependence of the races, and the absolute safety of justice, made him an easy convert to the principles of free trade. Exclusive rights, private privileges, local prerogatives and monopolies were his detestation. He believed that all mankind flourished and were happy together; no profit, he was sure, could be lasting or solid that was gained by a section, at the expense of the community. He ascribed to the teaching of Alvan Bronson his allegiance to free trade; but he must have come to it sooner or later by his unaided instinct. He could not have been a protectionist and remained, in other respects, what he was.

Why was he not, by a similar instinct of humanity, an advocate of the unqualified abolition of the penalty of death for the crime of murder? He was not. He gave money in aid of the advocacy of this reform. He favored its discussion, and would have been glad to be convinced by the arguments of its champions. But he stopped short of being persuaded, because the community was, in his view, of more consequence than the individual; safety demanded the suppression of crime, and the doom of death was the surest deterrent from crimes of the darkest character. The doctrine that vice was an infirmity of the blood to be pardoned, and crime a misfortune to be pitied, was a scandal to his moral

16*

sense. He believed in moral responsibility, in freedom
of choice, in the power of the roused will; and he believed, consequently, in the restraining force of punishment. His doctrine on this subject, so fully stated in
the address before the American Peace Society, at Boston, May 24, 1858, remained his doctrine to the end.

"The inviolability of human life! Much is said in favor of it, and
not a little very beautifully and strongly said; but after all the doctrine seems not to be reasonable. I readily admit that the life of
our brother is not to be taken unless there be the utmost necessity
for it. Even he who is convicted of murder should be led to prison
rather than to the gallows if thereby society shall be made equally
safe from him, and others shall be no less deterred from committing
the crime. But that he who has murdered has forfeited his life, and
placed it at the absolute disposal of the brotherhood I cannot doubt.
. . . To say the least, is there not a very disproportionate concern for the welfare of the murderer? His fellow-man into whose
hands his crime has put him, have their own welfare to see to; and
this they must do most thoroughly, be it at whatever expense it may
to him who has been guilty of invading it. The rights of the innocent must be maintained, cost what it will to the guilty. The common thief must be visited with a punishment adequate to restrain
his further violations of the sacredness of property. And so too,
must life go for life, if in that wise murder can be most effectually
prevented."

Gerrit Smith was one of the many petitioners to Governor Dix, in 1873, for the life of the convict Foster whom
he thought possibly guiltless of the crime of murder.
But he apparently had not the matter much at heart; for
the note was a very short one, without form of argument, or warmth of appeal. In a letter to his wife, he
merely alludes to the case: "So poor Foster must be
hung! I hoped the Governor would spare his life."
Many a loud voiced champion of the gallows, whose personal feelings proved, in this case, stronger than the

sense of duty to society, cried more pathetically over the
fate of the criminal than did this gentle, but just spirit.
His love of humanity was too sincere, and his abhorrence of evil too deep for him to grieve because a habitual disturber of the peace was removed.

Peterboro, Nov. 21, 1868.

Hon. M. H. BOVEE:

My Dear Sir — I have never taken the ground that human life
is "inviolable." Nevertheless, I have, for many years held that
there should be no capital punishment in a nation or state where
the imprisonment of the convict can be made sure.

I believe that capital punishment exerts a depraving influence on
the public mind ; and that, while it deters from the commission of no
crime, its tendency is to make all crimes more frequent. Still, should
it turn out that the safety of the innocent requires the taking of the
life of the guilty, then let it be taken ; for the safety of the innocent
is the first consideration. But I do not believe it will require it
where the guilty can be shut up beyond the power of escape.

I trust that you will be in Albany the coming winter to argue
with our legislature for the abolition of capital punishment.

With great regard, your friend,
GERRIT SMITH.

The changes in opinion that followed the abandonment of the Calvinistic theology were not confined to
the speculative region, or to the usual departments of
reform, but extended to the intricate problems of social
life. A few years ago, on the occasion of a celebrated
case of divorce and marriage, when a neglected and outraged woman found escape through the laws of another
state from the brutality of a drunkard, and married, on
his death bed, the man who had been her best friend,
and her deliverer in painful straits, Gerrit Smith espoused the woman's cause against an infuriated press
and an insane public opinion. At this time he wrote

and published an article declaring that his early convictions in favor of the severe limitation, if not the absolute prohibition of divorce had undergone revision and correction. He had come to think that the doctrine of the New Testament which he had held to be authority was, on rational grounds, open to criticism, besides being inapplicable to modern society. He had long been of the opinion that the ethics of Jesus, being adapted to a new state of things, being the moral code for the "Kingdom of Heaven" which He came to establish, must be modified and readjusted to meet the problems of our civilization. Some of the precepts, notably this one respecting marriage and divorce, were probably intended for the instruction of Jews, whose customs of divorce had become exceedingly lax. He regarded as illogical the practice of judging Western society by Eastern maxims, the usages and needs of the nineteenth century by the traditions of the first; and considered as "ludicrously inconsistent the tens of thousands who, in defiance of the whole Gospel, are willing that government should multiply without limit death-and-damnation-dealing dramshops, and protect slaveholders in making merchandise of men, and who are at the same time shocked at governments being so anti-Gospel as to allow a broken-hearted woman to be divorced from the drunken husband who beats her, and threatens and attempts to kill her."

The discussion of the Alabama treaty called from Gerrit Smith words of earnest confidence in the good will of the English people, and in the maintenance of peace between the two nations. They were printed in his own little paper, "The anti-Dramshop," and were probably read by few people ; but they were significant of the generous temper of the man.

"Come, England, make your offer ! Make it in a generous spirit, and it will be accepted in a generous spirit. Stand no longer on your interpretation of the treaty ! Stand no longer on your decision that it would be contrary to the dealings of the nations with each other to make these indirect losses a part of our account against you ! "

The cause of Cuba enlisted his warmest enthusiasm. To Miguel De Aldama, Thomas Jordan, and Charles A. Dana, he sent his cheque for one thousand dollars in 1873 : " This is neither the first nor the second time you have spontaneously given equal sums to the Cuban cause ;" the committee wrote. " But upon this occasion your donation is accompanied by such warm expressions of sympathy for the rights and afflictions of the Cuban people, that they must indubitably find an echo not only in the gratitude of the Cubans, but also in the hearts of all lovers of liberty and justice." At great pains he arranged public meetings in the aid of Cuba, at Peterboro and Canastota, writing and circulating hand bills, and making the occasions attractive by his hospitality. The ill success of these efforts gave him bitter pain. " What will these people do," he observed plaintively to a friend and neighbor, " when I am gone ! All my life, I have labored to interest them in the best things and the best people ; they allow me to do it, unassisted. I am old and soon shall leave them. Yet, even now, they take no interest."

What will they do indeed ! They did nothing. When he died, there were no signs of life remaining in them.

Earnest men in foreign lands showed more appreciation of the great-hearted American, than did his neighbors in the little village of Peterboro.

My Dear Friend, — I have been, from day to day, delaying my
answering you and acknowledging your very liberal gift of seventy-
five pounds sterling to our cause, hoping to find time for a letter such
as you ask, to your countrymen. I cannot write it *now*, and will not
delay any more sending a few words of gratefulness. I shall certainly write and send a letter for publication in a few days ; you may
reckon on it. But I am overwhelmed with work, and threatened
with giddiness and other ominous symptoms when I write too much.

I fancy your spontaneous gift will bring good luck to my plans.
I feel deeply grateful not only for the money, which is most useful,
but for the spirit in which it is given, and for the good, loving, and
earnest words which accompany it. Bless you !

I am absorbed in an actual crisis, and in the Roman question. I
hope that, with God's help, we shall solve it in a way beneficial not
only to ourselves, but to mankind.

Ever faithfully yours,
JOSEPH MAZZINI.

Feb'y 21-'67, 18 Fulham Road, London, S. W.

———

London, August 8.

Dear Sir — From my friend Bulowski and others I know how
our ideas concerning the immense advantages of a close alliance
between the republicans of the new world are harmonizing, and I
know that you belong to that class of men who understand that to
be a man is to be one in thought and action, to strive to embody
what we believe to be truth, into reality. The alliance proposed by
us and accepted by the New York and Boston Committees, is doubtless a good and great thought, but requiring, to bear fruit, a great
deal of active energy, and a capability for feeling the sacredness of
the principle and the practical way through which it can become a
powerful *fact.* You have both. Let me reckon on you as upon one
of the principal workers in and for the alliance. Lend a hand to
what I call the laying down of the *moral* Atlantic Cable. Your help
is needed.

The alliance wants organization, propagandism, a press, travellers, plenty of things requiring funds. Let us strike the coin of the

Republican Alliance. We have proposed to both the committees the issue of subscription notes for one, five, ten, twenty dollars, representing the admission to the Association, or the sympathy of those who will not, through some individual reason, formally belong to it. It seems to me almost essential that an American name should in these notes, be added to ours. The specimen of the note is by this time in the hands of the New York Committee; and I trust you will see it, think of it, and strongly advocate, with or without modifications, a speedy realization of the scheme.

Believe me, dear sir, ever faithfully yours,

JOSEPH MAZZINI.

---

18 Fulham Road, Nov. 5.

My Dear Sir — I come back from a three months' journey to Switzerland and Italy, and find such an arrear of work to be done that I have no time to write to you as I should wish. But I avail myself of the opportunity of my friend Mr. Linton leaving for the United States, to tell you that I am very grateful to you for your kind, good friendly letter, to tell you that I have read "The Theologies," and that I should feel ready to sign almost everything you say there, and that I value above all, the frank, fearless way in which you state what you believe or disbelieve in.

Mr. Linton, whom I beg to introduce to you, will inform you of our actual views and prospects as far as our *Alliance* is concerned. I feel disheartened at the prolonged silence of the two committees. I have never had an answer to my proposals. I regret it for both your sake and ours. To us a material help, just as that you speak of, would now be of the highest importance to yourself. The practical positive organization of the Alliance would be the initiation of a high, noble task, the fulfilment of which would strengthen you and consecrate as it were, even the internal struggle through which you now must go.

Do what you can in the right direction, and believe me, my dear sir, ever faithfully yours,

JOSEPH MAZZINI.

The little package containing these letters from the great Italian reformer, contains with them a copy of the circular announcing " The Universal Republic " which aimed " To maintain the right of every country to a republican government, and the consequent duty of all republicans to unite for a solidarity of republics." The needful information respecting means of efforts and rules of affiliation is given. The date is January, 1867. A scheme like this fired the imagination of Gerrit Smith. The vision of Utopia was always in view, gladdening and consoling. While toiling at the most unremunerative and disheartening causes in a " topsy-turvey world," he could contemplate a future when the vice of intemperance, the guilt of slavery, the brutality of war should cease ; when four hours of daily labor would be sufficient to supply man's natural wants, and the general cultivation of the intellectual nature should be carried joyously on.

CHAPTER X.

THE END.

GERRIT SMITH'S health was, to all appearances completely restored after his return from the asylum at Utica. The diary, which for many years recorded ailments, colds, hoarseness, giddiness, is nearly silent on the subject during the last ten years of his life. He called himself an old man, and spoke of the infirmities of his age more than was necessary; this was his habit. His friends rallied him upon it, as they had always done. His physical strength had visibly declined. His gait had become shambling, his movement slow; but his mind continued clear; his faculties worked easily; his feelings were warm, his impulses fresh and generous as of old. He was ripe, mellow and juicy; grander than ever in personal aspect, patriarchal in bearing and look, courteous in demeanor. He brought to mind the figures of ancient worthies who were at the same time priests and kings, their white beards betokening the dignity of the sacred office, their stalwart forms suggesting the sword and battle axe. His eye was soft, his skin ruddy, his voice deep and unctuous. As he stood, listening or talking, he was a man majestic and beautiful to look upon. On the 24th of December, 1874, he left his home in Peterboro to pass the Christmas holidays in New York, at the house of his kinsman, John Cochrane, 60

Clinton Place, leaving a paper on his desk giving directions about his letters and papers.   He was in excellent
spirits.   The Christmas eve was happy ; the Christmas
day was passed cheerfully in social chat.   At the dinner-
table he exhibited his usual liveliness, though it was remarked that he had less than his wonted readiness in
responding to " sentiments."   It was already his early
bed time when the company rose from table.   His day's
task was not completed.   Calling on his niece, Mrs.
Walter, to get her writing materials, he then dictated
four letters ; the first was to his old housekeeper at Peterboro, charging her not to neglect his poor in the village,
to see that the children of the orphan asylum had their
holiday supplies, and that papers were sent to the free
reading room which he maintained ; the other three were
kindly answers to applications for charity.   He then
went to bed, with plans in his mind to visit Thurlow
Weed, Charles O'Conor, and other old friends the next
day, and with pleasant thoughts about the happiness of
the day just ended.   The night was undisturbed.   He rose
as usual, at half-past six o'clock, and was dressing himself, when his wife, who had not risen, was surprised by
an incoherent remark that escaped him.   She raised her
head to look, and saw him feeling vaguely about in the
air.   She hastened to him, spoke but received no answer,
tried to move him, but he was inert.   Suddenly, with
his accustomed dignity of bearing, he rose from his chair
—walked unsupported to the bed, slowly, saying as if
to himself, " weak, very weak," laid himself straight, on
his back, his right hand at his side, his left hand on his
breast.   So he lay till he died, a movement of the left
hand in response to his wife's repeated and agonized cry

for recognition being the last sign of conscious life. The household was alarmed ; the family flocked in ; the physician came ; every brain was active in devising alleviations ; every hand and foot was ready to help him who had been hands and feet to so many ; he lay still, heavily breathing, unconscious. All day Saturday, all day Sunday, till Monday noon he lay thus. Then the glassy eyes started open to make the face look more soulless ; the head turned mechanically, and then sank heavily into the pillows ; the breath rallied for a final effort, then ceased. The man was dead. Fifty-three hours death had been extinguishing the vital spark. Slight premonitions of cerebral disturbance in the form of sudden wakings from sleep, nightmare, and fright, would have alarmed him, had they been more pronounced. As it was he had no apprehension or pain of dissolution.

The first mourner was Thurlow Weed, his old acquaintance who knew him in college, and stood by him when he made his first appearance in State politics, at Utica, in 1824. The next day—December 29—the body, surrounded with fresh flowers, the grand head embedded in roses, lilies, pinks, violets and ferns, was visited by troops of friends, Vice President Wilson, the President and Treasurer of Hamilton College, Highland Garnet, Christopher Brown, John D. Mulford, Peter S. Porter, Charles B. Ray, and other representatives of the black people, by Commissioner Echeverria, and General Queralto of the Cuban army, bringing expressions of respect and gratitude from their countrymen. Men of all the professions and laymen of every degree, came to look at the dead face of the philanthropist. A night train carried the body and a company of relatives to Canastota, where carriages were in waiting to finish the last journey.

In spite of the bitter cold—thirty degrees below zero —a crowd was collected at the railway station and at the house. The whole village was present at the mansion when the body arrived, men and women of all ages and degrees, the oldest and poorest being most conspicuous, because most bereaved. Flowers adorned the rooms; the Cuban cross stood on the table in the library, mottoes from the good man's speeches and letters hung in the hall, the library, and over Huntington's portrait in the parlor. The children of the Orphan Asylum, thirty in number, white and black—special wards of Gerrit Smith, inmates of an institution which he founded, came in, looked one after another on the face of their benefactor, and, ranged in a semi-circle about the coffin, sang a favorite hymn of his.

> Let us gather up the sunbeams
> Lying all around our path ;
> Let us keep the wheat and roses
> Casting out the thorns and chaff.
> Let us find our sweetest comforts
> In the blessings of to-day,
> With a patient hand removing
> All the briars from the way.

The funeral services were brief and simple. The family consulted the well known feelings of the dead, by excluding everything of a showy, expiatory, or penitential character. He regarded death as a natural and gracious ordinance, not as the doom for sin, or the result of transgression; not as the close of earthly probation, or the opening of the dreadful door to the Hall of Judgment; but rather as one passage in the human creature's career; a passage which all must pass through, and which one was as likely to pass through calmly as another. He had always considered the present as the fruit of the past and the seed of the future; had always been more concerned with what was than with what was to come. If he thought of the hereafter, it was with expectation and confidence, never with fear or foreboding. It is remarkable that, being the religious man that he was, he did not, even in his Calvinistic days, dwell on the hideous alternatives of death. Though the diary records the decease of many people, the saintly and the passionate, the good and the bad, the believing and the unbelieving, there is no allusion in it to the frightful hereafter, depicted by the popular creed. Often the departed is spoken of as having gone to heaven, as being with the Saviour, but never as having gone to hell, as being with Satan and his fiends. The natural faith of the man was unclouded by the views he professed. He anticipated in feeling the brighter day that has come when the Love of Christ is the heart of the Gospel and a gracious God is all in all.

Nothing was said at the house or grave, that was out of keeping with the benignant, beneficent life of the man. The Rev. S. R. Calthrop, a Unitarian minister of Syracuse, a liberal, cultivated, wise, and sympathetic man, the successor of the venerable Samuel J. May, the beloved friend of the deceased, read hopeful passages from Scripture, gratefully acknowledged the divine mercy and besought the heavenly peace, and addressed cheerful words to the mourners. A sentiment of mournful sympathy pervaded the house. The more bitterly bereaved broke into loud lament for their lost benefactor. The

relations and personal friends stood in the soft shadow
of recollections. Old "Aunt Betsy," the early protegée,
the confidential inmate and trusted friend, now past
eighty, stood, in complacent sorrow by the coffin, her
sense of bereavement being chastened by the universal
respect which all classes manifested towards her benefactor. The members of the village Sunday school sang
hymns from their song book which had been sweet to
the good man's ear, songs of kindness and compassion.
The lid of the casket was closed, and the procession followed the body, through the snow, to the unpretending
cemetery on the summit of a neighboring hill. Gen.
John Knox, of Knoxboro; Charles B. Sedgwick, of
Syracuse; Henry A. Foster, Dewitt C. Littlejohn and
Hamilton Littlefield, of Oswego; F. F. Petrie, Caleb
Calkins, John Campbell, Jeremiah Bump, and Noah
Brister, (colored) of Peterboro; William Kenny and
George Bland, (colored) of Geneva; Dr. Milton B. Jarvis,
of Canastota ; and Benjamin Chapman, of Clockville,
acting as pall-bearers. A plain block of granite, with
his name cut on it, marks the spot where Gerrit Smith
lies. Next him, covered by a similar block of granite,
lies the wife who survived him but three months. On the
other side a more ambitious, but less becoming, monument of marble indicates the burial-place of his first
wife Wealtha. At a little distance, a broad marble slab
commemorates his father, and two monuments his mother
and two brothers. The large plot has no enclosure
about it. The stranger's feet may stand there. It is
the one plot in the burial ground that is evidently tended
by careful hands. The rest are too little cared for, in
some instances overgrown with weeds and coarse grass.

Here the grass is closely cut, the weeds are eradicated, the dead leaves are removed as if in deference to the man who lived a sweet, open and cleanly life,

> With a patient hand removing
> All the briars from the way.

The death of Gerrit Smith excited a profound feeling in the community. All classes were touched. The press of the country, far and near, religious and secular, political, reformatory, social, took notice of him. The metropolitan papers devoted columns to a description of his life and character. His last hours and his obsequies were detailed with much minuteness by special reporters. The Board of Trade at Oswego met and passed resolutions in honor of him. The colored citizens of New York, with the old abolitionists, met in the Shiloh Presbyterian Church, on Sixth Avenue, to listen to a Memorial prepared by Highland Garnet, and to speeches gratefully celebrating the services rendered to the oppressed of all nations by the departed philanthropist. On all sides the tribute was paid to the man who loved his fellow-men. The politicians forgot their animosities, the reformers their jealousies, even the divines their rancor, and said a hearty, if a brief, word in praise of one who held party, reform and church connections subordinate to the welfare of humanity. The *Nation*, consecrated opponent of sentimentalism, quoted Dr. Channing's description of Mr. Smith, as " A man worthy of all honor for his overflowing munificence, for his calm yet invincible moral courage, for his Christian liberality, embracing men of every sect and name, and for his deep, active, inexhaustible sympathy with the

sinful, suffering and oppressed." "Words," added the
Nation, " which might well furnish an inscription for his
tombstone."

The letters of condolence need not be described.
They were legion ; and they differed from similar letters,
merely in the unaffected sincerity of their tone, and the
variety of conditions from which they came. A letter
of William Lloyd Garrison proves how entirely memories of dissension and bitterness will pass away when
death brings the fullness of a character into relief. The
two men had criticised one another severely. They had
not always been friendly, though at heart they had
been friends. A package of letters lies on the writer's
table tied up with red tape, and labelled " Disagreement
with W. L. Garrison and C. C. Burleigh ;—not unpleasant
with the latter but exceedingly so with the former."
They shall not be quoted. In a great campaign, leaders
will disagree, and the sharpness of the disagreement
will be in proportion to the earnestness of the men.
Brutus and Cassius are brothers. The disagreements
are for an hour. The sympathies are for all time. The
love grows and deepens as the years go on.

The following testimonial from the hand of William
Lloyd Garrison is proof of this :

"To-day, Dec. 28th, the impressive record is completed by the
telegraphic announcement of the decease of one who by reason of
his intellectual and moral force, his munificent liberality, his rare
self-abnegation, his stirring eloquence, his courageous and resplen-
dent example, his personal gifts and graces, his all-embracing philanthropy, made himself preëminent in the tremendous struggle for
the abolition of slavery. To whom can I refer but that great and
good man, Gerrit Smith ? His case is hardly to be paralleled among
the benefactors of mankind in this or any other country. The

language of eulogy, often so absurdly or tumidly applied, may in this instance, be used in its strongest form without danger of exaggeration. No description of sublime deeds can match their performance. Truly, in the Peterboro philanthropist and reformer was seen:

> 'A combination and a form, indeed,
> Where every god did seem to set his seal,
> To give the world assurance of a man.'

Of a man not only remarkable for the beauty and stateliness of his person, the suavity of his manners, and the charm of his social intercourse, but exceptional among millions in what he achieved in the matter of self-conquest over the strongest temptations and the most ample opportunities to lead a luxurious and purely worldly life."

There were tributes in verse, many; but wisdom counsels not to print them. Mr. Smith, besides meditating the Muse, himself, on a very slender reed, was an inspiration, all through his life, to the muse of others. Even those who were never suspected of indulging in poetic flights, ventured, in his honor, upon the empyrean. The book of family rhymes contains many an effusion which the authors would not care to see in type. Among the rest Miss Emily Faithful appears, in wonted prose rhythmically divided. The following sonnet, by a real poet, Miss Eliza Scudder, is an example of the best sentiment called out by this noble life.

TO GERRIT SMITH.

> Of all the days that gild the gladsome year,
> Not the first freshness of the vernal time
> Nor the refulgent pomp of summer's prime
> Giveth to me such warm and heartfelt cheer,
> As the sweet season that brings in the dawn,
> With roseate flush tempered with golden haze,
> And on the glowing woods and harvest lays
> The fabled splendors of an Orient morn.
> How like a life by purest goodness filled,

16

Its wise deeds like the ripe and garnered fruit
Its wild hopes chastened and its tumults stilled
In air serene of thought entranced and mute.
O friend! this hand in flattery unskilled,
For thee alone thus strikes the wandering lute.

Eliza Scudder.

Peterboro, Oct. 30, 1866.

The joined hands pictured at the end of the volume are the hands of Gerrit Smith and his beloved wife. They were modeled from life. Hand in hand the two went through life together, sharing and counseling, and supporting. The union was perfect. Both were large in brain and heart. The wife was the more poetical and delicate in mental structure, but she was equally simple and brave; equally earnest in her humanity and resolute in her devotion. Her interests and his corresponded in all respects. Their differences were as friendly and sweet as their sympathies. Her religion, like his, was interior and practical; but while his was the more practical, hers was the more interior. Her interest in Spiritualism pleasantly teazed, but did not vex him. They were in truth, all in all to each other. They left but two children, Greene and Elizabeth, (Mrs. C. D. Miller). Their grandchildren and great-grandchildren were precious to them as their own; and the memory of those that had died in infancy and childhood was so vivid as to keep them always near. Love ruled and blessed the home.

Few words are necessary to sum up the peculiarities of the character whose deeds have been described in the foregoing chapters. To say that Gerrit Smith was not a philosopher, a close scientific thinker, a student of theories about human society, or of human society itself as an organic product of time, is superfluous. The most careless reader of his life must perceive that he was not this. Neither was he a man of books, a literary man, largely acquainted with the achievements of the human mind. He neither fed on books, nor refreshed himself with books. His diary, which covers a space of more than forty years, mentions but two or three books as interesting him, and these were books of religious experience. Down to 1846 the only book named is The Life of Heinrich Stilling. In his political letters and speeches reference is made to such works as Hallam, Adam Smith, Vattel, the usual text-books in social science and constitutional law. The latest authorities were apparently unknown to him. Lysander Spooner was his authority on the Constitution of the United States. His writings on religion show vigor, acuteness, courage, a singular originality of view, but neither learning nor independent research. His library contained about eighteen hundred volumes, of a miscellaneous description, no works of value, no rare editions, no famous copies, nothing that a lover of literature might be tempted to carry away. It was strongest, though still not remarkably strong, in digests, volumes of diplomatic correspondence, state reports, and that semi-professional literature so useful to a public man. Of literature, in its highest sense, there was little or none. The Greek and Latin classics were conspicuously absent. An incomplete set of Bancroft's United States, Motley's Dutch Republic, Irving's Washington, Prescott's Ferdinand and Isabella, comprised the better portion of the history. Of biography there was none, or next to none. Of philosophy, natural or metaphysical, there was nothing. None of the great thinkers of the world, Greek, Latin, Italian, German, French or

English were there, not one, ancient or modern, original or translated. There were no essays, no treatises on the constitution of the human mind or on social ethics. Saving two popular volumes by Darwin, there was no science. A handsomely bound set of Campbell's British Poets comprehended all the poetry; and this, it may be observed by the way, was the only sumptuous looking work in the collection. It was apparently a gift copy, and had not been much enjoyed. There was no drama, no fiction, no travel. What *was* there? the astonished reader will ask. There was religious literature, so called, in good store; there were sermons, homilies, commentaries, the works of Wesley, the works of the "pious John Newton." Three or four of Renan's books in the bad English translation, were encountered; a set of Theodore Parker's writings; Mrs. Child's "Development of Religious Ideas;" some volumes by A. J. Davis; Jacolliot's "Bible in India," translated; Appleton's American Cyclopedia. It was a singularly unintellectual library, even for a small and miscellaneous reader, who desired only a superficial acquaintance with books. With the exception of a few primary books, there was nothing in any foreign tongue, ancient or modern. The books there were evinced no decided or distinctive taste. They were not selected, but were evidently picked up; many were sent by authors or publishers. It was not the library of a cultivated, educated, or deeply thoughtful man.

The truth is that Gerrit Smith was not a man of books; not a reader even of such books as he possessed; not a reader of reviews or of magazines. The newspapers, of which he took many, of all sorts, furnished his intellectual material. They made him acquainted with the events of the day, and, having a good memory, he was equipped for the chief emergencies of practical life. A faithful reader of the best of the daily papers will seem to be a wise and well-endowed man. It will be a mistake to call Gerrit Smith, on this account, a superficial man. That he was not, because his own mind was anything but shallow. He was gifted with extraordinary intellectual force. His resources were abundant and ready at command. His mental impulse was great. He was always awake and alive; eager to receive and to impart. His faculties played easily. To think, write, speak, cost him no effort; he enjoyed the exercise. His thoughts came quickly, faster often than he could arrange them. They crowded one upon another, pushed one another from the track of argument. He was massive and keen at the same time; with a perspicacity that a pleader might envy, and a momentum that would make a fortune at the bar. In business clearness, decision and despatch he was almost without a peer. The business men who knew him held him in the highest admiration. Constitutional lawyers acknowledged his preëminent ability in dealing with fundamental principles and interpreting nice questions. One who knew him well and long said of him: "Without doubt, his was one of the profoundest and most fertile minds America has produced, and viewed from any point which human vision can open, it is a great pity that he had to spend the rich aboundings of his nature in caring for wealth which in a large degree fettered his genius and cramped his powers, and without which both he and the world—so far as his influence in it is concerned—would have been better off this day."

To this unqualified judgment the biographer demurs
From one point of view opened by human vision, the
circumstances amid which Gerrit Smith lived, from boy-
hood up, were singularly calculated to develop his
genius. His wealth was his opportunity. His business
talent was part of his endowment, and not the least remarkable part of it. The work of increasing, investing,
administering money, was a professional occupation from
which he derived the advantages that a professional occupation gives. Nature made him a philanthropist, and
wealth enabled him to do what philanthropists love to
do. His name among men is, as a matter of fact, due to
his wealth, and to the use he made of it. The grandeur
of his character, as was attested by the universal tribute
that men paid him after death, consisted in his power to
master great wealth, to bind it to service, to make it the
instrument of his manhood, to extract from it the golden
quality, to " make friends of the mammon of unright-
eousness." He knew what it was to make money, and
so knew what it was to lose it. To be rich was not so
much a thing of course with him that he looked on
riches with habitual indifference bordering on contempt.
He knew what money was worth, and because he knew
it, thought it no mean employment to labor for it, and
no unworthy aim to consecrate it to the needs of humanity. Because he so prized its capabilities, he would
place none of it at the disposal of his lower nature, spent
nothing on pleasure, nothing on amusement, next to
nothing on dress. He bought no luxuries, ornaments or
trinkets, purchased neither pictures nor bronzes, forbade
needless household decorations, gave no holiday presents,
indulged his family in no expensive dainties. His per-

sonal expenses were absurdly small, even for a man of
moderate means, not for the reason that he was ascetic,
but for the reason that money, in his opinion, was worth
too much to be wasted on frivolities, on things that the
rust corrupted and the moth devoured. His house was
large, for it answered the demands of his hospitality.
His table was bountiful, as it must have been to feed the
people who came in from the highways and byways;
but there was never the least ostentation. There was
all that hospitality required, but nothing more. Mr.
Smith himself considered wealth to be an opportunity,
not a clog, and used to speak of it as the divinely appointed means of his influence.

As regards mental discipline and culture he had time
for that, had he been so disposed. His business engagements were no more engrossing than the business or
professional engagements of other men, lawyers, physicians, clergymen, journalists, writers. There was a period, lasting three or four years, when the cares of business consumed his whole time; but usually, it was otherwise. He attended conventions, made speeches, wrote
articles, published letters to people of all conditions. A
portion of the time spent in this way would have been
enough to make him accomplished as a man of thought
and letters. But his bent was not in this direction.
His mind was full and flowing. Not closeness and com-
pression, but looseness, and copiousness were his talent.
His was an urgency for expression, not an eagerness for
acquisition. He was a talker, not a student; more at
home on the platform, in the social circle, even in the
pulpit, the lecture-room, the Sunday school, than in the

library. His affluent mind supplied him with materials for public and private uses.

He was, essentially, a man of Heart. The deepest, most exacting element in his nature was Feeling. His warmth, exuberance, generosity, were conspicuous in his college days, and they were equally conspicuous in his maturity and age. His abounding, sympathetic, over-flowing disposition mantled in his countenance, suffused his eyes, beamed in his smile, imparted heartiness to his manner, mellowed the tones of his voice. His affections were ardent and constant. His lovingness had no changes of mood. His letters to his wife and children are perfect in their simplicity and natural overflow of expression. He had a passion for children. His eyes moistened at the least mention of suffering or sorrow. The mere thought of the divine goodness filled his cup of emotion to the brim. He was exceedingly sen-sitive to pain, in his own person or in that of others, even of strangers. He could not resist a tear. His wife having in one of her letters, spoken of the necessity she had been under to punish one of the children, he said in his answer: " The next time the necessity oc-curs, save the whipping for me." Like other and all men of heart, he allowed feeling to dictate and direct the movements of intellect. The wish was father to the thought. Feeling is positive, arbitrary, dictatorial; it speaks with authority, announces, proclaims, judges. Assertions are confounded with arguments; impressions stand for facts; sentiments are laws. Feeling is pro-phetic, overworks the categorical imperative, exaggerates the importance of the personal pronoun.

This quickness of sensibility made Mr. Smith an easy

subject for religious impression, and the religious impression moulded the sensibility. The feeling became most intense in the direction of God and Christ. The direction was given by his orthodox inheritance and education, but so strong was the element of pure natural feeling in him that the theology did not bar the passage to the divine love. The veneration, awe, holy fear it inspired were never qualified by terror, but filled his soul with reverence, trust and gratitude. Religion subdued and exalted all his emotions. A moral cast was given to his feelings. A sense of personal responsibility over-ruled passion. He was still the man of heart, but sanctified and consecrated. Love with him was all in all, but the love was heavenly, like the sunshine and the summer rain. God was the perfect justice; Christ was the absolute mercy, authenticating the instincts of his own bosom.

All his life, whatever his dogmatic opinions, whether orthodox or heterodox, presbyterian or rationalist, Gerrit Smith was a practical, earnest, hearty Christian, as good an example of a Christian man as our modern times afford. He made the Christian life his law; he accepted Jesus as his master; he aspired to be perfect after the standard set up in the New Testament. The Sermon on the Mount contained the sum of his philosophy; the Beatitudes kept before him the vision of happiness; the Golden Rule was his motto. He assumed the posture of a servant; his desire was not to be ministered unto, but to minister; he gave his goods to the poor; he fed the hungry, clothed the naked, visited the imprisoned, loosed the fetters of those who were bound. He forgave his enemies, blessed those that cursed him, prayed for

16*

those who despitefully used him, made himself poor
that the poor might be rich. An old friend testifies that
he never, but once, saw him in a fit of anger. Then he
begged him to pause an instant and repeat the "Lord's
Prayer." The bare recollection of the awful petition:
"Forgive us our trespasses as we forgive those that
trespass against us," subdued the wrath and melted the
man. The diary, entirely free from self-consciousness,
as unaffected a record as was ever penned, abounds in
expressions of touching humility. "Heavenly Father,
may the year on which I have entered, be my best
year!" is the usual opening of each twelve month. His
candor was perfect; so was his meekness. We came
across this record in the diary: "I preached this morning. This afternoon Mr. Copeland preached. Others
followed. Mr. Bliss spoke strongly against myself;
against my preaching politics on the Sabbath, and
warned Christians to cease from following me." The
scrap books contain insulting letters to himself, and his
replies. Here is a specimen:

Nelson, March 3, 1838.

Dear Sir — You will recollect that you sent four colored people
with your team to my house on Saturday, the 18th day of last month,
and left them on my premises, without inquiring whether I could
keep them or not, when you was well aware that they were paupers,
very poorly clad, and destitute in everything, and after your teamster
had left them on my hands and returned homeward, a man or a
priest informed and requested me, in your behalf, to keep and furnish
them until Monday morning. I told him I could not keep them any
longer than Sunday. I accordingly kept them until Sunday, and
furnished them with victuals and lodging at your expense, and for
which I charged you two dollars, and expect that you will send
the money soon, or at least will give an answer as soon as you
receive this.

N. B. In the first place, I should not have thought that you would have sent a filthy load of black paupers to a public house, to be kept over the Sabbath.

And in the second place, that a man who pretends to be as friendly to the blacks as you do, would have sent them away as needy as they were, without clothes to keep them comfortable.

Yours respectfully,
WILLIAM W. CLOUGH.

To which Mr. Smith replies as follows:

Peterboro, March 7, 1838.

MR. W. W. CLOUGH, Innkeeper, Nelson.

Sir — On my return home last evening from Albany, your letter was handed to me. I recollect that one of my hired men took my friend, Rev. Mr. Wilson, to Nelson two or three weeks ago. And I was told after they had gone, that a colored family had availed themselves of this opportunity to get thus far on their way to Cazenovia. I never saw this colored family, sir, more than a minute or two. They stopped at my house while on their way to Cazenovia, and stopped, so far as I know, simply to get their dinner. Mrs. Smith informs me that they ate their dinner, and that having received from her hands a present of a dollar, and of food sufficient to last them a couple of days, they left in the manner referred to. I knew nothing of this at the time. And, as I am much confined to my office, I know but little of many similar transactions in my family.

Whether, under these circumstances, I ought to pay you the two dollars which you say you have charged against me, I leave to yourself to decide. If you write me that in your judgment I should pay the two dollars, I will send you the money.

On the subject of your allusions to my having wronged and imposed on yourself, and to the sincerity of my professions of regard for my colored brethren, I have nothing to say. That we may both do justly and love mercy is the desire of

Yours respectfully,
GERRIT SMITH.

This man was subjected to something more than the common vulgar persecutions that are visited on the independent and unpopular. The prediction of the Master that his followers should have all manner of evil things said against them falsely, was fulfilled in him, and the blessing pronounced on them who receive it gently, was his also. We give a sample of the letters he received. There is a striking family likeness in all these productions, as every man has reason to know who has tasted the cup of public disfavor:

"It is impossible to find language to express the indignation and contempt with which every honorable man looks upon your conduct in regard to the election that has just passed. You mean, contemptible, fawning hypocrite, apostate; we can see through you as easily as we can through an old sieve. You are marked and will be attended to wherever you go." On which Mr. Smith remarks: "The whole letter makes it obvious that its writer, with whose plain dealing I must not be offended, is a Whig."

The publication of his religious opinions brought upon him attacks of the most virulent description, and from persons he loved and had worked with in causes of reform. He took them patiently, replying to the argument if there was any, acknowledging the courtesy, if it could be extracted, and keeping the insolence to himself. The broken friendships were grieved over in secret. The bitterness of hate was accounted for without casting reproach on men he had honored, and still felt that he must respect.

He was a Christian in believing that love was the fulfilling of the law, and that the kingdom of heaven, which is the reign of love, must come, as Jesus meant it should come, on earth. He was a Christian in believing that he must do his part in making that kingdom come. His was a genuine life, pure, obedient, trusting; manlike and childlike; honorable, chivalrous, spotless; a life of aspiration and of service. His faults were those of a large, full, self-assured, self-reliant nature. He was not sordid, or cunning. He had no private vices. He was proud, and confident, but neither arrogant nor overbearing. He asserted himself with the air and tone of authority that belong to men who are strong in feeling whether strong in intellect or weak; but being, himself, strong in intellect, his self-assertion had the self-sufficient cast that is easily mistaken for conceit. He seemed to dictate and lay down the law and don the imperial purple. But at heart he was simple, humble, sympathetic, unselfish. Perhaps, as is the way of men of his temperament, he associated somewhat too closely his private feelings with the Eternal will. But it was the Eternal will he revered. The beauty of such a character will hardly be disputed among thoughtful people. The value of such a life to society will be estimated differently according to the school of philosophy to which the judge belongs. By the scientific it will be pronounced nearly, if not altogether worthless. By some it will be called injurious to the permanent welfare of modern communities. To the professors of the latest current theories of social progress, the habitual service of others is harmful to their self-respect, and demoralizing to their self-reliance; the profuse expenditure of money in works of charity is wasteful, and productive only of idleness; the appeal to moral sentiment as the ground and authority for action, instead of to the generalizations of recorded fact, is set down as hopelessly misleading; the fundamental position that the issues of life are from the heart is dismissed as fanciful, in view of the discovery that progress, with all it implies, is the result of man's adaptation to his environment, and that this process of adaptation, slow and pain-

ful from necessity, must not be interfered with by indi·
viduals.   Herbert Spencer objects to the common, and
almost instinctive suggestion in cases of emergency that
" something must be done," that it is in precisely these
cases that *nothing* should be done; the meddlers should
retire, and allow matters to adjust themselves, or to remain for an indefinite time unadjusted.   Things it is
thought will instinctively work themselves into their places if let alone.   Hamlet fancies the world to be out of
joint and curses the fate that calls him to set it right.
Did he bless fate for so ordaining instead of cursing it,
the situation would not be improved; for the world is not
" out of joint;" it only looks so to Hamlet's diseased imagination.   The world is simply chaotic, immature, undeveloped.   No one is called to " set it right."   Every one
is called to keep his intrusive hands off, and let it come
naturallyright of itself.   The reformers and philanthropists do whatever is done to put the world " out of joint "
by their officious tinkering.   Men like Gerrit Smith, say
these philosophers, do more harm than good in the world
by their plans and efforts.   In proportion to their wealth,
their talent, their zeal, the nobleness and sincerity of
their character, is their mischievousness.   Their failure
is nature's repudiation of a method which is impracticable according to the laws of creation.   Take the fine
example of the man just portrayed.   His career was not,
to human vision, successful; for the reason that feeling
does not govern the world; goodness does not justify im-
providence or make error harmless.   His demand for
ideal perfection in men singly or combined was incompatible with sober expectation and reasonable performance.   His independence of such political organizations

as there were was glorious, but inoperative and weakening. He lost the attainable in striving for the unattain-
able. His " Liberty Party " was a chimera ; his " Anti-
Dram-shop Party " was a fanaticism. His negro colonies
wasted away; his runaway slaves came to no good in
northern cities ; he ruined his beloved Peterboro by excessive indulgence, doing so much for the villagers that
they became quite incapable of doing anything for themselves. His generosity dried up the sources of public
spirit and made men positively sordid. He proposed to
build and endow a public library there, and the owners
of desirable land sites were, all at once, misers, who held
their ground at prices so exorbitant that the scheme was
abandoned. He opened a free reading-room, and the
thirst for information, being anticipated, was discouraged.
He offered to erect a fountain on the common, and the
jealousy of the residents, each of whom wanted it in
front of his own house, caused a bitterness which the
waters of Bethesda would not cure. He presented a
town clock to the authorities and they grew at once so
parsimonious that he was requested to provide a man to
wind it up. The common railing was dilapidated, and
remained so, because he did not choose to repair it at
his own expense. The brood of parasites increased on
this branching oak. Tramps, swindlers, cheats multiplied. Liars sprang up like weeds. Beggars infested
the county. His bounty would in many cases, if not in
most, have been more wisely bestowed on the devouring
sea which it could not poison, or buried in the ground
where it would lie forever hid. The charity he most
congratulated himself on, the bounty given to worthy
widows and old maids, throve because it provoked stingy

people to provide better for their poor relations. He
set flowing the natural streams of good-will.

All this proves to the satisfaction of the social science philosophy that the life of Gerrit Smith was based
on a false principle, and could not therefore be productive of wholesome results. A conclusion which believers in the authority of the New Testament and in the
divine ethics there inculcated, will promptly repudiate.
For these it is sufficient that the rules he practiced on
were laid down by Jesus. Beyond or behind *His* word
they do not care to go. Their duty consists in obedience
to the written precept. The consequences of such obedience are not their concern. The consequences must,
indeed, be salutary since they proceed from divinely in-
stituted principles. The evils complained of must be
apparent only, temporary in their duration, and overbalanced by benefits that are out of sight. Of the constitution of society they profess to know little and doubt
whether any body knows much. The material aspects
of life are not the most important ; the material progress
of mankind does not chiefly excite the interest of men
deeply in earnest. At all events, they say, obedience to
the will of the Christ is commendable. The sentiments of
compassion, benevolence, kindness, pity, are the glory and
loveliness of human nature ; the impulse to help, to bestow, to serve, is worthy of universal praise ; the reformer,
the philanthropist, the saint, are held in veneration by all
mankind. Gerrit Smith succeeded because his obedience
to principle was universal. To mental eyes he seemed
to fail ; the work of his hands has perished. But he was
true to his orders. He fulfilled the law. He enacted
the Golden Rule. The Deity who disposes will see to

it that the water he poured upon the sands, becomes beneath them a living fountain to which fainting pilgrims will come in their thirst.

One other class of people will justify and glorify Gerrit Smith, the people who regard man as a spiritual and immortal being, with limitless capacities of moral development, and with dormant powers, which when stirred, will effect his personal regeneration. These, call them by what name you choose, have an invincible faith in human nature, in the worth and significance of the individual soul, in the potency of the spiritual laws. They have no patience with the ethics of expediency or the philosophy of circumstance. Utilitarianism, in its noblest form, is folly, in their opinion. Their hope of society lies in the prevalence of great ideas, the sudden quickening of the moral sentiments. They are revivalists, though not of the Methodistic or other " Evangelical " school. They trust in pentecosts of enthusiasm, in sudden outbursts and steady outgoings of religious feeling. They are disciples and apostles of Individualism in its spiritual form ; look on the world as lying in ignorance, apathy and sensuality, on men and women as imprisoned souls, on existence as a phase of the eternal being, on character as the fulness of divinity and the source of power. Such as these make little account of the apparent failures in a life like that of Gerrit Smith, but much account of his real successes as a stimulator of endeavor, an instigator of nobleness, a promoter of unadulterated justice and love.

It is not the biographer's province to decide which of these interpretations of life is the just one. His work is done when the character is delineated. Such it was.

Let men judge it as they will. It was original, unique, a singularly pure example of a type highly extolled in all ages, in Christian ages pronounced divine; a type reveringly looked back upon and, in its ideal form, worshipped under the name of the Christ. Separate traits of it, discernible here and there, are commended as saving graces in human beings otherwise wilful and corrupt, and are ascribed to the influence of the sanctifying spirit which works beneath the individual will. Of these traits Gerrit Smith possessed and combined more than any man of note in this generation, more, we may say than any man of note in this century of the world. No man, so well as he, illustrates the practical tendency of the ethics of the New Testament. On this account his life deserves to be written; for on this account his example is of general interest to mankind. The record, not otherwise especially important, is significant as bearing on the moral education of the age. His, in a certain degree, is a test character. Whether it tests the weakness or the strength of the principles it illustrates is a question worth raising and answering.

INDEX.